The Pedens of America

Being a summary of the Peden, Alexander, Morton, Morrow Reunion 1899, and an Outline History of the Ancestry and Descendants of John Peden and Margaret McDill; Scotland, Ireland, America, 1768 - 1900

By Eleanor M. Hewell

Published by Pantianos Classics

Cover: *Fairview Presbyterian Church in 2012*, photographed by Bill Fitzpatrick

ISBN-13: 978-1-78987-314-6

First published in 1900

Fairview Church in 1900

Contents

Part One - Peden, Alexander, Morton, Morrow Reunion 6

Part Two - The Pedens of America 41

    Chapter One - Ancestral Pride 41

    Chapter Two - Side Lights from Secular History 42

    Chapter Three - The Flitting 52

    Chapter Four - Our Fore-Fathers 56

    Chapter Five - The Peden in the Revolution 61

    Chapter Six - Migrations of the Peden 66

    Chapter Seven - Old Haunts and Homes 72

    Chapter Eight - Fairview and the Peden 78

    Chapter Nine – Peden — Christian, Patriot, Soldier 85

    Chapter Ten - The Founders of a House 113

    Chapter Eleven - House of Mary 117

    Chapter Twelve - House of James 127

    Chapter Thirteen - House of Jane 133

    Chapter Fourteen - House of Thomas 136

    Chapter Fifteen - House of William 149

    Chapter Sixteen - Elizabeth Gaston 152

    Chapter Seventeen - House of John 154

    Chapter Eighteen - House of Samuel 157

    Chapter Nineteen - House of Alexander 160

    Chapter Twenty - House of David 168

    Chapter Twenty-One - In Reminiscent Mood 181

Dedicated

Affectionately and Respectfully By the Author

to

Captain David Dantzler Peden

Acknowledged and venerated Chief of the American Pedens, with whom originated the idea of a family book, and through whose generosity it is now presented to the
Pedens of America.

Part One - Peden, Alexander, Morton, Morrow Reunion

Hon. John R. Harrison.

Capt. D. D. Peden.

Dr. H. B. Stewart.

W. H. Britt.

PEDEN--ALEXANDER--MORTON--MORROW REUNION.

To be Held at
Fairview Presbyterian Church,
Greenville Co., S.C.,
August 15th and 16th, 1899.

All descendants of John Peden and his wife Margaret (Peggy) McDill, who can possibly do so, are requested to join the undersigned in a family reunion at Fairview Presbyterian church, in Greenville County, S. C., on August 15th and 16th, 1899.

From the best information obtainable, the parents of John Peden refugeed from Scotland to the North of Ireland during the time of the religious persecution in the former country. He and his family came to the United States, first landing in Pennsylvania, settling in Bucks and Chester counties; just how long they remained there we cannot say. About the year 1768 he (John) removed to the Spartan District, South Carolina, settling near Nazareth church, in what is now Spartanburg County.

They had ten children. Sons — James, Thomas, William, John, Samuel, Alexander and David. Daughters — Hilary, who married James Alexander, Sr.,; Jane, who married Morton, after whose death she married Samuel Morrow; Elizabeth, who married William Gaston. (The latter left no children.)

As stated above, it is our design to have a reunion of as many of their descendants as possibly can attend at the place and time stated. It is our purpose to erect a monument in Fairview cemetery to the memory of these, our venerated ancestors, John and Margaret Peden.

Presuming that all of the descendants would consider it a privilege to take part in this good work, they are hereby requested to forward any amount (much or little) as they may feel able to give, to Mr. Adam S. Peden, treasurer, at Fountain Inn, Greenville County, S.C. The amount should be forwarded at once (this week, not next), as the cost, size and design of the monument will depend upon the amounts contributed. As the time will soon arrive for the reunion and much work will have to be done in the meantime, prompt action is absolutely necessary.

There will be a receptacle in the monument (in the nature of a cornerstone) in which will be placed a list of the names of all contributors, with amounts given by each.

We also request all descendants to bring or send individual or family photographs, with their names, post office address, etc., plainly written on same, to be placed in the receptacle alluded to above. This feature may prove to be of inestimable interest and pleasure to our descendants, say one hundred years from now. Also bring or send any relics to be placed on exhibition.

Kinsmen, remember the monument to honor our parents, who left us a good name is going to be erected, and if you wish to join us in the good work you must act immediately in forwarding your contribution.

We take pleasure in vouching for the integrity and thorough reliability of our treasurer, Mr. Adam S. Peden, who is an elder of the old mother church (Fairview) that has done so much for the cause of Christianity for more than one hundred years. The treasurer will promptly acknowledge receipt of all amounts sent to him.

Most interesting historical sketches and addresses will be heard; an elaborate program will be arranged for the occasion, and copies will be sent to all who express a desire or intention to attend the reunion.

Quite a number of the Pedens now spell their names P-a-d-e-n; of course, this invitation applies to them also; then there are a number of our kinsmen (Pedens and Padens) in the North and West, and elsewhere, they too, and all descendants connected by marriage, are cordially invited to join with us in the reunion ceremonies.

You are urgently requested to advise all other Peden, Alexander, Morton, and Morrow descendants, of your acquaintance, of the plans set forth, invite them to attend the reunion and kindly ask your local papers to publish notices of this invitation, for the name of Peden is legion, and the bearers of it are widely scattered, and it is our desire that none be overlooked. Those who hear of the reunion and attend it will be just as heartily welcomed as those known to us and to whom these circulars are sent.

It is very important that all who expect to attend should send their names as early as possible to Mr. A.S. Peden, Fountain Inn, S.C., so that the Arrangement Committee may provide entertainment for them.

RECAPITULATION

1st. Reunion of Peden descendants.

2nd. Place — Fairview church, Greenville County, S. C, (Railroad station, Fountain Inn, S. C.)

3rd. Time — August 15th and 16th, 1899.

4th. Contributions to be sent to A. S. Peden, Treasurer, Fountain Inn, S.C.

5th. Send photographs to be placed in the monument.

6th. Invite your descendants, and ask your local papers to print notices of the reunion.

7th. Importance of prompt action. Write the week you receive this notice; don't wait until next week of the week after.

We are respectfully your kinsmen,

Hooper Alexander, Atlanta, Ga.   M. C. Britt, Sparta, Ga.
R. B. Morrow, Demopolis, Ala.   S. M. Morrow, Somerville, Ala.
Miss Emma Morton, Lancaster, Texas.   Walter F. Morton, St. Paul, Minn.
Wm. D. Paden, Cameron, Texas.   D. D. Peden, Houston, Texas.
J. W. T. Peden, Van Vleet, Miss.   Wm. Peden, Richburg, S.C.
J. T. Peden, Graycourt, S.C.
Adam S. Peden, Treasurer, Fountain Inn, S.C.

Mrs. C. A. Shannon.

Mrs. D. M. Peden.

Rev. M. C. Britt.

A. S. Peden.

ORDER OF EXERCISES

PEDEN - ALEXANDER - MORTON - MORROW REUNION

To be Held
August 15th and 16th, 1899.
Fairview Presbyterian Church,
Fairview, Greenville County,
South Carolina.

COMMITTEES

Executive, On Monument,
On Invitations, On Addresses,
On Music, On Reception,
On Badges, On Relics,
On Finance, On Entertainment.
On Amusement for Children.

EXECUTIVE COMMITTEE

Dr. H. B. Stewart, Chairman.   J. T. Peden.   D. D. Peden.
Adam S. Peden.   Jno. R. Harrison.

COMMITTEE ON ADDRESSES

Rev. M. C. Britt, Chairman.   Dr. H. B. Stewart.   M. P. Nash.   Jno. T. Peden.

COMMITTEE ON INVITATIONS

Hon. Hooper Alexander, Chairman.   Rev. M. C. Britt. Wm. D. Peden.
Rev. R. B. Morrow.   J. W. T. Peden.
Miss Emma Morton.   Thomas Peden.
D. D. Peden.   J. T. Peden.   A. S. Peden.

COMMITTEE ON MONUMENT

Capt. D. D. Peden, Chairman.   W. Stewart Peden.   J. Stewart Peden.
L. Hayne Templeton.   J. Wistar McDowell.

COMMITTEE ON MUSIC

W. Hewell Britt, Chairman.   Dr. H. Boardman Stewart.
Miss Eugenia Dunbar Hewell.   Mrs. Nannie Stewart Peden.
Miss Lillie Helen Harrison.

COMMITTEE ON RECEPTION

Hon. Jno. R. Harrison, Chairman.   T. W. McDowell.   J. Wistar Stewart.
A. S. Peden.   J. M. Peden.   W. H. Britt.   J. R. West.

COMMITTEE ON BADGES

Adam S. Peden, Chairman.   Dorroh D. Peden.
Capt. David D. Peden.   James F. Peden.

COMMITTEE ON RELICS

James F. Peden, Chairman.   M. White Fowler.   Mrs. M. E. Britt.
Mrs. E. M, Peden.   G. Calvin Anderson.   Jefferson D. McKittrick.

COMMITTEE ON FINANCES

Adam S. Peden, Chairman.   W. S. Peden.
Jas. M. Peden.   Jas. F. Peden.   Jno. T. Peden.

COMMITTEE ON AMUSEMENT FOR CHILDREN

Jones R. West, Chairman.   W. S. Peden.   Mrs. Calvin Anderson.
Mrs. J. T. Peden.   Mrs. Sue West.

COMMITTEE ON ENTERTAINMENT

Mrs. Caroline Peden, Chairman.   Mrs. A. S. Peden.   Mrs. H. B. Stewart.
Mrs. Eliza Peden.   Mrs. M. Emily Britt.   Mrs. T. W. McDowell.
Mrs. M. Caroline Templeton.   Mrs. Jas. F. Peden.   Mrs. Ella Armstrong.
Miss Isabella H. Stenhouse.   Miss Effie Fowler.
Miss Cathie Stewart.   Miss Lillie H. Harrison.

FIRST DAY— AUGUST 15th, 1899

1. Meeting called to order promptly at 10. o'clock a. m. by Hon. Jno. R. Harrison. — Welcome Address.
2. L. M. Doxology — Old Hundred.
3. Prayer — Rev. H. W. Burwell.
4. Election Permanent Chairman.
5. Election Secretary.
6. Election Assistant Secretary and Historian.
7. Psalm 148, 4th part — Autumn.
8. Address — Hon. H. Alexander of Atlanta, Ga. Subject: "The Scotch-Irish and their Achievements."
9. Hymn 119 — Coronation.

10. Address — Rev. R. B. Morrow of Demopolis, Ala. Subject: "Pedens and Presbyterianism."
11. Hymn 235 — Protection.
12. Adjourn with benediction by Rev. M. C. Britt, Sparta, Ga.

Afternoon to be spent in social intercourse until 4.45 p. m.
13. Meeting called to order at 4.45 p. m. Opened with music.
14. Unveiling of Monument.
15. Music and Benediction.
16. Adjourn until 9.00 a. m. tomorrow.

Peden Monument

SECOND DAY— AUGUST 16th, 1899.

1. Meeting called to order at 9.00 a. m.
2. Prayer.
3. Hymn 117 — Fount.
4. Address — Capt. D. D. Peden of Houston, Texas. Subject: "History of the Peden Family."

5. Music — "Singing on the Old Church Ground," composed for the occasion by Rev. H. W. Burwell, pastor of Fairview church.

6. Report of Treasurer and collection to defray expenses on Monument, and other necessary expenses.

7. Hymn 121 — Loving Kindness.

8. Address — Judge J. R. Alexander of Thomasville, Ga. Subject: "Reminiscences."

9. Hymn 472 — Varina.

10. Adjournment until 4.45 p. m.

11. Meeting called to order.

12. Music — "Holy is the Lord."

13. Short addresses.

14. Hymn composed by Rev. H. W. Burwell to Trinity.

15. Adjourn sine die with benediction.

UNVEILING HYMN.

(Tune — "Tentingon the Old Camp Ground.")

1. We're gathered to-day on the old Church ground
    Where our forefathers dwelt;
   And with songs of praise we bow before
    The Throne at which they knelt.

Chorus:
Many are the years that have past away
   Since they to Fairview came,
And with joyful hearts we join today
   To sound abroad their fame.
Singing to-day, singing to-day,
   Singing on the old Church ground.

2. That they might serve and worship God
    As taught within His Word,
   Our fathers turned from Scotland's shore
    And fled the tyrant's sword.
Chorus.

3. 'Twas God's own hand that led them safe
    Across the ocean wide,
   And to this day His blessings free
    On their offspring abide.
Chorus.

4. Here where they worshipped, loved and died,
    A marble shaft we raise,
  That generations yet to come
    May know and sing their praise.
                            Chorus.

5. And now to God whose hand has led
    Us on in grace and love,
    Till we join the saints above.
  Our grateful thanks we'll raise through life,
                  (Chorus after last verse.)

  There all our loved ones who've passed away
    We'll meet to part no more.
  And never a cloud shall cast its blight
    Across that shining shore.
  Safe in the hope we're singing today,
    Singing on the old Church ground.
  Singing to-day, singing to-day.
    Singing on the old Church ground

PARTING HYMN

(Tune— "Trinity.")

1. Come brothers ere we part,
  Come, let us raise our hearts
    To our great God.
  We praise Him for His love
  Which like a heavenly dove
  Rests on us from above,
    Holy, adored.

2. We praise Thee for the joy
  Which now our hearts employ
    While here we dwell.
  And as we turn away.
  Be, Lord, our strength and stay,
  That we from day to day
    Thy love may tell.

3. For Thy rich blessings free,
  Our Father, now to Thee,
    Our thanks we bring.
  Give what Thou seest best,
  Then shall we all be blest,

We bow to Thy behest.
   Thy praise we sing.

4. As on we go through life,
   'Mid peace and joy, or strife,
      Be Thou our guide.
Then may th' eternal light,
So guide our souls aright.
That we, in garments bright,
   Stand near Thy side.

Fairview Church Arranged for Reunion

The Reunion of 1899

Fairview! what a thrill; what a crowd of tender memories cluster round thy name, thou cradle of the Peden race on America's soil.

Nature seemed in accord with the clan Peden on the dates set for their great gathering in August, 1899. Never shone the sun brighter; never was the blue dome of heaven clearer; never the native forests in denser, greener leaf — even the woodland singers seemed inspired with the spirit of the occasion, and myriads of throats made the welkin ring.

The bustling little town of Fountain Inn was filled with pilgrims, and every train heralded the arrival of some Peden, bound for the shrine of his or her forefathers. A busy committee of reception threaded their way in and out among the crowd, distributing visitors among waiting hosts, or eagerly scanning strange, new faces for the familiar lineaments that mark the Peden. Long lines of carriages with Pedens, and their belongings were speeding along over the excellent country road towards their Mecca (Fairview). Now and then meeting an empty, returning carriage, driven by some Peden host, who must be delayed for a word of greeting, or a speedy introduction to some strange kinsman.

The drive is a little over four miles, then a swift curve brought the white columns of Fairview church into view, up the gently sloping hill, through an avenue of stately oaks and pines, to her wide, open portals, her snowy columns bathed in the mellow radiance of the August sunlight, she seemed like a mother welcoming home her long lost children. Away down the hill slope to the left, under the shadow of the trees, gleamed the white tents of the encampment, edged by a white sanded road, which, like a silver ribbon separated the camp of the living from the silent bivouac of the dead, within the grey rock-walled church yard, where generations of Pedens were at rest.

Near the center stood mysterious in its drapery, the shrouded form of the Peden monument.

After a brief rest at the temporary home, the writer and party strolled up the hill towards the church, and memory was busy with other days, other times, and other actors gone beyond ken. Within the house of God busy committees were putting the finishing touches to their labor of love. The Pedens being Scotch-Irish-Americans, the decorations were emblematic of these peoples, and blended under the artist's hands into beautiful harmony. Those of Scotland and Ireland combined with the stars and stripes of America, were draped from ceiling to floor, along the long galleries in festoons and sweeping folds of color.

The sacred desk was banked with ferns, palms and potted plants of most luxurious growth and foliage, while rich colors lent their aid to the scene. The stairs and entrances were adorned and guarded by immense sheafs of Scottish thistle, so woe, to the unwary intruder, whose unconsecrated foot sought sacrilegious hold, (to the Peden the pulpit is sacred). Above this, and covering the entire wall floated the colors of the three peoples, the purple red and orange of Scotland, the emerald green of Ireland, with the red, white and blue of the United States, formed a back-ground for the golden letters:

JOHN AND PEGGY PEDEN,
Founders of the House.
PEDEN-ALEXANDER-MORTON-MORROW REUNION
1760.   1899.

"The base and foundation of the church and nation is the family."

Along the walls, galleries and pillars were life size portraits of the Pedens of past generations, among them their life-long pastor. Rev. Clark B. Stewart, Mrs. Rebecca (Peden) Westmoreland, David Martin Peden, John McVey Peden, and others.

The relic corner, too, was specially attractive. (The writer hopes that some clay a mortuary chapel may be built of iron or bronze within the walls of the church-yard, these relics all be collected and placed therein in perpetuity.) A stack of rifles borne through the Revolutionary war by the seven brothers Peden, their rusty hunting knives, bayonets, swords, spurs, powder horns. All were not there, as some have wandered away to far off States, or lost; some old colonial coins when George the Third was King, one or two dating back and bearing the curled, cruel head of Charles First; old bits of crockery, pewter spoons and pans, ancient mirrows. or "shaving glasses," old andirons and many articles of feminine handicraft, coverlets, quilts, fringes, laces, yellow with age, old pictures; but missing was Peggy's treasured china with its varied history (it has passed out of the race); John's stick and his arm-chair, which David Morton made him, has since been found, but unattainable. Each article has its history, its tradition, which if told would make a small volume. Leaving the relic corner with its hallowed memories, and passing out at the eastern door down the slope towards the camp .under the lengthening shadows, where the evening fires glowed the nostrils were greeted with savory odors of coming supper, such as the Peden housewives knew how to prepare. In the camp were gathered representatives from the houses of Mary, James, Thomas, John, Alexander and David, while were sadly missed any from the houses of Jane, William and Samuel.

The evening and far into the summer night was spent in that sweet communion and interchange of thought which is known only to those bound by ties of blood.

On the morrow the arranged program was rendered as planned. The great church was filled to overflowing. Hon. John R. Harrison made the welcoming address in his usual stately, gracious manner which met the courteous response of Hon. Hooper Alexander.

Mr. Chairman, Kinsmen and Friends:

I thank you heartily in behalf of the visiting kin for your words of welcome, but it is just as useless for me to respond as it was for you to put into words the generous welcome that breathes in the very atmosphere about this old church. I never felt more at home in my life than I did from the first moment I drove up to this splendid grove and began to be introduced around to all these magnificent, big-boned, blue-eyed Peden men and all this galaxy of handsome Peden women.

Your reference, Mr. Chairman, to Rob Roy is especially in harmony with my feelings ever since I have been on this hill. He was a McGregor of the Campbell clan, but because of the turbulent spirit of the McGregors they had been forbidden to bear the name, and in the lowlands answered by law to the name of Campbell. Going up into the mountain from Glasgow, a companion addressed him as Campbell, to which he angrily retorted as he crossed the highland border: "Campbell me no Campbells; my foot is on my native heath and my name is McGregor."

And so today I feel here that though I never was at Fairview before, I am at home. And I want all you Pedens to understand that I am just as much a Peden as any of you. It is true that I bear another name and a name that I have no desire to drop even for the name of Peden, but all we Stewarts and Harrisons and Vernons and Celys and Shannons and Salmons and all the rest have just this much advantage of you, that we come down from the good looking Peden girls, the best part of the family, and that's why we go by other names.

I never saw so many people of the same name in my life. Down in my country, in Georgia, we have got a big batch of the Pedens, and good folks they are, too, and if you come to Georgia we can make very substantial additions to your lists of kinsfolks with our Casselses and Kings and Shannons and Gordons and Rounsavilles and Pegues and Salmons and lots of others; but I am obliged to confess that this is the first time I ever found enough kinsfolks to stock a whole county at one time. I never will get them straight. There is your Tom Peden and your Dick Peden, your long Jim Peden and your short Jim Peden, your Bill Peden and your Hugh Peden, and such another list of Pedens that I don't know how you ever found names enough to go round.

Verily, John Peden of old had the blessing of Abraham, whom God called out of the Chaldees and promised to make him father of many nations. Surely you are like the old darkey said about the patriarchs of old — the forgetfullest people on earth — for, said he, "dey forgot deir own chillun. Abraham forgot Isaac and Isaac forgot Jacob and Jacob forgot a hole lot of his boys." Verily the Pedens are a forgetful race.

Mr. Chairman, I thank you again for your cordial words of welcome.

Scotch-Irish and Their Achievements

Mr. Alexander, having concluded his address in response to the welcome, entered into his speech on "The Scotch-Irish and their achievements." For almost an hour Mr. Alexander held his kinsmen spellbound with his eloquence, and every word that came from his lips during his discourse fell upon attentive ears.

In part he said:

Every incident in human history is a separate knot in the intricate meshes of eternity's net work, the constituent cords of which reach forward, diverging to an unknown future. Every action of men, whether isolated from their fellows or in connection with them, is potent for influence, good or bad, on human civilization. Every separate occasion in the affairs of men bears fruit in its own future and finds the springs of its own occurrence ramifying back through uncounted ages of the past.

The beneficent Father of us all gave us every good and perfect gift, whose covenant has stood through the ages to declare that He will show mercy unto thousands of those that love Him and keep His commandments, has not seen fit to give us any glimpses of the future that lies before, nor allowed us to look forward and forecast what consequences shall flow from this coming together of men and women to do honor to the memory of one sturdy man and one virtuous woman. But it is permitted that we look back and trace out the steps that have preceded and made possible this occasion. Let us this day exercise for a while the privilege of retrospection and find what lessons of the past may serve to make us better men and better women and stand as staunch witnesses to the future for virtues of an honorable past.

If we seek backward into history for the mainspring of the present occasion, all the threads of research lead indeed to John Peden, Ulsterman, Presbyterian and elder, and to Peggy McDill, faithful helpmate to a worthy man and mother of many generations, proudest office ever given to a woman. But we shall fail to measure up to the full significance of the present occasion if we stop with the frontiersman and go not back to a remoter past, rich as his own life, in every inspiration for the patriot, the parent and the Christian.

Go with me today and I will carry you back along the pathway of a peculiar people, who, whether we find them fighting for their firesides as Carolina Whigs, or staunchly standing amid the Shamrock boys of Ireland for the right to worship God according to the dictates of their own consciences, or leagued together in solemn covenant in the shadow of Scotland's heathered hills, in every condition and under all circumstances have steadfastly stood for the rights of mankind and sturdily maintained their faith toward God and men. From such a people and such stock John Peden drew his lineage.

It is true indeed that no virtue and no glory of ancestry can redeem any present from its own unworthiness. It is true indeed that every present must stand or fall by its own record. True is it indeed that no present condition can find atonement for its own unworthiness by pointing to an illustrious past. It is always true that honorable ancestry only aggravates the blame for a degenerate present. But it is also true that it is at all times wise and proper to illuminate and study the virtues of past ages if we purpose in so doing to set them before us as a model to imitate for the future.

In such a spirit and with such a purpose let us trace out today the history that drove stalwart John Peden to leave his home in Ireland, and like a patriarch of old, with his children and childrens' children around him, become part of that splendid band of empire builders who carved out of this primeval wilderness the corner-stone and pediment on which is still being upreared the temple of the best civilization of the nations.

Story of Persecution

The speaker then proceeded to develop the story of the persecution of the Presbyterians in Scotland, the great migration and settlement of Scotch Presbyterians in the northern province of Ireland at the invitation of King James, and the persecutions to which they were there subjected, the ingratitude which was shown by the English kings, parliament and church for their splendid services in building up law, order and industry there; their final disappointment at the continued persecutions and oppression in trade, schools, marriages and religion, and their final abandonment of Ireland in swarms for the American colonies.

Speaking of their final disappointment in the conduct of the House of Hanover, the speaker read this striking passage from James Anthony Froude, the great English historian:

"And now recommenced the Protestant emigration which robbed Ireland of the bravest defenders of English interests and peopled the American seaboard with fresh flights of Puritans. Forty thousand left Ulster on the destruction of the woolen trade. Many more were driven away by the first passing of the test act. The stream had slackened in the hope that the law would be altered. When the prospect was finally closed men of spirit and energy refused to remain in a country where they were held unfit to receive the rights of citizens; and thenceforward, until the spell of tyranny was broken in 1782, annual ship loads of families poured themselves out from Belfast and Londonderry, The resentment which they carried with them continued to burn in their new homes; and in the war of independence England had no fiercer enemies than the grandsons and great grandsons of the Presbyterians who had held Ulster against Tyrconnel."

This reading finished, the speaker resumed his discourse, concluding as follows:

And now, kinsmen, I have finished. Long as the story has been, I have had bare time to scantily outline the record of the Scotch in Ireland and their influence on America. Columns have been written on each several item of their spirit-stirring epic, and how could I hope with my feeble tongue to do justice to such a theme. Take it with you to your homes when we separate, and take with you the proud consciousness that you spring from honorable lives. Teach the story to your children and your children's children, to remotest generations, and let them understand that the splendid heritage they have through John Peden and Peggy McDill entails on them the high duty to be worthy always of its faithful traditions.

No man knows what is in store for us yet. The future is big with uncertain issues. The peace that Ulster won under James was followed by the massacre of '41. Derry and Enniskilen and Boyne water gave no immunity against the eighteenth century. The tranquility of a subdued American wilderness did not exempt them from the high duties of Alamance and Mecklenburg and King's Mountain.

The treaty of Paris had to be paid for by the statesmanship of the Constitution builders, and so today, with religious toleration established and old Fairview the center of a land of tranquil religious history, no man here may know where next it shall please God to try our souls as the souls of our ancestors were tried before us.

Let every man go to his respective home, resolved that when that day comes there shall not be written on our walls the tekel upharsin of an unworthy generation.

At 4.30 o'clock in the afternoon the clan again gathered in the church, a vast conclave, for a few brief words, then, at the command of the Chairman, descended the hillside to the sacred enclosure where stood tall, mysterious in its white drapery, the Peden Monument, on the sunrise corner of the old, brick church, in the very heart of the solemen, last home of many Pedens.

During the singing of the unveiling hymn the veil was dropped by the four dear little girl cousins selected for the honor. These lovely little ones shall go down into Peden history, in letters of living gold, "fair as poet's dreaming" are they; bonny, rosy, bright-eyed, lassies of the House of Alexander: Jane Armstrong, Lucy Allen Peden, Lauribelle Peden, Lulu Templeton.

The monument stood revealed; a marble shaft pointing heavenward, rising sixteen feet from the pedestal, being four feet broad at the base, a pedestal of some feet between base and shaft, on which is engraved in large letters the name

PEDEN.

This on the north side, and above it is the dedication:

In Memoriam.

"This monument is placed by their grateful descendants, gathered from far and near, and who are as the sands by the seashore, and stars of heaven for multitude."

August 17, 1899.

On the eastern or sunrise side:

John and Margaret Peden,

Founders of the House in South Carolina.
1768   1899.
Born in Ireland.
Emigrated to America.
Died in Chester, S. C.

"Lord thou hast been our dwelling place in all generations." Ps. 90:1.
[Said to have been the last audible words of John Peden.]

On the southside and overlooking long rows of Peden tombs, are placed the arms of the adopted State — South Carolina. That grand old commonwealth, whose freedom from tyranny was dearer to John Peden and his seven sons than life itself. All of whom, as well as the three sons-in-law, and numerous grandsons, bore arms in defense during the dark days of the American Revolution. As is fitting, the arms are entwined and surrounded with the thistle of Scotland, the shamrock of Ireland, while in the midst, proud and stately, stands the imperishable palm.

While on the western side, facing the broad iron gates, presented by Capt. D. D. Peden, are inscribed the names of the children of John and Margaret Peden.

SONS OF PEDEN
James. Thomas. John. William. Samuel. Alexander. David.
DAUGHTERS OF PEDEN
Mary (Peden) Alexander. Jane (Peden) Morton-Morrow.
Elizabeth (Peden) Gaston.

These, for want of correct information at the time, are not placed in their proper order, later and authentic information gives the following table:

Mary, born 1732; died ___.	Elizabeth, born 1750; died 1824.
James, born 1734; died 1811.	John, born 1752; died 1810.
Jane, born 1737; died ___.	Samuel, born 1754; died 1835.
Thomas, born 1743; died 1834.	Alexander, born 1756; died 1841.
William, born 1749; died 1817.	David, born 1760; died 1823.

The second day of the reunion was intended to be strictly historical, but owing to the enforced absence of Rev. R. B. Morrow, the time allotted to his theme was courteously given to Rev. S. R. Preston, D. D., of Chicora College, Greenville, S. C, who spoke fluently for Christian Education.

Capt. David D. Peden, acknowledged chief and leader of the clan, in his usual happy, courtly style gave the history of the race.

Address of Capt. D. D. Peden.

My Friends and Kinspeople:

Your committee on addresse has assigned to me the task of writing a history of the Peden family. I doubt not this work could have been done in a much more attractive and interesting manner by a number of those who are present here today. However that may be, I will do the best I can and bespeak your kind indulgence.

Tradition tells us that the name Peden appears in the annals of the old Culdee church, on the western coast of Scotland, located on the little island Iona, and near to Ayrshire, the home of some of the Pedens to this day. The Culdee church is said to have been one of the purest types of the Protestant religion. In fact, it is claimed to be a continuation of the Apostolic church, (See history of "The Culdee Church" by Rev. T.V. Moore, D.D., published by our committee at Richmond, Va.) The Peden referred to is said to have been a shepherd, an honest and honorable calling. What relationship there is between the Shepherd Peden and our ancestors is, of course, conjecture, though we may reasonably suppose we are his descendants.

The first authentic mention of the Peden name, that I have been able to find, after considerable research and correspondence, was during the persecution of the Protestant Christians by the Roman Catholics under the Stuarts in Scotland, a period embracing the year 1680, when "The Declaration and Testimony of the True Presbyterian, Anti-prelatic, Anti-Erastian. persecuted party in Scotland," and known as the "Sanquhar Declaration," was adopted. (See Traditions of the Covenanters, next page.)

The Pedens were an Ayeshire family, in the west of Scotland, (where to this day it is still quite a common name). In the middle of the sixteenth century a number of the Peden families went to the North of Ireland to escape the persecution then raging in Scotland. About the beginning of the seventeenth century some of these families and their descendants returned to their native land, some remained in the land of their adoption, while our ancestors sought civil and religious freedom in the wilds of the American forests.

I will leave this branch of the subject for the moment, returning to the religious persecution of Scotland. Rev. Alexander Peden, sometimes called "Peden the Prophet," bore a conspicuous part during the times referred to in 1680, in encouraging the Protestants to be steadfast in adhering to their faith and doctrine, many of whom, in order to do so, had to endure many hardships and deprivations, even martyrdom. During the reign of the Stuarts the persecution was both cruel and relentless, under the inhumane Claverhouse and his minions. In order to worship God according to the dictates of their consciences, they had to meet oftentimes at night or in the dense forests and on the wild mountain sides. Their ministers, especially, were hunted like wild beast and had to take refuge in caves, caverns and the moss hags and mountains.

The following is taken from his "Life and Death," published in Belfast, in 1790:

"Alexander Peden, late minister of the gospel at Glenluce, in Galloway, who died the 28th of January, 1686, being about sixty years of age. He was born in the parish of Sorn, in 1626, in the Sheriffdom of Ayr. After that he passed his courses in college, he was employed for some time to be school master, precentor and session clerk to Mr. John Guthrie, minister of the gospel at Tarboltown. He had no family and was never married. He was a man of sincere and deep piety; he was a brave man and possessed the courage of his convictions in a very remarkable degree."

Traditions of the Covenanters

I will read some extracts from a little volume, the title of which is "Traditions of the Covenanters," by the Rev. Robert Simpson, Sanquhar, Scotland:

"About the commencement of the persecution in Scotland, nearly three hundred and fifty ministers were ejected from their churches, in the severity of winter, and driven with their families, to seek shelter among the peasants.

"The desolation and distress of many a family, after the standard of the gospel was reared in the field, were unutterable. The tender hearted wife knew not how it fared with her husband traversing the waste, or lodged in the cold, damp cave; and many a disconsolate hour did she spend in weeping over her helpless children, who had apparently nothing before them but starvation. The affectionate husband, far from his dearly cherished home, was full of the bitter remembrance of his beloved family, and picturing to himself their many wants which he could not now relieve, and their many sorrows which he could not soothe, and the many insults from which he could not defend them. But, notwithstanding all this, they had peace; for God was with them. And though their hearts sometimes misgave them, yet, through the grace of Him with whose cause they were identified, their faith recovered its proper tone, and their despondency vanished.

"One of the most renowned of those worthies who persisted in preaching the gospel in the wilds of his native land, at the constant hazard of his life, was the venerable Alexander Peden, whose history is familiar in almost every cottage in Scotland. Every incident of any importance in the life of this good man has already been collected, so that scarcely anything new can now be added. Still there is to be found a stray anecdote of him here and there in the remote parts of the country, and which, for his sake, may be deemed worthy of record. Few persons possessed a more saintly character than did this man of God. He was full of faith and of the Holy Ghost. Entirely devoted to his Master's service, he counted not his own life dear unto him, that he might maintain the cause of truth in the face of the abounding iniquity of a degenerate age. His solitary wanderings, his destitutions, his painful perseverance in preaching the gospel, the peril in which he lived, his prayerful spirit, and the homeliness of his manners, greatly endeared him to the people among whom he sojourned. He had no home, and therefore he spent much of his time in the fields. The caves by the mountain stream, the dense hazel wood in the deep glens, the feathery brackens on the hill, the green corn when it was tall enough to screen him from observation, afforded him by turns, when necessary, a retreat from his pursuers, and a place for communing with his God.

"On one such occasion he had fixed his eye on a cottage far off in the waste in which lived a godly man with whom he had frequent intercourse, and there being nothing within view calculated to excite alarm he resolved to pay his friend a visit. With his staff in his hand he wended his way to the low grounds to gain the track which led to the house. He reached it in safety, was hospitably entertained by the kind landlord, and spent the time with the household in pious conversation and prayer till sunset. Not daring to remain all night, he left them to return to his dreary cave. As he was trudging along the soft foot path and suspecting no harm, all at once several moss troopers appeared coming over the bent and advancing directly upon him. He fled across the moor, and when about to pass the torrent that issues from Glendyne, he perceived a cavity underneath its bank that had been scooped out by the running stream into which he instinctively crept and stretching himself at full length lay hidden beneath the grassy coverlet waiting the result. In a short time the dragoons came up, and having followed close in his track, reached the brook at the very spot where he was ensconced. As the heavy horses came thundering over the smooth turf, on the edge of the little rivulet, the foot of one of them sank quite through the hollow covering under which the object of their pursuit lay. The hoof of the animal grazed his head, and pressed his bonnet deep into the soft clay at his pillow, and left him entirely uninjured. His persecutors having no suspicion that the poor fugitive was so near them, crossed the stream with all speed, and bounded away in quest of him whom God had thus hidden as in his pavilion, and in the secret of his tabernacle. A man like Peden, who read the hand of God in everything, could not fail to see and to acknowledge that Divine goodness, which was so eminently displayed in this instance; and we may easily conceive with what feelings he would return to his retreat in the wood, and with what cordiality he would send up the voice of thanksgiving and praise to the God of his life.

A Memorable Deliverance

"It is recorded in the Scots Worthies that he was favored with a memorable deliverance from the enemy who were pursuing him and a small company with him somewhere in Galloway after he came out of Ireland. When their hope of escape was almost cut off, he knelt down among the heather and prayed, Twine them about the hill. Lord, and cast the lap of Thy cloak over old Sandy and these poor things and we will keep it in remembrance and tell it to the commendation of Thy goodness, pity and compassion what Thou didst for us at such a time.' Thus he prayed, and his supplication was recorded in heaven, for he had no sooner risen from his knees than dense volumes of snow-white mist came rolling down from the summit of the mountains and shrouded them from the sight of their pursuers who, like the men of Sodom when they were smitten with blindness, could not grope their way after them."

I quote again from the same book:

"This occasion is related by old Patrick Walker in the following words: 'After this, in Auchengrouch muirs in Nithsdale, Capt. John Mathison and others being with him, they were alarmed with a report that the enemy were coming fast upon him, so they designed to put him in some hole, and cover him with heather. But not being able to run hard by reason of age, he desired them to forbear a little until he prayed, when he said: 'Lord, we are ever needing at Thy hand, and if we had not Thy command to call upon Thee in the day of our trouble, and Thy promise of answering us in the day of our distress, we wot not what would become of us; if Thou hast any more work for us in Thy world, allow us the lap of Thy cloak this day again: and if this be the day of our going off the stage, let us walk honestly off, and comfortably through, and our souls will sing forth Thy praises to eternity for what thou hast done to us, and for us.' When ended he ran alone a little, and came quickly back, saying, 'Lads, the bitterest of this blast is over; we will be no more troubled with them this day.' Foot and horse came the length of Andrew Clark's, in Auchengrouch, where they were covered with a dark mist. When they saw it they roared like fleshly devils, as they were crying out:

'There's the confounded mist again! we cannot get these execrable whigs pursued for it.'"

Banished to America

I could continue to quote many other interesting incidents, but I must not consume too much of your time, as some of you, at least, are perhaps familiar with them. I will mention one incident taken from the "Life and Death of Alexander Peden."

During the time of the persecution, he and a number of covenanters were captured by the enemy and were sentenced to banishment to the English plantations in America. "When brought from the Bass (prison) to Edinburgh and sentence passed on him and sixty others, in December, 1678, to go to America, never to be seen in Scotland again under the pain of death. He several times said: 'The ship was not yet built that would take him or these prisoners to Virginia, or any other of the English plantations in America.' When they were on ship board, in the road of Leith, there was a report that their enemies were to send down Thumbikins to keep them from rebelling. At the report of this they were greatly discouraged; he came above deck and said, 'Why are you so cast down? You need not fear there will be Thumbikins nor Bootekins come here; lift up your hearts and heads, for the day of your redemption draweth near; if we are once in London we will all be set at liberty.' This remarkable prophecy was literally fulfilled, for when the skipper who was to take them from London to Virginia came to see them, they being represented to him as thieves, robbers and evil doers, he refused to take them aboard. When he found they were grave Christian men, banished for Presbyterian principles, he said, 'I will sail the sea with none such.' In this confusion, that one skipper would not receive them and the other would keep them no longer, it being expensive to maintain them, they were all set at liberty. Both skippers, it is said, 'got compliments in London for releasing them.' They went to Ireland and then returned to Scotland, in face of the threat that, if he did he would be punished with death, thus evincing courage and devotion to duty that cannot be surpassed. Many other thrilling and even marvelous incidents could be given regarding this remarkable man."

I must forbear, however, and return to our immediate ancestors. You have already been told that some of the Pedens came from Ireland to America to seek religious and civil liberty. Among that number were our ancestors, John Peden and wife, Margaret. We are assembled here today to pay homage to their memory. We have representatives here from the Pacific to the Atlantic oceans, all the way they have come, from the golden shores of California, on the Pacific, to dear old South Carolina, whose shores are washed by the Atlantic, and which was the home of these aged saints. Their ashes lie buried in her bosom. I suppose there is scarcely a State or Territory in the United States that does not contain descendants of John Peden.

Settled In Pennsylvania

Tradition tells us that he settled in Pennsylvania, probably Chester County. Our ancestors, having several sons who had preceded them to this country, and settled in what in now Spartanburg County, S.C., they and other members of their families came and settled in the same place, not far from old Nazareth Presbyterian church, about the year 1768. (See Dr. Howe's "History of Presbyterianism in South Carolina," but more particularly the centennial celebration of old Fairview church, in September, 1886; specially the address of our kinsman. Rev. M. C. Britt, and an historical sketch by Mr. Savage.)

It is sad to relate, that these venerable people, with their seven sons, three sons-in-law and their families, were not granted the privilege of enjoying the civil liberties they had traveled so far and risked so much to obtain. They had scarcely settled in their new homes before the Revolutionary War was begun. We are told that all of the sons and sons-in-law were Revolutionary soldiers. I have heard also that the venerable John was himself a soldier. I have some doubt on this point as tradition tells us that by reason of the incursions of the Indians and Tories, the old people, with the younger members of their families, refugeed to Chester County, near the old "Catholic Presbyterian Church," for safety. At the close of the war in 1783, we are told also, on account of their age, they remained in Chester County after the close of the Revolutionary War, where they died and were buried near the old "Catholic Presbyterian Church." The others returned and settled near this church, with the exception of the second son, Thomas, who returned to and settled near the old homestead in Spartanburg. Some years afterwards, one son, probably Samuel, and the second daughter, Jane, with her second husband, Mr. Samuel Morrow, moved to Alabama. All of the ten children, except Elizabeth, who married Wm. Gaston, raised large families. The descendants of the Pedens, Alexanders, Mortons and Morrows are almost as the sands by the sea shore in numbers.

Nearly All Were Farmers

For the most part, the descendants are, as were their honored fathers before them, engaged in agricultural pursuits. It is said that when our ancestors (to honor whose memory we have erected the handsome monument in the old cemetery near by where the ashes of so many of our loved ones are buried) left the coast of Ireland to seek their homes in this country that the father of us all set his face steadfastly towards the west, refusing all entreaties to take a parting look at the Emerald Isle as it faded out of view. On the contrary, our mother, Margaret, who is said to have been a beautiful as well as a good woman, shed tears as the isle, which had been her home, sank out of sight behind the eastern horizon. The passage over the broad Atlantic was a long and tiresome one at best in those days, and their voyage was specially disagreeable on account of severe weather and lasted many days.

Our ancestors were cabin passengers on this memorable trip from the Emerald Isle to the then comparatively new world, and they fared of course much better than did the steerage passengers on this long and stormy passage.

I exceedingly regret that both time and lack of information prevent me from giving somewhat in detail, at least, brief sketches of each of the ten children of our venerable and venerated ancestors. Their record, however, is a glorious one — one in which we can take a pardonable pride. First, and best of all, they were God-fearing men and women; all strong adherents to the "true Presbyterian, Anti-Prelatic, Anti-Erastian, persecuted party of Scotland," of which "Peden the Prophet" was such a determined and fearless advocate and to which church, I presume, at least nine-tenths of their descendants are still adherents.

The Other Tenth

The above remarks, I wish it distinctly understood, means no reflection to the remaining tenth. I know of my personal knowledge of some of our kinspeople who have united with other Protestant churches in the communities to which they had moved. Others, again, married into families of other denominations and in that way became separated from us. Others, perhaps, joined other churches through choice. Just so long as they are Christians and are fighting under the banner of the Cross, we are all brethren, friends, kinsmen, and are all most affectionately and cordially welcome to this love-feast of relatives. If there is a family in this great and glorious country of ours (the United States of America) who can honestly and truly feel a glow of pride in the part taken by their Revolutionary sires in the memorable struggle that won our independence from England, that family is the Peden family. "There are others," but we yield the palm to none unless they can successfully prove their claim.

Seven sons and three sons-in-law, and a number of grandsons, and probably the old father, from one family, is a record not easily beaten. Several of the sons and grandsons, and perhaps sons-in-law, held commissions.

A Revolutionary Hero

My grandfather, David Peden, was the youngest of the ten children, and, no doubt, a private soldier. There is not a particle of doubt that he took an active part in the revolution that brought independence to the United States. I have here the positive proof, it being a grant from the State of South Carolina for nine hundred acres of land, signed by Governor Charles Pinckney, 20th of February, 1792. Rabun Creek, the head-waters of which you cross coming from Fountain Inn here, runs through the property, on which stream one of the first grist and saw mills erected in this part of the country was built by him. He and his two wives are buried in the cemetery near the monument erected in honor of his father and mother, John and Margaret Peden. He was the father of thirteen children, my father, Rev. Andrew G. Peden, being next to the youngest. For a more detailed history of the ten children of John and Margaret Peden, and their descendants, we will have to look to our historian, who will take up Peden History, etc.

More Pedens and Padens

Before concluding I wish to say that there are a number of Pedens and Padens in the United States who are doubtless related to us, but who are not descendants of our ancestors. John and Margaret Peden. There are Pedens and Padens in Pennsylvania, Virginia, Kentucky, North Carolina, Texas and perhaps other States, whose ancestors came direct from Scotland. I have in my possession a copy of a singular letter written by Dr. Alexander D. Peden, giving a graphic and tragic account of the great flood on the coast of Texas about twenty-four years ago.

An Entire City Engulfed

Indianola at that time was a prosperous seaport town; in fact, was a rival of the city of Galveston in point of commerce, trade, etc. The city was literally swept from the face of the earth — the waters from the Gulf were driven by the fury of the winds many miles inland. Dr. Peden's family was on his ranch (or farm) some distance from the city. His wife and children were drowned, except three children. One son was assistant keeper of the lighthouse, one daughter was absent (at school, perhaps), one small son took refuge in a cedar tree which was about to be submerged. Seeing his pet pony swimming by, he called to him. The pony turned and came immediately under the tree and the boy dropped on his back, and was thus miraculously carried to a place of safety. Dr. Peden was serving on a jury some distance from home, consequently was unable to aid his family in making their escape. Speaking of himself, Dr. Peden says he "sprang from an ancient family of Pedens in Scotia's isle."

Further says he was "the son of Alexeander Peden, deceased, merchant of Wilmington, N. C. He, in turn, was son of Mingo Peden, merchant, in Irvine, Ayrshire, Scotland," and adds that he had been at the grave of Alexander Peden, "the prophet in Scotland. A thorn bush grows at his head, as he prophesied." Archie Hoye, Chester, S. C, says the grave is at Cumnock, Scotland, and that two thorn bushes grow at the head of his grave, one bearing a white and the other a red bloom. Mr. Hoye's statement is borne out by books from Scotland. I could continue to give various interesting incidents, sketches, etc., but time admonishes me that I must give way to those whose addresses will be much more interesting than this historical sketch.

A Plea for Education

Before taking my seat, however, I want to beg, insist and entreat one and all to pay more attention to the education of your children. Out of our vast relationship, running into the thousands, we should and ought to have representatives in all the branches and walks of life. We should aspire to have a president, or, better, presidents of the United States, presidents of colleges, universities, governors of States, United States Senators, members of congress and legislatures, men eminent in theology, law and physics, science, arts, mechanics and in other walks of life.

The farmer's life is an honorable one, none more so, but we must not be content to be all farmers. Recognize talent in your children and encourage them to develop it; for heaven's sake, don't suppress it; don't discourage them by belittling their efforts. I haven't the least doubt but there have been Pedens and descendants by other names, if they had been encouraged and educated, could and would have occupied the positions mentioned above. They simply lacked the opportunity, and the lack of a good education barred them from the opportunity.

In conclusion, I want to mention a little incident that occurred within a short distance of this spot, quite recently. I was invited to visit one of our kinsmen. The weather was intensely hot; we were sitting in the yard in the shade of the trees. The father directed his little son to step across the road and see if the peas sown in the corn were coming up. The little fellow promptly obeyed. Returning, he plucked a "may pop" about the size of a large hen's egg. He reported "the peas are coming up all right, sir." He then commenced cutting into the "may pop," and in a few moments had fashioned it into a perfectly proportioned basket. He held it up by the delicate handle and looked it over. He then began work on the outer sides of the basket. I was watching him, and the thought occurred to me that, boy-like, he was going to cut it to pieces, but he didn't; instead he was ornamenting it, by tracing a vine and leaves into the green rind of the "may pop." I then asked to see it. He seemed surprised that I should notice what he regarded so simple a thing. I remarked to the father: "There is talent in that boy, you ought to encourage him."

A Young Genius

The father then told the boy to bring and show me the "scraper" he had made. He soon returned with the front wheels of his toy wagon, an iron rod, a piece of chain, a piece of discarded steel, that had been used by the convicts in working the roads. With this material he had constructed a miniature road machine that does beautiful work. The little fellow showed me a little sidewalk or roadway he had built at right angles to the road and adjoining the front yard. The work is there to show for itself. In passing the home of Mr. James Peden going from here, look on the far side of the yard, and you will see as perfect a little road bed as Mr. Sanders, manager of the convicts, can construct. The lesson is: Encourage and educate the boys and girls.

Upon the conclusion of his address Capt. Peden introduced little Lee Peden to the members of the, family, and the little fellow was given an ovation by his kinspeople.

The great reunion of 1899 is now of the past. Many have crossed over beyond our ken, in the few years that have intervened, some sleep in faraway tombs, some rest under the shade of the trees at Fairview, under the shadow of the monument they helped to rear, while the march "Homeward" and Heavenward!" is steady — there are equally, or more, tiny crafts launched on the turbulent ocean of this life, to fill up the vacant places, and advance with the progressive spirit of the New Century.

Minutes of the Peden-Alexander-Morton-Morrow Reunion

Fairview, S. C, August 15th, 1899.

The reunion exercises of Peden, Alexander, Morton, Morrow was called to order at 10 o'clock a. m., by Hon. Hooper Alexander, of Atlanta, Ga., who nominated Hon. Jno. R. Harrison as chairman. He was unanimously elected and made a capital address of welcome; so we felt at once so perfectly at home that "it was good to be there." The meeting began with grand Old Hundred to the long meter doxology; then a prayer by the pastor of Fairview church. Rev. H. W. Burwell, (who, while not of the Peden race, has been closely identified with its interests). After which the election of a permanent chairman was in order, resulting in the unanimous election of Hon. John R. Harrison, of Fairview, South Carolina.

Then the following vice-presidents were elected from the different States represented:

1st — Rev. R. B. Morrow, Demopolis, Ala.
2d— J. W. T. Peden, Van Vleet, Miss.
3d — Capt. D. D. Peden, Houston, Tex.
4th— M. S. Paden, Woodstock, Ga.
5th — Louis Salmons, Valley Center, Cal.
6th — Judge J. Wister Stewart, Fairview, S.C.

[None of the other States having representatives present, the election of vice-presidents was discontinued.]

On motion, W. M. Stenhouse, of Sterling, S. C, was elected Secretary, and Eleanor M. Hewell, of Greenville, S. C, was elected as Assistant Secretary and Historian.

After the election of permanent officers Dr. H. B. Stewart, of Fairview, S. C, presented to the Reunion a beautiful gavel, made from a root of a black walnut tree taken from "Alexander Peden's place." The venerable tree was planted by him, over a century ago, soon after he located on his land.

Dr. Stewart is the present owner and a great-great-grandson-in-law of Alexander Peden.

His words were very appropriate in presenting the gavel, finding an echo in all our hearts, while he held the full attention of the large gathering. A well chosen hymn to Autumn followed, after which the Reunion had the pleasure of hearing Hon. Hooper Alexander, of Atlanta, Ga. Subject: "The Scotch-Irish and their Achievements." [Hon. Hooper is a typical Alexander. A man who has given the clan every reason to be extremely proud of his achievements in the legal profession.] His address was received with enthusiastic applause, and followed by grand, inspiring old Coronation, "All hail the power of Jesus name."

The Rev. R. B. Morrow was unavoidably absent, therefore the Reunion was deprived of the pleasure of seeing and hearing this gifted son of the Church. His subject, "The Pedens and Presbyterianism" was omitted and the time allotted used otherwise.

The closing hymn was sung to Protection. The Chairman then announced that at the afternoon session we would unveil the Monument, and as soon as the unveiling took place the afternoon session would be declared adjourned. Meeting then adjourned with benediction by pastor.

(Signed.)   W. M. Stenhouse,
Secretary.

Afternoon Session

Meeting called to order by Chairman, Hon. Jno. R. Harrison. After singing the Chairman announced that the Reunion would repair to the church yard to witness and take part in the unveiling of the Peden Monument.

After the unveiling the meeting is adjourned until 9 A.M. tomorrow.

(Signed.)   W. M. Stenhouse,
Secretary.

Second Day— Morning Session

Fairview, S. C, August 16th, 1899.

Chairman Hon. Jno. R. Harrison called the Reunion to order at 9 o'clock a. m. Meeting opened with prayer, after which we sung the old familiar hymn, 117, to the tune Fount.

The Chairman then introduced Capt. D. D. Peden, of Houston, Texas, to whom the Reunion is very much indebted for its success. Capt. Peden was listened to with great interest and pleasure while he traced the Peden family back to an early century.

The choir then rendered very beautifully the hymn composed for the occasion by Rev. H. W. Burwell, "Singing on the Old Church Ground."

Dr. S. R. Preston, President of Chicora College, Greenville, S. C, then gave a very able talk on Christian Education, filling the space allotted to the venerable Judge John R. Alexander, of Thomasville, Ga., who was debarred from coming to the Reunion by the infirmities of age, so his "Reminiscences" were omitted, to our keen regret.

Reports were called for and Adam S. Peden, treasurer, read his, which was quite satisfactory, therefore unanimously adopted by the Reunion.

Meeting then adjourned to meet at 3.45 P.M. Benediction pronounced by Rev. S. R. Preston, D. D., of Chicora College, Greenville, S.C.

(Signed.)   W. M. Stenhouse,
Secretary.

Afternoon Session

Meeting called to order by the Chairman, Hon. Jno. R. Harrison, and opened with singing of the grand tune of "Loving Kindness," and it was the pleasure of all to hear addresses by the following: J. Ripley Westmoreland, of Woodruff, S. C, and Rev. John C. Bailey, Jr., of Summerton, S.C. [These two gifted young men represent the present generation, and give bright promise of future usefulness in their professions.] They were followed briefly by Col. J. A. Hoyt (editor of the oldest newspaper in Greenville County, "The Mountaineer," which has been in existence for nearly a century, under several names. He is also of Scotch-Irish descent, therefore in strong sympathy with the Peden race).

Dr. H.B. Stewart made a feeling response to his call and paid a loving tribute to the memory of one of the best beloved pastors of old Fairview church, who in life and death was a faithful shepherd of the flock, Rev. Clark B. Stewart.

Adam S. Peden then read, by request, a letter from the venerable and beloved Mark S. Peden, of Woodstock, Ga., stating that his advanced age only kept him away, and requested to be kindly remembered to all present.

The closing address, which was a grand burst of oratory, was given by Hon. Hooper Alexander, after which the parting hymn, composed by Rev. H. W. Burwell, was sung standing. The Chairman announced the grand Reunion of Peden Alexander, Morton, Morrow, adjourned to meet another day.

Rev. H. W. Burwell pronounced the last benediction.

(Signed.)   W. M. Stenhouse,
Secretary.

These minutes are inserted as part of the Reunion of 1899. They will be corrected and adopted by the next Reunion of Peden, Alexander, Morton, Morrow.

Eleanor M. Hewell,
Assistant Sec. and Clan Historian.

List of Contributors to the Peden Monument - Fairview, South Carolina, 1899.

Capt. D. D. Peden, Houston, Texas $144 00
E. A. Peden, Houston, Texas 50 00
D. D. Peden, Jr., Houston, Texas 37 50
Allen Vernon Peden, Houston, Texas 12 50
John M. Peden, Hubbard, Texas 5 00
J. W. T. Peden, Van Vleet, Miss 5 00
M. W. Fowler, Fountain Inn, S.C. 50
J. C. Bailey, Greenville, S.C. 5 00
Mrs. Harriet Peden, Westminster, S.C. 3 00
Mrs. L. M. Peden, Westminster, S.C. 50
Mrs. Bettie Wasson, Westminster, S.C. 50
Mrs. Corrie Anderson, Westminster, S.C. 1 00
Mrs. E. M. Peden, Fairview, S.C. 5 00
Miss I. H. Stenhouse, Fairview, S.C. 5 00
T. W. Peden, Troy, Miss 1 00
J. T. Peden, Graycourt, S.C. 5 00
J. F. Peden, Fairview, S.C. 5 00
Mrs. A. G. Peden, Pedenville, Ga 1 00
Mrs. Dora Sullivan, Pedenville, Ga 1 00
Hon. Hooper Alexander, Atlanta, Ga 10 00
L. H. Templeton, Fairview, S.C. 2 00
Mrs. Jane Terry, Lickville, S.C. 1 00
Rev. Thos. P. Pressly, Miss Belle Pressly, Troy, Tenn 5 00
Mrs. B. E. Babb, Babbtown, S.C. 1 00
Miss Mag Thompson, Babbtown, S.C. 1 00
Mrs. M. A. Salmons, California 1 00
J. W. Peden, Springtown, Texas 1 00
Mrs. W. A. Haynes, Spartanburg, S.C. 1 00
Mrs. M. E. Putnam, Fountain Inn, S.C. 1 00
Mrs. Emma Alexander, California 1 00
Thos. Peden, Bascomville, S.C. 3 00
Rev. J. C. Bailey, Summerton, S.C. 1 00
Mrs. W. F. Pearson, Due West, S.C. 1 00
Mrs. Mary Stewart, Atlanta, Ga 1 00
Claud S. McNeely, Atlanta, Ga 50
H. L. Peden, Spartanburg, S.C. 1 50
Jas. R. Peden, Kansas City, Mo 5 00
Mrs. Janet P. Stenhouse, Sterling, S.C. 5 00
H. W. Cely, Greenville, S.C. 1 00
Mrs. J. J. Vernon, Wellford, S.C. 1 00
J. R. Westmoreland, Woodruff, S.C. 1 00
W. B. Westmoreland, Woodruff, S.C. 1 00
Jno. R. Harsison, Fairview. S.C. 5 00
Miss Jane Harrison, Fairview, S.C. 50
Miss Lillie Harrison, Fairview, S.C. 50
Angus McQueen Martin, Laurens, S.C. 50
Mrs. Mary H. Martin, Laurens, S.C. 50
Mary H. Martin, Laurens, S.C. 25
John H. Martin, Laurens, S.C. 25
M. L. Thompson, Fairview, S.C. 1 00
Drayton Babb, Fairview, S.C. 50
J. P. Simpson, Fairview, S.C. 50
Mrs. D. M. Peden, Fairview, S.C. 5 00
W. P. Fowler, Fairview, S.C. 1 00
Mrs. Jane McDowell, Fairview, S.C. 2 00
Herbert Hammond, Greenville, S.C. 1 00
Mrs. M. M. Thompson, Fairview, S.C. 25
M. P. Nash, Fairview, S.C. 1 50
Mrs. Mary McKittrick, Fairview, S. C 1 00
W. H. Britt, Fairview, S.C. 1 00
J. M. Peden, Fairview, S.C. 1 00
J. T. Woods, Fairview, S.C. 25
J. S. Peden, Fairview, S.C. 5 00
G. C. Anderson, Fairview, S.C. 50
Walter Peden, Fairview, S.C. 25
Dr. H. B. Stewart, Fairview, S.C. 5 00
W. C. Harrison, Fairview, S.C. 50
W. S. Peden, Fairview, S.C. 5 00
A. S. Peden, Mrs, N.S. Peden, Bessie B. Peden, Annie S. Peden, J. C. Peden, Fountain Inn, S.C. 18 00
J. T. Fowler, Fountain Inn, S.C. 50
Nellie West, Greenville, S.C. 50
Carrie Peden, Graycourt, S.C. 50
Lours Peden, Graycourt, S.C. 50
Annie West, Greenville, S.C. 25
Mrs. Laura West, Greenville, S.C. 2 00
Miss Ethel West, Greenville, S.C. 1 00
Eugene Peden, Graycourt, S.C. 25
Lucy Peden, Graycourt, S.C. 25
D. D. Peden, Graycourt, S.C. 2 00
C. L. Peden, Graycourt, S.C. 1 00
Peden Anderson, Westminster, S.C. 50
Geneva West, Fountain Inn, S.C. 25
Eleanor West, Fountain Inn, S.C. 25
Mabel West, Fountain Inn, S.C. 25
Robbie West, Fountain Inn, S.C. 25
Wm. West, Fountain Inn, S.C. 25
Mrs. J. R. West, Fountain Inn, S.C. 1 00

Mrs. Dr. Westmoreland, Woodruff, S.C. 1 00
J. Alarvin Peden, Fairview, S.C. 25
Calvin Peden, Fairview, S.C. 25
Maggie Peden, Fairview, S.C. 25
Lee Ross Peden, Fairview, S.C. 25
J. E. Peden, Fairview, S.C. 25
Jno. McDowell Peden, Fairview, S.C. 25
Jas. Stunt, Fountain Inn, S.C. 50
Crayton Stunt, Clifton, S.C. 1 00
J. W. Stunt, Fairview, S.C. 1 00
J. W. Anderson, Fairview, S.C. 1 00
A. L. Peden, Fairview, S.C. 1 00
Jno. S. Hammond, Welford, S.C. 1 00
Mrs. Nancy Hammond, Welford, S.C. 1 00
Mrs. Mary Woodruff, Welford, S.C. 1 00

Register Peden-Alexander-Morton-Morrow Reunion of 1899.

*(Those marked with an * died since the reunion.)*

Alexander, Hon. Hooper Atlanta, Ga.
Alexander, Claude L. Bold. Spring, Ga.
Anderson, W.P. Westminster, S.C.
Anderson, Corrie M. Westminster, S.C.
Anderson, Wm. P., Jr Westminster, S. C
Anderson, Frank P. Westminster, S.C.
Anderson, T. Peden Westminster, S.C.
Anderson, J.L. Walnut Springs, Texas
Anderson, Ora B. Walnut Springs, Texas
Anderson, Marvin C. Walnut Springs, Texas
Anderson, Lang Walnut Springs, Texas
Anderson, Forrest Walnut Springs, Texas
Anderson, G.C. Fairview, S.C.
Anderson, Hattie M. Fairview, S.C.
Armstrong, Mrs. E.A. Simpsonville, S.C.
Armstrong, Jane Simpsonville, S.C.
Armstrong, Ernest Simpsonville, S.C.
Armstrong, Charles Simpsonville, S.C.
Armstrong, John Simpsonville, S.C.
Aughey, Rev. Jno. H. Leavenworth, Kan.
Aughey, Mary P. Leavenworth, Kan.
Babb, Mrs. Elizabeth Babbtown, S.C.
Babb, J. Drayton Babbtown, S.C.
Babb, Mrs. Mary T. Babbtown, S.C.
Baker, A.R.W. Springtown, Texas
Baker, Mrs. Nancy Springtown, Texas
Baker, Beulah M. Springtown, Texas
Baker, Samuel R. Springtown, Texas
Baker, John T. Springtown, Texas
Baker, Wm. P. Springtown, Texas
Baker, Jessie J. Springtown, Texas
Bailey, Rev. J.C. Summerton, S.C.
Boyd, H.Y. Fountain Inn, S.C.
Boyd, Mrs. Eula L. Fountain Inn S.C.
Boyd, Fowler Fountain Inn, S.C.
Boyd, Pearl Fountain Inn, S.C.
Boyd, Ivy Fountain Inn, S.C.
Britt, Rev. M.C. Sparta, Ga.
* Britt, Mrs. Lizzie Sparta, Ga.
Britt, Mrs. M.E. Sparta, Ga.
Britt, W. Hewell Sparta, Ga.
Brooks, Mrs. Alice Simpsonville, S.C.
Brooks, Bertie Lee Simpsonville, S.C.
Brooks, Marie Simpsonville, S.C.
Brooks, Gertrude Simpsonville, S.C.
Brooks, C. Peden Simpsonville, S.C.
Bugbee, Mrs. Lou Paris Texas
Carson, Mrs. J.M. Carnesville, Ga.
Clark, Mrs. Marion Atlanta, Ga
Cely, H.W. Greenville, S.C.
Cely, T. Lake New York
Cely, W. H Greenville, S.C.
Cely, Mrs. Alice Greenville, S.C.
Cely Eleanor Greenville, S.C.
Cely, W.R. Greenville, S.C.
* Cleveland, Vannoy. Marietta, Ga.
* Ferguson, Mrs. A.K. Chariton, Iowa
Ferguson, Mary Chariton, Iowa
Fowler, J.T. Martins Mills, Texas
fowler, Mrs. Serena Martins Alills, Texas
Fowler, R. Elizabeth Martins Mills, Texas
Fowler, F. Franklin Martins Mills, Texas
Fowler, Robert W. Martins Mills, Texas
Fowler, Moses M. Martins Mills, Texas
Fowler, Nancy R. Martins Mills Texas
Fowler, Jno. T. Martins Mills, Texas
Fowler, Harris L. Martins Mills, Texas
Fowler, Albert T. Martins Mills, Texas
Fowler, F.F. Martins Mills, Texas
Fowler, Mrs. Delpha Pass Martins Mills, Texas
Fowler, M. White Simpsonville, S.C.
Fowler, Mrs. O.A. Simpsonville, S.C.

* Fowler, D.S. Simpsonville, S.C.
Fowler, Mrs. Eliza Simpsonville, S.C.
Fowler, Hattie Simpsonville, S.C.
Fowler, Mattie Simpsonville, S.C.
Fowler, Thomas Simpsonville, S.C.
Fowler, William Simpsonville, S.C.
Fowler, Effie Simpsonville, S.C.
Fowler, David Simpsonville, S.C.
Fowler, Arthur Simpsonville, S.C.
Fowler, Stewart Simpsonville, S.C.
Fowler, Grady Simpsonville, S.C.
Fowler, W.P. Crescent, S.C.
Fowler, Mrs. W.P. Crescent, S.C.
Fowler, Moses T. Crescent, S.C.
Fowler, Grover P. Crescent, S.C.
Fowler, Wells Crescent, S.C.
Fowler, Annie Crescent, S.C.
Fowler, W.R. Crescent, S.C.
Fowler, Mrs. Dora T. Crescent, S.C.
Fowler, Ethel May Crescent, S.C.
Fowler, Robert S. Crescent, S.C.
Fowler, Wm. H. Simpsonville, S.C.
Fowler, Mrs. W. H Simpsonville, S.C.
Fowler, S.A. Fairview, S.C.
Fowler, W.A. Fairview, S.C.
Garraux, Charles Fairview, S.C.
Garraux, Mrs. Belle Fairview, S.C.
Garraux, Cora Fairview, S.C.
Garraux, Annie Fairview, S.C.
Garraux, Belle Fairview, S.C.
Garrett, F.L. Commerce, Texas
Garrett, Mrs. Mary J. Commerce, Texas
Garrett, Henry H. Commerce, Texas
Garrett, Waddy L. Commerce, Texas
Garrett, Rose E. Commerce, Texas
Garrett, Nancy B. Commerce, Texas
Garrett, Florence T. Commerce, Texas
Garrett, W.P. Fountain Inn, S.C.
Garrett, Mrs. Hattie Fountain Inn, S.C.
Garrett, Crayton Fountain Inn, S.C.
Garrett, Annie R. Fountain Inn, S. C
Gaston, Amzi W. Zebs, S.C.
Gaston, J.W. Zebs, S.C.
Gaston, R.W. Zebs, S.C.
Gaston, A.C. Zebs, S.C.
Gaston, J.S. Zebs, S.C.
Gaston, T.C. Zebs, S.C.
Gaston, N.R. Zebs, S.C.
Gaston, D.H. Zebs, S.C.

Gaston, F.H. Zebs, S.C.
Gaston, M.E. Zebs, S.C.
Goldsmith, Mrs. M.E. Cedrus. S.C.
Goldsmith, Helen Cedrus, S.C.
Goldsmith, Sarah Cedrus, S.C.
Goldsmith, Thomas Cedrus, S.C.
Goldsmith, Edwin Cedrus, S.C.
Hammond, Jno. S. Welford, S.C.
Hammond, Mrs. Nancy T. Welford, S.C.
Hammond, Adelia C. Welford. S.C.
Hammond, T. Herbert Greenville, S.C.
Hammond, Mrs. T.H. Greenville, S.C.
Hammond, A.P. Greenville, S.C.
* Hammond, Ethel P Greenville, S.C.
Hammond, Leila Greenville, S.C.
Hammond, Nannie Greenville, S.C.
Hammond, Ernestine Greenville, S.C.
Hammond, Edna Greenville, S.C.
Hammond, Mary Ella Greenville, S.C.
Hammond, Jno. H. Greenville, S.C.
Hammond, Margie Belle Greenville, S.C.
Hammond, Thos. Alexander Greenville, S.C.
* Hammond, S.G. Spartanburg, S.C.
Hammond, Mrs. M.E. Spartanburg, S.C.
Hammond, J. Oeland Spartanburg, S.C.
Hammond, E.B. Spartanburg S.C.
Hammond, Samuel R. Spartanburg, S.C.
Hammond, Margaret E. Spartanburg, S.C.
Hardin, F.M. Atlanta, Ga.
Hardin, Mrs. Mary J. Atlanta, Ga.
Hardin, Mary T. Atlanta, Ga.
Hardin, H. Frank Atlanta, Ga.
Harrison, Dr. W.A. Reidville, S.C.
Harrison, Edward B. Reidville, S.C.
Harrison, Jno. H. Marietta, Ga.
Harrison, J. Wade Columbia, S.C.
Harrison, R.P. Reidville, S.C.
Harrison, Eugene S Reidville, S.C.
Harrison, W.C. Reidville, S.C.
Harrison, Mrs. Maggie Reidville, S.C.
Harrison, W. Sloane Reidville, S.C.
Harrison, Norman A Reidville, S.C.
Harrison, Lloyd B Reidville, S.C.
Harrison, Jno. R Reidville, S.C.
Harrison, Hon. Jno. R Laurens, S.C.
* Harrison, Jane Fairview, S.C.
Harrison, Lillie H. Laurens, S.C.
Haynes, J. L. Spartanburg, S.C.

Haynes, Mrs. Welthy A Spartanburg, S.C.
Haynes, Annie Spartanburg, S.C.
Haynes, Norman Spartanburg, S.C.
Haynes Guy Spartanburg, S.C.
Hewell, Dr. J. W Greenville, S.C.
Hewell, Mrs. Meta McJ. Greenville, S. C.
Hewell, Marion McJ. (1898) Greenville, S.C.
Hewell, Elizabeth (1900) Greenville, S.C.
Hewell, Barbara (1902) Greenville, S.C.
Hewell, E. M. Greenville, S.C.
Hewell, Eugenia Dunbar Greenville, S.C.
Knight, Mrs. Martha Princeton, S.C.
Knight, Alma Princeton, S.C.
Martin, Angus McS. Laurens, S.C.
Martin, Mrs. Mary E. Laurens, S.C.
Martin, Helen Laurens, S.C.
Martin, John H. Laurens, S.C.
* McDowell, Mrs. Jane Fairview, S.C.
McDowell, T. Whitner Fairview, S.C.
McDowell, Mrs. T. Whitner Fairview, S.C.
McDowell, James S Fairview, S.C.
McDowell, Corrie E. Fairview, S.C.
McDowell, Laura E. Fairview, S.C.
McDowell, Thomas H. Fairview, S.C.
McDowell, Jno. L. Fairview, S.C.
McDowell, Mrs. Gertrude Fairview, S.C.
McDowell, Frank H. Fairview, S.C.
McDowell, ____ Fairview, S.C.
* McDowell, Mrs. Eugenia Fairview, S.C.
McDowell, Eva Fairview, S.C.
McDowell, Jennie Fairview. S.C.
McDowell, Peden Fairview, S.C.
McDowell, Minnie Fairview, S.C.
McDowell, Hettie Fairview, S.C.
McDowell, Thomas Fairview, S.C.
* McKittrick, Mrs. M.A. Fairview, S.C.
McKittrick, Jeff. D Fairview, S.C.
McKittrick, Mrs. Nannie Fairview, S.C.
Nash, M. Perry Rapley, S.C.
* Nash, Mrs. C.E. Rapley, S C.
Nash, L.B. Rapley, S.C.
Nash, N.J. Rapley, S.C.
Nash, S.R. Rapley, S.C.
Nash Essie M. Rapley, S.C.
Nash, E.M. Rapley, S.C.
Neal, Lillian E. Carnesville, Ga.
Parsons, Mrs. Sam Woodruff, S.C.
Parsons, Lucy Woodruff, S.C.

Parsons, Lillie Woodruff', S.C.
Parsons, Bruce Woodruff, S.C.
Pearson, Mrs. E.E. Due West ,S.C.
Pearson, A.A. Due West, S.C.
Pearson, J.T. Anderson, S.C.
Pearson, Mrs. J.T. Anderson, S.C.
Pearson, W. G. Anderson, S.C.
Pearson, Paul C. Anderson, S.C.
Paden, Mark S. Woodstock, Ga.
Peden, J. W. T. Van Vleet, Miss.
Peden, Mrs. Sue Van Vleet, Miss.
Peden, Henry S. Van Vleet, Miss.
Peden, Dora Van Vleet, Miss.
Peden, Capt. D.D. Houston, Texas
Peden, Edward A. Houston, Texas
* Peden, Mrs. Ione Houston, Texas
Peden, Allen Vernon (1899) Houston, Texas
Peden, Edward David (1901) Houston, Texas
Peden, D.D., Jr. Houston, Texas
Peden, Mrs. A.G. Pedenville, Ga.
Peden, Thomas Chester, S.C.
Peden, Mrs. Irene Chester, S.C.
Peden, J. M. Chester, S.C.
Peden, David M. Chester, S.C.
Peden, William Chester, S.C.
Peden, Margaret Chester, S.C.
Peden, Mrs. E.M. Fairview, S.C.
Peden, Adam S. Fountain Inn, S. C.
Peden, Mrs. Nannie S. Fountain Inn, S.C.
Peden, Bessie Belle Fountain Inn, S.C.
Peden, Annie S. Fountain Inn, S.C.
Peden, J.C. Fountain Inn, S.C.
Peden, J. Stewart Fairview, S.C.
Peden, Mrs. Mamie M. Fairview, S.C.
* Peden, Samuel Fairview, S.C.
* Peden, Robbie Lee Fairview, S.C.
Peden, Henry Burwell Fairview, S.C.
Peden, Lila and Lizzie Fairview, S.C.
Peden, Mrs. Caroline Fairview, S.C.
Peden, Jno. Thomas Graycourt, S.C.
Peden, Mrs. Mary Graycourt, S.C.
Peden, David Dorroh Graycourt, S.C.
Peden, Chas. L Graycourt, S.C.
Peden, Carrie Sue Graycourt, S.C.
Peden, Thos. Eugene Graycourt, S.C.
Peden, Lucy Allen Graycourt, S.C.
Peden, W. Stewart Fairview, S.C.

Peden, Mrs. Rixie Fairview, S.C.
Peden, Fred S. Fairview, S.C.
Peden, Nettie C. Fairview, S.C.
Peden, Laura Belle Fairview, S.C.
Peden, David M. Fairview, S.C.
Peden, Mrs. Eliza Mc Fairview, S.C.
Peden, Irene Fairview, S.C.
Peden, Walter Fairview, S.C.
Peden, May Fairview, S.C.
Peden, Archie I. Fairview, S.C.
* Peden, Mrs. Janie Fairview, S.C.
Peden, Earle L. Fairview, S.C.
Peden, Floride Fairview, S.C.
Peden, Harry Lee Fairview, S.C.
Peden, Mrs. Margaret Richburg, S.C.
Peden, Andrew Richburg, S.C.
Peden, Jno. M. Hubbard, Texas
* Peden, Mrs. Mary J Hubbard, Texas
Peden, Jas. Rufus Hubbard, Texas
Peden, Jos. Whitner Hubbard, Texas
Peden, Eleanor E Hubbard, Texas
Peden, Ora May Hubbard, Texas
Peden, Mary A. Hubbard, Texas
Peden, Hugh B. Hubbard, Texas
Peden, Corrie M. Hubbard, Texas
Peden, Miss Elizabeth Fairview, S.C.
Peden, Hugh L.W. Spartanburg, S.C.
Peden, Mrs. Hugh L.W. Spartanburg, S.C.
Peden, Jas. F. Fairview, S.C.
Peden, Mrs. Ella M. Fairview, S.C.
Peden, Maggie Fairview, S.C.
Peden, Joseph Thompson Fairview, S.C.
Peden, Lee Fairview. S.C.
* Peden, Jno. P. Fairview, S.C.
* Peden, Mrs. Emma V. Fairview, S.C.
Peden, Janie Fairview, S.C.
Peden, Eva Fairview, S.C.
Peden, Cora Fairview, S.C.
Peden, Roxie Fairview, S.C.
Peden, Edgar Fairview, S.C.
Peden, Eliza Fairview, S.C.
Peden, Jessie Fariview, S.C.
* Peden, David M. Babbtown, S.C.
Peden, Mrs. Mary J. Babbtown, S.C.
Peden, Leila Babbtown, S.C.
Peden, W.S. Babbtown, S.C.
Peden, Essie Babbtown, S.C.
Peden, Maggie Babbtown, S.C.
Peden, Stacie Babbtown, S.C.

Peden, Robert D. Babbtown, S.C.
Peden, Mary Babbtown, S. C.
Peden, J.D. Babbtown, S.C.
Peden, Mrs. Elizabeth Babbtown, S.C.
Peden, Nancy Babbtown, S.C.
Peden, Mary Babbtown, S.C.
Peden, Myra Babbtown, S.C.
Peden, Janet Babbtown, S.C.
Peden, William Babbtown, S.C.
Peden, Rosa Babbtown, S.C.
Peden, Ellen Babbtown, S.C.
Peden, Earle Babbtown, S.C.
Peden, Grace Babbtown, S.C.
Peden, Mrs. H.M. Westminster, S.C.
Peden, Mrs. Elizabeth Westminster, S.C.
Peden, James M. Fairview, S.C.
Peden, Mrs. M.C. Fairview, S.C.
Peden, Minnie Thomason Fairview, S.C.
Peden, Emma Turner Fairview. S.C.
Peden, Marvin Fairview, S.C.
Peden, A. Calvin Fairview, S.C.
Peden, Mrs. Annie Fork Shoals, S.C.
Peden, John T. Fork Shoals, S.C.
Peden, Charles T. Fork Shoals, S.C.
Peden, Alice Fork Shoals, S.C.
Peden, Andrew Fork Shoals, S.C.
Peden, Edward Fork Shoals, S.C.
* Peden, Fred Fork Shoals, S.C.
Pollard, A.P. Simpsonville, S.C.
Pollard, Mrs. Elizabeth A Simpsonville, S.C.
Pollard, Fred Simpsonville, S.C.
Pollard, Mattie Simpsonville, S.C.
Pollard, Geneva Simpsonville, S.C.
Pollard, Ethel Simpsonville, S.C.
Pollard, Zelema Simpsonville, S.C.
Pollard, Sara Simpsonville, S.C.
Putnam, Mrs. M.C. Fountain Inn, S. C.
Putnam, Jas. R. Fountain Inn, S.C.
Putnam, Jno. W. Fountain Inn, S.C.
Putnam, Sara K. Fountain Inn, S.C.
Putnam, Thos. Alex Fountain Inn, S.C.
Putnam, Mary Fountain Inn, S.C.
Richardson, Mrs. M.C. Simpsonville, S.C.
Richardson, James C. Simpsonville, S.C.
Richardson, Walter Simpsonville, S.C.
Richardson, Maggie Simpsonville, S.C.
Richardson, Marie Simpsonville, S.C.
Richardson, J.M. Simpsonville, S.C.

Richardson, Mrs. Mary J Simpsonville, S.C.
Richardson, T.W. Simpsonville, S.C.
Richardson, Freeman Simpsonville, S.C.
Richardson, Pearl Simpsonville, S.C.
Richardson, Carrie Simpsonville, S.C.
Salmons, Mrs. Mary Valley Center, Cal.
* Shannon, Mrs. Cynthia Harmony Grove, Ga.
Shannon, W. Alexander Harmony Grove, Ga.
Snead, Mrs. Elizabeth Martins Mills, Texas
Snead, Jno. R. Martins Mills, Texas
Snead, Laura E. Martins Mills, Texas
Stanton, Dr. Jno. H. Chariton, Iowa
Stanton, Mrs. Jno. H. Chariton, Iowa
Stanton, Gertrude E. Chariton, Iowa
Stanton, Sara McCalla Chariton, Iowa
Stenhouse, Miss Isabella Fairview, S.C.
Stenhouse, Wm. M. Sterling, S.C.
Stenhouse, Mrs. Jeannette Sterling, S.C.
Stenhouse, Elizabeth Sterling, S.C.
Sprouse, Mrs. Mattie Fairview, S.C.
Sprouse, Mary C. Fairview, S.C.
Sprouse, Lucinda Fairview, S.C.
Sprouse, William W. Fairview, S.C.
Stewart, Judge J.W. Fairview, S. C.
Stewart, Mrs. J.W. Fairview, S.C.
Stewart, Leila Fairview, S.C.
Stewart, Katherine Fairview, S.C.
Stewart, Anderson Fairview, S.C.
Stewart, Dr. H.B. Fairview, S.C.
Stewart, Mrs. Mattie E. Fairview, S.C.
Stewart, Frennie F. Fairview, S.C.
Stewart, Bessie Britt Fairview, S.C.
Stewart, Rosa R. Fairview, S.C.
Stewart, Clifford C. Fairview, S.C.
Stewart, Mack M. Fairview, S.C.
Stewart, Hoke H. Fairview, S.C.
Stewart, Calvin B. Fairview. S.C.
Stewart, Mrs. Mary Atlanta, Ga.
Stewart, Claud M. Atlanta, Ga.
Sullivan, Mrs. Stella Houston, Texas
Sullivan, Leonora Houston, Texas
Sullivan, Margaret Peden Houston, Texas
Sullivan, Luther M. Houston, Texas
Sullivan, Andrew Peden Houston, Texas
Sullivan, W. Edward Houston, Texas
Sullivan, Frances E. Houston, Texas
* Sullivan, Mrs. Eudora E. Pedenville, Ga.
Sullivan, Malcolm McKay Pedenville, Ga.
Sullivan, Annie Eudora Pedenville, Ga.
Sullivan, Ruth Peden Pedenville, Ga.
Sullivan, M. Lucile Pedenville, Ga.
Sullivan, Wm. Bartlette Pedenville, Ga.
Sullivan, Julia A. (1900) Pedenville, Ga.
Templeton, Mrs. M.C. Fountain Inn, S.C.
Templeton, L. Hayne Fountain Inn, S.C.
Templeton, Mrs. Mary C. Fountain Inn, S.C.
Templeton, Lutie M. Fountain Inn, S.C.
Templeton, Lula M. fountain Inn, S.C.
Templeton, Jas. H. Fountain Inn, S. C.
Templeton, David Peden Fountain Inn, S.C.
Templeton, Carrie E. Fountain Inn, S.C.
Talley, Olin B. Fairview, S.C.
Talley, Mrs. Olin B. Fairview, S.C.
Talley, Elizabeth N. Fairview, S.C.
Thomason, Rev. D. L Fairview, S.C.
Thomason, Mrs. Therese M Fairview, S.C.
Thomason, Sam W. Fairview, S.C.
Thompson, M.L. Townville, S.C.
Thompson, Mrs. M.L. Townville, S.C.
Thompson, L. Grace Townville, S.C.
Thompson, Maggie Townville, S.C.
Thompson, Leila White Townville, S.C.
Thompson, W.H.L. Fairview, S.C.
Thompson, Mrs. M.M. Fairview, S.C.
Thompson, R.V. Fairview, S.C.
Thompson, A.B. Fairview, S.C.
Thompson, B.B. Fairview, S.C.
Thompson, M.L. Fairview, S.C.
Thompson, L.M. Fairview, S.C.
Thompson, W.S. Fairview, S.C.
Thompson, S.L. Fairview, S.C.
Thompson, N.E. Fairview, S.C.
Thomason, Mrs. Alice Simpsonville, S.C.
Thomason, David E. Simpsonville, S.C.
* Thompson, Nina Lee Simpsonville. S.C.
Thomason, Annie May Simpsonville, S.C.
Thomason, Francis C Simpsonville, S.C.
Vernon, J.J. Welford, S.C.
Vernon, Mrs. J.J. Welford, S.C.
West, Jas. I. Greenville, S.C.
West, Mrs. Laura F. Greenville, S.C.
West, Charles D. Greenville, S.C.
West, Casper S. Greenville, S.C.
West, Ethel Greenville, S.C.

West, Nellie M. Greenville, S.C.
West, Annie Greenville, S.C.
West, D. Peden Greenville, S.C.
West, Jones R Greenville, S.C.
West, Mrs. Sue Greenville, S. C,
West, Geneva Greenville, S.C.
West, Eleanor Greenville, S.C.
West, Mabel Greenville, S.C.
West, Robbie Jones Greenville, S.C.
West, Wm. D.P. Greenville, S.C.
Westmoreland, J.R. Woodruff, S.C.
Westmoreland, Mrs. Maggie Woodruff, S.C.
Westmoreland, J. Ripley Woodruff, S.C.
Westmoreland, Nannie P. Woodruff. S.C.
Westmoreland, Goldie L. Woodruff, S.C.
Westmoreland, Bettie Barbara Woodruff, S.C.
Westmoreland, Fred S. Woodruff, S.C.
Westmoreland, W.B. Woodruff, S.C.
Westmoreland, Mrs. Minnie E. Woodruff, S.C.
Westmoreland, Rebecca Peden Woodruff, S.C.
Whiten, H.T. Fountain Inn, S.C.
Whiten, Mrs. Ellen Fountain Inn, S.C.
Whiten, Alvin C. Fountain Inn, S.C.
Whiten, Cora Fountain Inn, S. C
Whiten, Nannie Fountain Inn, S.C.
Wilson, Rev. S. L. Westminster, S.C.
Wilson, Mrs. M.M. Westminster, S.C.
Wilson, Frank Pearson Westminster, S.C.
Wilson, Park T. Westminster, S.C.

Eleanor M. Hewell

Part Two - The Pedens of America

Chapter One - Ancestral Pride

A godly ancestry is the best heritage that can be given to man. Only within the last few years of the present century has the new world awakened to the sad fact that the very founders of its history were fast sinking into utter oblivion, leaving not the faintest trace of their achievements. One of the curious and interesting evolutions of the day is the organization of societies founded upon ancestries connected with the earlier history of the country, and happy is that family who can boast of forefathers whose arrival in the new world ante-date the Revolution. These Historic societies are steadily on the increase, a list would be almost interminable, for the fever is spreading yearly until it is becoming an epidemic.

The tracing of this ancestry, while laudable in itself, is involved in great obscurity; therefore attended with uncertainty for it cannot always be told what is at the far distant end, or very beginning of the line, consequently many mistakes are made. Yet in the majority of cases those of this day and time who can go back to their ancestors who stood boldly, bravely and loyally for the defense of civil and religious liberty in the Revolution of 1776 have every reason to be fully satisfied with results; for no people, no nation, ever had a finer race of progenitors than the Americans of these United States. Their record, compared with the average royal lineage, is as white, compared to very deep brown, if not black of a mournful hue. As Lowell says of them: "God hath sifted the nations for the wheat of this planting."

Of these, the Scotch-Irish, the last and heaviest sifting, have produced the strongest growth. Little did James Stuart dream when he so carefully selected and transplanted his staunch, Presbyterian, Ayreshire Pedens and their compeers to his barren Irish wastes, that he was merely the tool in the hand of God for the furtherance of the Divine plan, that he was promoting the very cause he was striving to eradicate by simply garnering and treasuring the golden grain of civil and religious freedom for the planting of the untried fields of the new land with a sturdy race whose influence is now dominant.

Practical good comes from the new movement, for it increases respectful admiration and appreciation approaching reverence for the lives and labors of glorious ancestors, thereby leading to a deeper study of national history.

The point, in its modern application, is that every one who can trace his or her line back to any defender of this grand land stands upon the same social level, whether that defender was a simple private or a high officer, whether a farm hand or cavalier, whether a carpenter or an aristocrat. The fact that he fought loyally for his country entitled him to equal distinction with the most illustrious of his day.

The prospect is amazing standing at the dividing line between two centuries a glance backward shows what has come of the past, and a forward look shows the promise of the glorious future. While it is the duty of the present to treat the heroes of the late war well, while they yet live to give them that sympathy and recognition they so well deserve, admire heroism and sacrifice to principle in the fast vanishing veterans, as well as to worship it a century ago.

In the bloody civil war the name Peden-Paden was written deep with the life-blood of many a young hero "in the rank and file" on both sides. It is in honor of this mighty race, now scattered over this glorious Union and in far lands, that this volume is written; also to rescue the Scotch-Irish-American name of Peden from the oblivion which threatens to engulf it, giving it a place beside its compeers among the Scotch-Irish race in America.

Of its antiquity as a race there can be no question. As Col. Hooper Alexander and Capt. D. D. Peden, in their able addresses at the great clan reunion, under the ancestral oaks, at Fairview, S. C, in 1899, brought out the strong character and fervid religious nature of the race in the old world, with a few additional side lights thrown from secular history, the threads will be taken up where they laid them down, imposing the dutiful task of tracing the Peden in the new world and writing an honored name in a book upon the author; therefore with considerable trepidation of heart that mighty weapon, the pen, is taken in her woman's hand with the apology in advance that there will be many unintentional mistakes, many missing links, many broken, tangled threads, left to be rectified by some gifted historian of the future, who will gather and garner the truths as they emerge from the depths of the dust covered folios of long forgotten lore, redolent of dead rose leaves, thyme, lavender and cedar of the past.

In following the Peden in America through his many wanderings it was deemed advisable to appoint a family historian from each of the nine families representing the race. This however has not proven a success generally, and the author has been thrown almost entirely on her own resources, which involved a voluminous correspondence wherever an address was obtained, so if some are left out they will understand it was not the author's intention, for she has certainly a superabundance of ancestral pride and race love; therefore "I have gathered me a posie of other men's flowers, and nothing but the thread that binds them is mine own."

Chapter Two - Side Lights from Secular History

"Gently draw aside the curtain of the Past, and gaze reverently adown the dim-litten vistas of Time."

Far back in the misty realms of tradition, ere Time's footprints were lighted by the lantern of written history, the human race became divided into three great families or septs. The cradle of man was the elevated plateau of western Asia; thence they were dispersed eastward, southward, westward. The last migration to leave the cradleland were the great Aryan division, who swept westward with mighty strides of civilization, crossing in time over into Europe after founding the Perso-Phoenician races, thence founding the grand colony of ancient Greece. Legend tells that about the time of the call of Abraham, when the race still dwelt in tents, a number of the Aramites began the westward march over the arid plains toward the setting sun, finally settling in Greece where they dwelt in the "open country because of their great flocks of sheep and cattle." These people were called Pedens, or dwellers of the "open fields," and students of patronymics state that the name Peden in all its various changes signifies "a field." Taking up the line of march northward this tribe or sept finally became merged into the Aryan race, eventually forming the great Germanic nation which proved such invincible foes to conquering Rome, forming an impassable barrier between that all powerful empire and the coveted shores of the northern sea. The story of Arminus or Herman gives the indomitable love of liberty, so strong in the Peden race, as a marked characteristic in the days of Caesar as well as of today.

All modern students of history and patronymics are agreed that the Scotch-Irish people, so distinctive now, are not, as have been generally received, of Gallic or Celtic origin but of Germanic. A large number of authorities can be quoted bearing on this subject. Suffice it to say that the earliest trace of the Germanic in the British Isles is in Ireland which being the more fertile land was more attractive to these tent dwellers of the open field than the rugged rock-bound coast of Scotland; however, it was not long before the narrow channel was crossed and they found permanent hold in Ayrshire.

The surname was a product of the Norman invasion, and the Scot, like the American Indian, derived his from his surroundings, his locality. For example the famous name Douglas, under whose leadership many a Peden fought for Scotland's freedom, signifies "the blackwater" — the river Clyde. Holmes means the "low lands" or land along the margin of streams. Dunbar is from a stone and a barrier, otherwise stonewall. It was an olden custom to call a man John, of Holmes; James, of Douglas; George, of Dunbar; and as Alexander is so emphatically a Peden name it is supposable that Alexander, of Peden, was the founder of the race. The saving "Back to Alexander" is thus defined.

"Quehein Alexander our king was dede,
  That Scotland led in lane and le
Alwayes was sons of ale and brede
  Of wyne and wax, of gamyn and gle," ect.

The time of Alexander the Third thus alluded to by the earliest Scottish poet corresponds to the days of the English Arthur and his table round, and is almost regarded as mythical; however, there is far better proof of the existence of Alexander than of Arthur. A mystery envelopes the founders of the English monarchy which does not exist regarding the Scottish. "Thirty kings" preceded the Bruce, all of whom sleep on the sacred Isle of Iona, Macbeth, the Usurper, being the last Culdee king, for the Bruce rings in the Norman blood, and with it the church of Rome, first established by St. Margaret, wife of one of the Alexander fine, which became extinct in the Alaid of Norway.

The name Peden existed in the time of the first Alexander, for a shepherd of that name brought the king "a lammie wrapt in his plaidie." The story runneth thus: "Alexander the good king being wearied from the chase in Ayr loitered behind his band, and was lost; a storm coming tip the king sought shelter of a shepherd's hut or "shealing." The shepherd, ignorant of the rank of his guest and seeing his forlorn state bade him "rest a wee," and wrapping himself in the shepherd's dry plaidie thc king lay down and slept a lone while, but was awakened by savory odors in the air. His host seeing him awake presented a part of a freshly roasted lamb with a bannock or oaten cake which the king ate eagerly. He then inquired the name of his h.ost. "Alexander, of Peden," was the reply. Then said the good king, "What dost thou most desire?" Peden replied "The freehold of the stead whereon I dwell." Then the king, on further questioning, discovered that the desired possession was within his gift said, "On this condition, that from this time forth thou and thv descendants shall hold the stead of Auchin-by-the-ford by presenting yearly a young lamb to the king of Scotland." This was religiously kept until the kingdoms were united under James Seventh.

Tradition also states that the third Alexander, and the greatest of the line, expired on the breast of "one faithful yoeman, Paiden of the hags." In the year 600 the king of Northumberland applied to the Culdees for men to come and make his country Christian. Oswald, who had been banished to the land of the Picts, was a Culdee, so when restored to his kingdom prayed the church at Iona to send one of their number to his court. A man named Conan was sent but he was soon so disgusted with English manners and morals that he retired to the sacred island and his brethren. Then Aidan or Paidan went and devoted his life to the task which Conan had found so distasteful. He taught and toiled among them with great zeal which Oswald the king rewarded and warmly seconded. He was the founder of the little church of Lindisfarne on the bleak Northumbrian shore.

These Culdee priests were often married and fathers of families. It is recorded that Duncan the Good was the son of the Abbot of Dunkeld, and a daughter of Malcolm the Second. It is also stated that a natural son of Alexander the First bore the name of Peden and gave his brother the king much trouble. Considering the rude morality of those dark times he possibly had as good right to be king as his brother David.

In 1160 the Peden name occurs on a list of Culdees to whom Donald, ninth Earle of Mar, granted land to build a Culdee church. The title of Mar is the oldest in the English peerage. .

"On the eve of the battle of Bannockburn 'tis said that from out the Scottish host there stepped 'a tall piper of so marvellous likeness to the king that many wondered greatly thereat, and as he doffed his bonnet their wonder increased for the king embraced him warmly' and thus they held each other for a space as though loath to part asunder. Then they walked together out of ear-shot and without the guard, and some of the nobility cast dark glances at the tall, martial figure in the tartan and bonnet with the eagle feather, but the marvel ceased when it was told that the stranger was Peden, of Cadzow, the favorite piper of the king; that he had come hither at the Bruce's desire, for none else in the kingdom could so well play the "Logan Water" which was to inspire the army on the morrow in the desperate battle for liberty against England's chivalry and power. When the sun rose the king rode bare of bonnet in front of the humble Scottish army on a mean, little horse, the Abbot of Dunkeld walking in front holding aloft the cross, the tall piper stalking at the horse's flank the host of Scotland knelt as they passed. The English cried "Behold, they kneel!" Their leaders replied, "Yes, but not to us." The stirring notes of the piper followed the prayer. On came the charge." The story of Bannockburn has oft been told and need not be reiterated. It is of the tall piper we sing. "When the battle was over the tall piper lay stiff and stark on that gory field of carnage. Then came the king, and in the wild abandonment of grief, threw himself on the sward beside the dead corpse with the wild lamentation, 'Is it thus, my brother, that we part, I thought to have clapt on thy spurs and dub thee Knight of Cadzow, but alas." The scene is from "The Bruce and Wallace Wight."

History tells us that Cadzow and its desmense passed after Bannockburn into the possession of the Hamilton, it being a fief of the crown, therefore within the king's gift; also the three sons of the piper became the wards of the crown. Only one grew to man's estate. He lived and died in Ayr.

Until the House of Stuart came to the throne Scotland enjoyed great freedom both civil and religious. Later history tells that on a certain occasion Angus, Earl of Douglas, refused to sleep within the walls of a captured castle saying that "Better hear the lark sing than the mouse squeak." The said Lord Angus, "Bell the Cat," was a scholarly man, an illegitimate son of the old earl, whom he succeeded, by right of his great superiority to his lawful brothers, so he was legitimatized and given the title, and well worthy he proved. Tradition says his mother was Margaret, of Peden, a woman of great personal beauty.

The ancient name does not, so far as ascertained, occur again in secular history until the days and times of the Covenanters. That its bearers were strangely shielded by the crown during those bloody periods is a remarkable proof of not only esteem, but of some strange claim, together with the fact that the family or sept were ever vassals of the crown of Scotland, never of any petty lord, though there were times when they fought under the leadership of Douglass and Hamilton; in covenanting days under Cameron. It is the purpose of this chapter to throw the secular light, not the religious, which is the strongest feature of the Peden character. Another pen has portrayed their adherence to the reformed religion.

When that strange sifting for the planting of the wastes of North Ireland under James Seventh took place, he showed great preference for the house of Peden, granting them many privileges not accorded to others. This transplanting took place 16001602. During a space of nearly two centuries the Pedens with their compeers were engaged in making the Irish desert blossom as the rose with their industry and skill. They had gathered together a fair share of possessions, except land ownership, which is and was impossible to Irish tenantry; they could only obtain long leases; when these leases, at first extremely liberal, expired, owing to their own vast improvement of the wastes they were raised exorbitantly by owners, oft-times absentees, but more frequently oppressive landlords at home. In addition to increased rents their woolen and linen manufactories were suppressed by enaction of harsh laws. The spirit of the Peden revolted. The historians Froude, McCauley and others give graphic pictures of the times of both civil and religious persecutions covering the last ninety years of their sojourn in Ireland. The name does not appear, but the race was there. At the close of 1668 began the attack on Londonderry. The story is a familiar one, but the names of the brave "thirteen apprentices," Scottish boys, seem unattainable. Tradition states that the Pedens descend from one of them. This may be on the maternal side. It matters not, if only it can be proven will be a descent worth far more than royal blood. It was an act of bravery unparalleled in modern history.

The Peden was now called upon to choose between the Protestant religion and the House of Stuart. What that choice was is the pride and glory of their descendants. Foremost among the men of Ulster he is found side by side with the Leslie, Mills, McDill, Gaston, Alexander, and the exiled Morton, as well as many another honored name that would swell the list interminably. Among the band that surrounded William of Orange in the mid-stream of that Irish river, running red with blood, the tide was flowing fast, his charger could scarcely keep his feet, and was almost swimming, when his bridle was seized by a young soldier, Peden by name, and led to shore where his arrival decided the fate of the day. He held his sword in his left hand. One of the Enniskilleners, thinking him an Irish leader, was about to fire, William gently pushed the carbine aside asking, "What, do you not know your friends?" "It is his majesty," said their leader. Then rose from the ranks a mad shout of joy, "Men of Ulster, 1 have heard of you, let me see something also, you shall be my guards today." And truly they proved worthy, but the brave young soldier Peden fell in the Battle of the Boyne. There were three others, brothers also, there on that proud occasion fighting under the Dutch General Schomberg, who fell that day. The name of Gaston occurs among his men. "Men of the rank and file were the Peden." After this famous battle they seem to have led quiet, religious lives until the accession of George the Third and passing of the infamous law that made them exile themselves. For the finger of God pointed westward, their hearts heard the command "Go forward!"

[Note. — As some of the clan seem desirous of a royal beginning the Historian adds to this chapter a few lines from the best recognized Scottish historians, Tytler, McArthur and McKenzie.]

The name Scot is Celtic and signifies a rover or wanderer. At some remote period, not now possible to obtain dates, there came from Spain into Ireland a party of these Celts, who took the liberty of making themselves very much at home. Vigorous and powerful they were and quite capable of planting themselves wherever they wished; even down to the present day this element is dominant; however, they very soon took possession of Ireland and drove out the native Irish wherever they wished possession. This was about the third century. Here they remained until about the sixth century when a small colony of them crossed over to Scotland and settled in what is Argyleshire, spreading into Ayreshire and Galloway, where they flourished, and in the year 700 A.D. founded the little kingdom of Dalraida, a long struggle for existence against the Picts, both north and south and the Scottish kingdom of Dalraida united them under her king Kenneth McAlpin. This king was elected to the throne about 770 A.D. He was the founder of the Scottish monarchy and the father of a large family. A long list of the most prominent Scottish names could be given as his descendants, but only a few will be culled. Alexander of the fields, or Peden, Grant, Dunbar, Cameron, Campbell and all the Mcs.

Kenneth McAlpin and his successors down to Bruce, 1314 A.D., were buried on Iona, the Sacred Isle. All these Scots were Culdees, having embraced Christianity at the beginning of the second century, Jesus having been preached among these Scots by refugees from persecution. "Whoever they were that first sowed the gospel seed in Scotland all recollection has perished. They are known alone to Him from whom they are receiving their rewards, some information, however, we have about the most remarkable of those primitive missionaries, who at a later date aided in extending the worship of God over Scotland. We see these men as trees walking, but true men they were, in heart and life." They preached a simple faith, the faith of the Culdee. The first was Ninian, a young prince who visited Rome about the latter part of the fourth century. The Bishop of Rome, who had not yet swollen into a Pope, found the young Briton well skilled and taught in divine truth, ordained him and sent him to preach to his countrymen. He landed at Whitehorn, in Galloway, where he built a little church — the first in Scotland. It was called the White House. "To that little white-walled church, peacefully looking from its bold headland, over the racing tides of the wild Solway, he taught the pagan people to go up to hear the words of eternal life." The humble White House in after years formed the site of a stately Abbey which bore the same name, but not a trace now remains of either, A few years later came Palladius and founded the church in Ferdon, in the Mearns (Ayeshire), which Burns has immortalized in Tam O'Shanter as Auld Alloway's Kirk. He was a powerful preacher and his converts were very numerous. The greatest evangelist was Columba, who came about 545 A.D. to Iona in a curraugh a boat made of hides stretched on a keel and ribs of wood; very frail, but it stood the stormiest seas and bore over Colum, or Columba, and twelve companions. Here they built a church of posts, wattled with reeds and plastered with clay, also a few huts, and supported themselves by cultivating the soil. This was the first theological seminary or missionary college. Starting from this point they made their way over rugged mountains and through pathless forests; they endured hardships like good soldiers; suffered violence, and sometimes death, at the hands of the Druids. They pursued their way, and wonderful success was given them. What a life of strange adventures theirs must have been. At nightfall waking the echoes of the gloomy forests with songs of praise, or prostrated on the grass reading their Latin Bibles; now driven from the gate of some mighty chief; now preaching in his huge oaken hall; now standing in the midst of the village telling the story of the cross; now in the warrior's camp preaching the Prince of Peace; now teaching various mechanical arts, for they were well skilled in manual labor. Columba fell asleep at a very great age, but his work was not suffered to lag and went on growing and increasing for generations, until their persecutor arose in the fair St. Margaret, queen of Malcolm Canmore, who loved not their simple faith, but desired the gorgeous ritual of Rome.

To return. The followers of Columba were called Culdees (servants of God). Their churches and schools were established at Alernethy, Dunblane, Scone, Brechin, Dunkeld, Lochleven, St. Andrew's, and, in fact, all over Scotland. Their religion was the pure and undefiled religion of the Bible, free from the corrupt doctrines and practices of the church of Rome. They owned no rule but the word of God. They had no worship of saints or angels; no prayers for the dead; no confession to the priest; no sacrifice of the mass. They hoped for salvation from the mercy of God alone, through faith in Jesus Christ. They had no bishops or prelates, and their only office bearers were ministers and elders. The little island settlement grew into fame and grandeur, for ages it was the great light of the north, for centuries Scotland's kings were buried in its soil, even the royal dead of other lands were brought to rest in its sacred soil. Nothing now is to be seen except a square tower and roofless walls. The unceasing roar of the sea's wild waves as they dash against the granite cliffs is the only sound that breaks the stillness of the desolate scene. The church of the Culdees flourished long but the days of persecution came and as the ages passed it was reduced to a mere handful who kept the faith even through the stormy days of the Reformation, as late as 1494 it is stated. The first Archbishop of Glasgow had thirty persons, mostly of prominence, arrested for being Culdees, and many of them from Ayrshire.

The origin of the name Peden has two traditions, one has been already given, belonging to the Culdee sketch. The following has just reached the author: Among the knights who accompanied the Norman Conqueror, William to Britain in 1066, was one named Sir Hugh de Pothein; and in confirmation of this Norman theory is quoted from Johnson's Appreciation of Alexander Peden, the Prophet of the Covenant, these notes from his "Lives of Six Saints."

"Alexander Peden was registered at the university as Peathine, and he sometimes wrote his name as Pedine. Other forms of the family name occurring in writs or to be found on old heirlooms are: Pothein, Pothoin, Pothin, Pethine, Peathine, Petein," and in the sixteenth century as Peden.

"In the list of 'rebels and fugitives from our laws' appended to the royal proclamation of the 5th of May, 1684, the following names belonging to the same locality, Mauchline, Ayrshire; Alexander Peden, of Blockerdyke; John Peden, portioner of Holehouse; Robert Peden, son to Hugh Peden in Waulkmill of Sorn, and also ____ Peden, his son."

"The father of the distinguished Covenanter was a small proprietor in the district, and he himself (Alexander Peden) seems to have been the eldest son of the Laird of Auchencloich."

In Dr. Hay Fleming's notes to the lives of "Six saints" we learn that "Alexander Pethein was retoured heir to his grandfather (Alexander Pethein) in Hillside of Sorn, on the i6th of March, 1648; and on the same day heir of Auchencloich. And so, like a considerable number of the Covenanting ministers, Alexander Peden belonged to the lesser (Lairds) gentry of Scotland."

"The Covenanters have been looked upon," writes Lord Moncrieff, in "Church and State," "as a somewhat uneducated, rude, fanatical body of the lower order, and people seem to contrast them with the better birth and manners of the royalists. I believe there is in all this a very great delusion. The inception of the Covenanters embraced the largest portion of the upper ranks, and whole body of the people. Whatever of birth, of culture, of manners, and of learning or intellectual power of Scotland could boast was at that time unquestionably to be found in the ranks of the Covenanters."

To like purpose the words of Jas. Dodds: "Whether it was from early connection, or from subsequent acquaintance he (Alexander Peden) was honored with the friendship of the Boswells, of Auchenleck, in his immediate neighborhood, an old and respected family from whom descended the biographer of Samuel Johnson. Indeed, it is manifest from many incidents that Peden was on terms of endearing friendship with many of the best old families of the West. I mention this in passing, not because in itself it made him any better, but to remove an impression which has been propogated, that he was some obscure, ranting vagrant — half-crazed nondescript. In the best sense Peden was a gentleman and through life the companion of gentlemen."

From "Heroes and Heroines of the Scottish Covenanters," by Dr. J.M. Dryerre, F.R.G.S.: "The strangest man of the Covenanting struggle was Alexander Peden. Around his name has grown a multitude of stories, in which people have tried to express the wonderfulness of his character. Laying aside such as have need of verification, we still have the picture of a strange man, spiritual in mind and heart, noble in character, keen of insight, and fully justified to the title which people gave him of the 'Prophet.' We must not deny the term, then, to Peden, because he died in his bed. This was not the fault of his enemies. To the hour of his death they hunted him, but failed to shed his blood. Peden was a native of Ayrshire, being born at Auchencloich, in Sorn, about 1626. His father, Hugh Pethein, was a small proprietor, and left his son a fair patrimony. His social position gave him the entrance into the best society, and we find him often at the Boswells, of Auchenleck, and at the Baillies, of Jerviswoode, and the houses of all the gentry round about. From an early period he felt called to the ministry, and cared nothing for earthly honors, or glory. His prayers were conversations with a Personal Friend. His sermons were visions of the glory of God, which had come to him in his meditations, and filled the people with awe. His talk was about God and His will in regard to down-trodden Scotland. Tall in stature, and well-built, as he proclaimed his message of God he must have been intensely impressive."

Another writer describes him as of "fair and ruddy countenance, with beaming eyes when in repose, stern and flashing like the eagle's when denouncing the enemies of the Lord and Scotland." (Wilson.)

A description of his birth-place, also the cradle of the American line, will not be amiss here:

"Belonging at present to Sorn, Auchencloich (field of stones); at the time of our story (1626) was situated in Mauchline parish. Sorn was not able to boast of a church of its own till 1658, nor had it a separate existence as a parish till 1692, when it was disjoined from Mauchline. The interest of the story therefore, at the outset, centers in Mauchline.

"The village of Sorn stands on the river Ayr, about three miles from Catrine and five from Mauchline. As the birthplace of Peden it is famous. Sorn Castle, not far off, has a charming situation. Pity that its association should be so dissimilar, for under Scotland's reign of terror the castle was taken possession of as a fort-a-lis of the royal forces and made the seat of a garrison for overawing the Covenanters. Yet, after all, what does it matter?" aptly remarks the author of "Mad Sir Uchtred of the Hills (R. L. Stevenson), as he says, "thro' all the sou-west not a bairn's prayer is changed for all the fusillades of Claverhouse, and for all the tramplings of his squadrons."

"Auchencloich, the birth-place and death-place of the Prophet Peden, is a hamlet in Sorn, 2 miles N.E. of Mauchline. The derivation of the name, and historical facts connected with the place will be found in Mr. Todd's 'Homes and Haunts.' The present tenant (1902) is Mr. David Bone, reputed a good man and true and very much pleased to show Peden's birth-place to all comers. Too much must not be expected, however, for the building is a very humble one, having been converted into a byre for cattle."

"The Peden name is a common one in the Mauchline registers, the other Peden homes, Auchen lon-ford and Tenshilling, are not far away, also Blockerdyke, Waulkmill, &c.

"In the kirk records, session of 1682, there is an entry to the effect that the sum of twenty-four shillings was given by the church to a poor man recommended by a Mr. Alexander Peden. 'It is just probable,' writes Dr. Edgar, in Old Church Life, 'that the Alexander Peden who gave the recommendation may have been the famous Covenanter of that name, who was well known doubtless to both ministers and elders of Mauchline.' The minister of

Mauchline at the time of Peden's birth and baptism was John Rose, who died in 1634, and was succeeded by Geo. Young the following year."

"Alexander Pethein was retoured heir of his grandfather, Alexander Pethein, of Hillheid Sorn, on the i6th of March, 1648. [Inquistiones Generales, No. 3433.] and on the same day was retoured his heir in the half-merk lands of Auchenlonfuird, in the lands of Bruntishiell and Lairdship of Kylemuir [Inquistiones Generales, Ayr, No. 418]. This last little lairdship had apparently been in the hands of a good many Pedens for on the 29th of April, 1611, Hugh Pethein was retoured heir of his father, Alexander Pethein, in Sorn in the half-merk lands of Auchenlonfuird within the lands of Bruntishiells and Lairdship, and regality of Kylesmuir. [Ibid, No. 176. J

"William Cunningham, one of the foremost scholars of his age, and author of several works on Theology was 'a descendant of the Covenanting Pedens,' his mother being a sister, or niece of the Prophet, and to whose influence and godly upbringing her famous son owed much of his beauty of character. She is described as 'a tall, stately woman, of noble mein, of unswerving fidelity to the tenets of the Covenanters, and her son, whom she reared and educated despite many and sore trials, proved worthy of her and her race, the ancient and honorable Pedens.' William is said to have been a reproduction of his venerable relative, the Prophet, both in personal appearance and mental vigor. He is described as a giant mentally, physically and spiritually, of commanding appearance, stern of countenance, yet with a manner and smile so winning that the 'weest bairnie' gladly nestled in his broad bosom, or sought shelter in the lap of his 'plaidie.' While no picture of the Prophet Peden exists, the strong, gentle, handsome face of William Cunningham can be found somewhere in broad Scotland."

Statement of Charles Peden, engine driver, 29 Union Place, Dundee, Scotland:

I am sixty-three years of age. Have resided in Dundee for the last twenty-three years. I came to Dundee at the opening of the first Tay Bridge and was driver of the first through passenger train from Dundee to Glasgow. This train consisted of ten carriages, containing between two and three hundred passengers. I have a family of four daughters and one son. I was born at ____. My father's name is also Charles Peden. He worked in the freestone quarries and on farms as a laborer. My grandfather's name is James Peden. He lived some years in Stirling and was between sixty and seventy years of age at the time of his death. The following particulars are contained in a document which was found among my grandfather's papers:

The first notice of the Peden family is in 1648. On the 16th of March of this year Alexander Peden, the Prophet, became heir to the estate of Auchin-longford, Ayrshire, on the death of his grandfather, also named Alexander Peden. James Peden, father of Mingo Peden, came into the property in 1693. His wife was Agnes Miller. He was succeeded by his son, James, in 1723, whose wife was Isabella Robb. Their son James succeeded to the estate in _____ and sold it to a Mr. Bones, of Stowe, near Edinburg, and it is still owned by the Bones family. This James Peden, who was the last successor to the estate Auchin-long-ford of the Peden name, died in 1775. [Was he father, brother or cousin to John Peden who was born in 1709 and emigrated to America in 1768-1770?]

Alexander Peden, the Prophet, was born in 1626; died in 1686 (two years before the Reformation), in a brother's house in Auchinleck, a few miles from Sorn. His estate consisted of three small farms and was situate about three miles from Sorn. He was never married. He had two brothers (from one of whom the Pedens of America descend, presumably James). Their names are James and Mingo. Both had families.

A few years ago I had the pleasure of seeing the Bible of the Prophet. It was in the possession of a family in the vicinity of Dundee, who had purchased it in Edinboro for twenty guineas. This Bible was the means of saving his life. The cave in which he usually hid (under Peden's stone) himself to elude his enemies who were searching the country for him having been discovered, he forsook it and fled to his brother's house (James). His sister-in-law (Agnes Miller) said to him, "What are ye doing here, the enemy will be upon ye?" In a very few minutes the soldiers were seen approaching. In haste the Prophet took shelter in the byre or small barn, his sister-in-law accompanying him, there he laid down, his Bible clasped to his breast. She covered him with straw and retired. The soldiers searched the house in vain, then one proceeded to the byre, only a pile of straw was seen so, thinking he might be beneath it, the soldier plunged his sword down through the straw; the point of the weapon was arrested by the leathern cover which it but slightly touched, leaving scarcely a mark on the outside board of considerable thickness. Being satisfied that no man was hidden beneath the soldier withdrew and joined his comrades, thus the worthy man again escaped his enemies miraculously.

The above was furnished by Mr. T. Y. Miller, of Dundee, who personally saw Charles Peden.

Chapter Three - The Flitting

"Religion stands on tiptoe, in our land
Ready to pass to the American strand."

— Herbert.

Down one of Ireland's greenest of green lanes, bordered on either side with neatly clipped hedges of hawthorn, white with blossom, carpeted with velvet sward, studded with oxeyed daisies; over head floated soft, fleecy clouds in a sea of blue ether; no sound save the droning of bees among the flowers; the cawing of a colony of rooks in the castle woods; distant lowing of cattle. A study fair of white, blue, gray and green. A calm Sabbath in May, in the year 1750. The sound of voices, and lo, a long procession of men women and little children, following like sheep an old, old man whose long silvery locks fell in rippling curls on the stooping shoulders. He walked very slowly, aided by a shepherd's crook.

The lane ended at the foot of a knoll on whose summit stood, and perhaps still stands, a gray stone church overgrown with ivy, which grows more luxuriantly in Ireland than elsewhere, because tradition as well as history tells us that Ireland was once "one vast battle-field." From the crest of this hill nature spreads out a fair landscape of hill and dale; a wide stretch of country, grim, old castles in ruins, farm houses nestling in the midst of smiling farms, with here and there a native hovel to mar the beauty of the scene. In the distance flashed the silver waters of the Lough in their basin of emerald and gray stone. The exiled Scots loved this fair spot where they had found a brief refuge from persecution and had named their church Fairview.

On this day their awakening was to come; a rude one it proved, for as they reached the open door of the church, passing through the sweet God's acre where so many of their race were sleeping the long sleep ere the final waking. Here and there among the grass and daisies lay white stones like a scattered flock of sheep. Sounds of war issued from the sacred portals and instead of prayer and psalm came the din and clash of arms and spurs, while horses grazed in the church yard. The procession paused. The officer in command bade them disperse in the king's name. Undaunted they stood; the blood of martyrs flowed in their veins, the old fire only smoldered. The Sabbath calm would have been broken by carnage had not the aged pastor (William Montgomery) raised his voice for peacefully retiring; resistance was useless. The officer held a writ of ejectment; the ejected band turned and followed their leader slowly down the hill away from the green graves of their sires and little ones, the women weeping, the little children full of wonder, the men full of a stern resolve. They had borne much, their fathers more, for their faith's sake driven hither and thither through Scotland, and finally out of fair Ayreshire into the desert wastes of Antrim, driving before them the wild natives of Tyrone and Tyrconnel.

Again out of the darkness came the command of "Go forward!" With prophetic gaze they beheld the distant shores of the new world, far beyond the storm-tossed ocean where some of their brethren had already gone and built altars and homes amid primeval forests, finding the savage red-man and wild beasts more merciful foes than those at home under the sway of the ruling house. His eloquent appeal for peace was the last oration of the old pastor — that night he was apprehended while at his devotions, but ere he reached his prison "The hand of God touched him and he slept."

Leadership thus devolved upon the eldest elder who bore the time-honored name of Peden, tradition says James, an old man who had seen many trials, but was staunch and steadfast in the faith; and well he fulfilled his part to the bereft flock. He was the father of five sons, Thomas, William, James, Robert and John. Of these Thomas returned to Scotland (there is some uncertainty as to whether his name was Thomas or Samuel), Robert remained in Ireland, where his descendants are to be found today (1900), John, the founder of this house, was at the time of this ejectment nearly fifty years of age. James Peden and Mary Mills, his wife, were old, and the old tree does not bear transplanting, so after many prayers he revealed his plans to them advising them to seek homes with others of their faith in America, where the demand for skilled labor, especially in the Southern colonies, was steadily increasing, and where many were still going from persecution, both civil and religious, with every outgoing tide, gentleman and yeoman, to people that far new world. The heavy emigration which nearly decimated Ireland's population lasted nearly a score of years ere it was checked, from 1758 to 1770. It is said of the Scotch that only one motive, that of gain, will induce him to leave Scotland, so strong is the love of country.

While the sojourn in Ireland was not more than a century in length, it had the effect of weaning and preparing for a still further flitting. In 1770, John Peden having helped lay his aged parents away to sleep 'til the resurrection, called his now large family around him and told them of his long cherished hope of emigrating to America, whither two sons had preceded him. He was now growing old, but like Moses, his strength was not abated, his eye was not dim, he had a great spirit within him. Verily the heaviest sifting was this last great harvest of golden grain for planting in America in 1770.

"At long anchor in Belfast Bay lay a great sea-going ship; two others were gliding away under the light of the harvest moon; their decks were black with people, so were the shores, and skiffs plied busily to and fro between ship and land. There was a great sound of lamentation on land and shore, the people mourning and crying last farewells to one another so as to pierce the heart; the emigrants put out their hands beseechingly towards the land until the captain, nearly beside himself, gave orders to sheer off. Then the friends on the beach took up a wild lament like that for the dying, and were joined by the exiles on ship-board." Presently, however, the passengers on one ship took up the Hundredth Psalm, and among the voices joining therein was that of old John Peden and his family. The name of the vessel is lost. Her log-book, too, lies possibly at the bottom of the sea until it gives up its dead and buried treasures, but it is an assured fact that with John Peden and his wife, Margaret McDill, there came over, James Peden, his wife and five children; James Alexander, St., his wife and several children; Jane Peden, widow of James or David Morton, and her five children. It is a mooted question whether these came with or preceded their father. The following is unquestioned, Thomas and his wife and an infant child, Mary; William Gaston and his wife, Elizabeth Peden; the five younger brothers, William, John, Samuel, Alexander, David, ranging from eighteen to ten in years. Other kith and kin were among the passengers, names now famous in America. The vessel was crowded "fore and aft, cabin and steerange." No pen can describe the sufferings of the emigrants, the long tedious, dangerous voyage, the sickness and death. All brought what they could of cattle, goods for household needs in the new world. The men the tools and implements of their trades. John Peden was a wagon maker, James a miller, Thomas a miller, John a gunsmith, Samuel a blacksmith; James Alexander was a man of letters, a merchant or farmer, William Gaston was of high lineage, but followed the trade of weaving silk and wool. The women brought their flax-wheels, their hackles, their looms and other necessaries. It is told that Margaret McDill brought over in a bottle a tiny root of the pink moss rose which grew in the castle garden at Broughshane, and that old John brought some apple scions from the trees that grew in the old orchard at home; anyway, there are yet to be found a peculiar juicy white and red apple at Fairview known as "Grandfather's apple" by the children of the seventh son, David.

The last vessel with the Pedens on board had not proceeded far when a cry arose from the deck, "A man overboard!" A boat was lowered and the man rescued amid a shower of musketry from the shore. The adventurous youth gave his name as Robert Mills, and was promptly taken in charge by his kinswoman, Peggy McDill, and her brothr, Thomas McDill. The young man was pursued by the "press-gang" and made his escape by slipping under a fallen tree, his pursuers being mounted had to make their way around the tree, lost time and he cast himself into the sea. His subsequent history belongs to the McDill family who have preserved their traditions, and it is a well known name in the history of South Carolina.

Thomas McDill was destined to be the hero of the voyage, and it may not be amiss to tell of his act of heroism as it saved the vessel and its valuable cargo of souls to bless the new world. He was somewhat of a sailor and fond of the sea and soon became a favorite with the crew; a mutiny was imminent; the "good captain" thrown overboard and the first mate took command; he was unprincipled and took the part of the mutineers, who proposed to take the passengers to the Bermudas and sell them into slavery, turn pirates and scourge the seas. They took Thomas McDill into their confidence, proposing that he should join them; but he was cast in a different mould and with the help of his friends succeeded in putting the crew in irons. Providence was guiding this vessel for a divine purpose, for Thomas McDill, totally ignorant of the coast he was nearing, piloted them safe into harbor. It was not the harbor of their destination, however, but a safe one. "So they tarried awhile in the Land of the Friend." History is not clear on this point as to whether they really landed in Pennsylvania first, or Charlestown. There are two versions so, for the benefit of the doubtful, both are given. Anyway the Pedens bore titles from King George to lands in South Carolina. Unfortunately these old titles have been lost. However many believe that they tarried in Pennsylvania and prospered there until the great tide of emigration swept southward, when they too came to their possessions in what is now Spartanburg County, South Carolina. The other version is that they were landed at Charlestown and there John Peden put together the wagons they had brought and buying a few horses and a few supplies they turned their faces bravely toward the wilderness of upper Carolina, sending in advance some to "blaze" a path. At some points they found a road, but most of the, way they found there were streams to cross, perils to meet. They subsisted on game that their rifles brought down, fish from the rivers, green corn bought of the red-men and had often to dodge swift arrows sent after them by hidden foes. At night they built great fires to protect them from wild beast, and committing themselves to God lay down to rest in a strange land.

> "Tho their hearts were sad at times, and their bodies weary
>   Hope still guided them on,
> 'Patience!' whispered the oaks from oracular caverns of darkness;
> And from moonlit meadows a sigh responded — 'Tomorrow.'"

Note — Later information states that the emigrant ships were the "Eagle Wing," "Morning Star" and "Adventurer," each 150 tons burden. Each emigrant was entitled to 100 acres of land (some more none less) by a grant from the king, for which was paid about seventy-five cents, with the agreement to bring under cultivation a certain number of acres within the year. These old grants bear the date 1768.

Old records of the Alexander family show that they landed in New York in 1768, coming to South Carolina in 1770, tarrying in Penna. for two years; also that James Alexander, Sr., David or James Morton, and James Peden came first with their families settling in Penna., while Thomas Peden with his father and five younger brothers, and William Gaston, his wife, Elizabeth, came later in 1770, direct from Philadelphia to South Carolina, making no stop in that state. Among their fellow emigrants were these names, Lee, Garrett, McQueen, Hughes, White, Brown, Hemphill, Jackson, McQuestion, McClintock, McDonald, McDill; these found homes in Chester and comprised almost an entire congregation, while to Spartanburg came Anderson, Alexander, Barry, Caldwell, Coan, Collins, Dodds, Gaston, Jamison, McMahan, Miller, Moore, Morton, Morrow, Pearson, Penrey, and others.

Chapter Four - Our Fore-Fathers

> "What sought they thus afar?
> Bright jewels of the mine?
> The wealth of seas; the spoils of war?
> They sought a Faith's pure shrine."

[Note — For much of this chapter the writer is indebted to Rev. R. H. Reid, venerable pastor of Nazareth church, also to Mr. A. W. Gaston, lineal descendant of Thomas Peden, who still owns the old home, and last, but by no means least, to the fine memory of her own maternal grandmother, Eleanor G. Dunbar, who was the youngest daughter of David Peden, the seventh son of John the Founder, who was a girl of fifteen when her father died, so she had the precious privilege of hearing the dear, old brothers talk of perils past in which conversation they delighted to while away the long winter evenings around their firesides. A custom which they kept up until death entered the charmed circle was to meet at one of their homes Saturday evening and spend their Sabbaths under one roof-tree. This they did in rotation. Eleanor G. Dunbar was a woman whose veracity could not be questioned, for, like her venerated father, she abhorred a lie. She rejoined the great host gone before in May, 1899, a few weeks prior to the Peden reunion at Fairview, S.C., and would have attained her ninetieth year on June 16, 1899. Consequently she remembered her father; her grandfather, John, dying before her birth.]

It was long past mid-summer when John Peden and his family reached the place of their final sojourn in the new world and there was already a suspicion of frost in the air.

Some eight or ten families who had come down through the pathless woods from the land of Penn. and had settled on the branches of the Tyger river in what is now Spartanburg County, S.C., as early as 1761. The place chosen for their church was equally distant between the two settlements known as the "upper" and "lower," in order to be accurate the distance was stepped by two old men. The first house of worship was of roughhewn logs, built in 1765. It was this rude temple that greeted the sight of John Peden when he and his tired band emerged from the woods into the clearing. It is said that he reverently bared his head as he passed, his sons following his example; here too they were met and welcomed by their brethren all joining in a service of praise to the Great Father, who had brought them together after many perils by sea and land at the altar reared by pious hands, on the sacred hill where the old church now stands, though the rude log one was replaced by a spacious brick one long ago.

"The solemn voice of praise then broke the stillness which had reigned upon it since creation. In "the virgin forest, amid the vistas through which they walked as through long drawn aisles of some vast temple, while above them hung the dome of heaven, fretted with stars. From the green isle beyond the sea, and from Scotland's glen and heather came the children of the martyrs, who had sealed with blood their testimony for Christ's crown and covenant. Edging their way along the slopes of the Alleghenies, the watershed of a great continent, their weary feet rested at length upon the fertile banks of Enoree and Tyger, founding upon this venerable spot a plantation for God. By obscure bridle paths through tangled woods, across rocky fords, over which wild streams yet dash their shallow floods they came singly and in groups to this rude sanctuary in the woods."

Here too John Peden and his family found food and rest. These friends kindly ministered to their needs ere they passed on to the hillside where John Peden reared his first cabin home. When their first camp fire was kindled and ere an axe was laid to fell a tree, or stone was placed, John Peden brought from the depths of his wagon the "Book" Seating himself on a huge flat rock, with his wife beside him, his children and grandchildren around him, Davie with his tired head on his mother's knee watching the smoke curl up, and sparks lose themselves among the trees, striving to keep his sleepy eyes wide open. The father opened at the ninetieth psalm, which he read slowly and impressively, offered a fervent prayer, and they all joined in singing "Old Hundredth," after which they partook of "hominy" and laid themselves down to sleep regardless alike of wild beast and yet wilder redman, knowing well that "He who keepeth Israel slumbers not nor sleeps." Thus the Peden reared his altar ere he built his home.

These early pioneers held grants or deeds to lands on the Tygers and Enoree rivers for several hundred acres of land. Of only one of these documents is there any trace and unfortunately it is lost, being an heirloom in the family of Thomas Peden, second son; a deed for five hundred acres of land lying along what is known as Ferguson's creek, bearing the signature of George the Third, king of England, &c. The price paid was seventy-five cents per hundred acres, equal to three dollars and seventy-five cents for the whole five hundred acres, with the understanding that a certain portion was to be put in cultivation within a given time, one or two years. This tract is now in the possession of his descendant, Mr. A. W. Gaston, who has many of the characteristics of his forefathers. It is generally accepted among the Pedens that John Peden purchased a larger number of acres because of his four younger sons, they all being under age. However all traces of these earlier boundaries are lost, for after the War of the Revolution, all these lands were regranted and only Thomas Peden remained near the old site. Where once stood the first cabin home of John Peden is the bare hillside and the disused spring at its foot. This pioneer home differed in no wise from its neighbors, being simply a kind of pen of roughhewn logs, the spaces filled in with clay to keep out the wintry blast and too curious gaze of the red-men. Its size was 20 x 20 feet, one entire end filled by a huge fire-place of stone and clay, here swung the crane and pot-hooks of rude manufacture; here was baked the Johnny cake and ash-cake of Indian meal; here was roasted the wild game from the woods, and fish from the streams. In one corner stood the loom, near-by the flax wheel, brought across the sea. The furniture was of the rudest description, and what need for better in a wild land, where the torch of the red-man was so often applied and they had to flee for refuge to some fort or blockhouse. Old Fort Prince will serve as a description of all the others as there was no essential difference in the style of these places of safety. It was named for Wm. Prince, an old settler. There were several others equally distant, Poole's, near Glendale, Nicholls, near "Narrow Pass," on the David Anderson place. Blockhouse, Earle's, Thicketty. Which of these afforded safety to the Peden in times of danger is lost to tradition.

The historic Fort Prince was built near the famous Blackstock road (once the route used by armies of the Revolution, and during the troublous days prior to 1776, also in the piping days of peace noted persons have traveled its length), about three-fourths of a mile from Mt. Zion church, two and one-half miles from the present town of Fairforest, near the stream now known as Gray's creek, one of the tributaries of North Tyger river. This stream is the only water crossing the Blackstock road between Motlow's creek, one of the prongs of the South Pacol'et river, and the Tyger river at Blockstock ford, a distance of forty miles. "The fort was circular in shape, of heavy timbers from twelve to fifteen feet high; surrounding this was a ditch or moat the earth from which was thrown up against the walls of parapet height. This was secured in front by an abatis of heavy timbers making when completed a respectable place of defense against the enemy. In the upright pieces portholes were cut one and one-half inches by four inches in diameter for the riflemen inside." (Landrum's History of Colonial and Revolutionary South Carolina.)

Oftentimes their bedding and clothing were concealed for weeks in hollow trees, where great piles of brushwood hid the openings, at the mercy of mice, squirrels and other sharp-toothed wood folk. Many valuable records were lost in this way. Their food was also buried under ground for days, the cattle driven off to the cane-brakes, or captured by the foe, their barn-yards depopulated of poultry and hogs; yet they returned and took up the burden anew, enjoying even a temporary lull of hostilities. Within a few years they gathered about them a few of the rudest comforts of life, happy and content to have the freedom to worship as they chose.

One thing they missed sadly and that was schools for their growing youth. The older members were not, as is generally supposed, ignorant, this idea is erroneous in the extreme. The Scotch-Irish were well educated as a race, and some of those wonderfully preserved old yellow documents show a scholarship remarkable even at this late day. They seldom had the "preached word" for only occasionally during those early days did a minister reach them traveling by bridle paths from the older settlements or the coast, which was extremely hazardous and tedious. The first mentioned was the Rev. Joseph Alexander, who came from Philadelphia to minister to his brethren in the wilderness. It is presumed that he was related to that James Alexander, husband of Mary Peden. Why no preacher came over with the Pedens is a source of some comment, as one generally came with each ship-load, history is silent — possibly he was lost at sea, for many died on ship-board, or he may have been on one of the other two ships from which they were separated and which subsequent events proved reached the Jersey shore. The intensely religious nature of the Peden did not suffer from this want for he had his Bible and his catechism, and was not a worshipper of creed, marking out straight paths by the light from the word, he walked therein regardless of man.

Troubles were brewing too across the sea; the heel of oppression was grinding the colonies; vague rumors reached them through occasional travelers, or when one of their number made the perilous trip down to Charleston. The Pedens, never remarkable as talkers, did a great deal of thinking, and when the fulness of time gave opportunity proved them men of action. While these distant thunders were muttering in the distance, the Pedens on the Tyger and Enoree were clearing their lands, attending to their trades and attending strictly to their own affairs. Their women were teasing wool, hackling flax, spinning yarn, weaving long webs of cloth, clothing their households, if not in purple and fine linen, at least warmly. The costume of a pioneer ancestress may not come amiss. She wore short comfortable skirts, blue stockings, heavy, home-made shoes, a short, full sacque, always different from her skirt, this was belted down, a kerchief around her neck, and after motherhood a cap over her sunny or raven hair. These caps were curious things, a bit of snow-white linen cloth folded square, a seam, a slight pucker, a pair of ties, a hem and they were done, and fair and sweet was the face they framed. The dress of the men was truly pioneer in appearance. They wore the hunting shirt, belt, powder horn and knife, heavy boots, coming well up over their homespun trousers, the three cornered hat, and always carried their rifles. When at work they removed the outer or fringed deer skin hunting shirt, and wore the homespun one provided by the thrifty wife at home. For Sunday or holiday occasions they shone out in brave attire and were quite splendid in cues and powder, lace and buckles. The women were always soberly clad like the mother birds.

[Note — According to Howes' History, the settlements on the North and Middle Tygers did not take place earlier than 1755. This was the year of Governor Glenn's treaty, and the statement is corroborated by Ramsey, who refers to the colony as following Colonel Clark and settling in Spartanburg County in 1755. (Ramsey's *Hist. S.C.*, page 118.) Among these settlers are the present familiar names, Moore, Barry, Jordan, Nesbit, Vernon, Collins, Peden, Nichols, Caldwell, Wakefield, Anderson, Snoddy, Miller. Mills says in his statistics, "This section was settled between 1750-1760, but from its exposed situation, it did not much increase in population until 1776. These first settlers were from Virginia, Pennsylvania and North Carolina." There was positively no communications with the eastern or sea-board colonies earlier than 1775. "They were a brave, noble set of pioneers, well worthy to be the entering wedge of civilization in the upcountry of South Carolina. They came to confront the Indian tomahawk and scalping knife, with a true heroism and patriotism, a spirit of energy and progressiveness, which they transmitted to a noble posterity. They braved all dangers and difficulties, and their humble efforts to better their condition, and to lay the foundation for the generations that succeeded them have been crowned with success. Therefore it becomes a solemn, a sacred duty to —

"Cherish their memory,
 Glory in their triumphs,
Emulate their virtues,
Avoid their mistakes,
Faithfully discharge the trusts.
Committed by them to our keeping —"

Chapter Five - The Peden in the Revolution

"Hail Independence! heavens's next best gift To that of life, and air and an immortal soul."

— Thompson.

With long, low mutterings the ominous clouds of war were ready to burst over the infant colonies. The Pedens were too fresh from the land of the oppressor, the house of bondage, to forget their wrongs. They had breathed in the spirit of Freedom during their brief sojourn in the new world: so were ready — among the first to cry, with the Virginia orator: "Give me liberty — or give me death!"

The Pedens being men of action, not of words, were ready long before the call came, thinking and thinking deeply, so when the cry came echoing down from Boston, and Dan Morgan called for men they were ready to respond. An old author says: "There came into the camp, among the first recruits, a company from over the Carolina mountains of Scotch-Irish settlers along the Tygers and Enoree rivers. Among them an old man with long locks, white as snow, and eyes that flashed like the eagle's. He was tall and somewhat bent, as one who had stooped much. He was driving the company's wagon and with his seven sons were enlisted; as well as some sons-in-law and not a few grandsons. These men fought through the war to its close in rank and file, but braver soldiers never were in any army."

The name of this old man was not given, but there is every reason to believe it to be John Peden, as the company was a picked one from the famous Spartan regiment. Col. John Thomas, Sr. In regard to this regiment it may be of interest to give some historic authority in this place, so two are quoted. quoted.

"I had this day (August 21, 1775) a meeting with the people in this frontier. Many were present of the other party (Tory), but I have the pleasure to acquaint you that those became voluntary converts. Every person received satisfactory reasons and departed with pleasure. I finished the day with a barbecued beef. I have also ordered matters here, that this whole frontier will be formed into volunteer companies, but as they are at present under Fletchall's (Tory) command, they insist upon being formed into a regiment independent of him; and I flatter myself you will think this method of weakening Fletchall, to be considered sound policy. These people are active and spirited; they are staunch in our favor; are capable of forming a good barrier against the Indians, and of being a severe check upon Fletchall's people. For these reasons and to enable them to act with vigor, I shall take the liberty of supplying them with a small quantity of ammunition, for they have not an ounce, when they shall be formed into regular companies. Several companies will be formed by this day week." (Drayton's Memoirs, vol. I., page 374.)

This regiment, known as the Spartan Regiment, was formed on September 11, 1775. A letter from Col. John Thomas follows:

"Spartan Regiment, Sept. 11, 1775.

"To the Honorable Wm. H. Drayton, Esq.:

"May it please Your Honor: I this moment received Your Honor's favor of the loth inst.; and very fortunately, the command for this district (Spartan), was just assembled at my house in order to address the Council of Safety almost on the very purport of Your Honor's letter, as we had all the reason in the world (and still have) to believe from good information, that the malignants (Tories), are forming the most hellish schemes to frustrate the measures of the Continental Congress, and to use all those who are willing to stand by those measures in the most cruel manner. Your Honor will be fully convinced of the truth of this by perusing the paper transmitted herewith, to which I refer Your Honor.

"I shall comply with Your Honor's orders as far as is in my power; Your Honor must suppose it impossible to raise the whole regiment, as several have families, and no man be left about the house, if they should be called away. I shall take as large a draft as possible from every company, and in short, do everything to the utmost of my power, and when encamped shall transmit to Your Honor as quick as possible, an account of my proceedings.

"John Thomas." (Col.)

These quotations show the patriotism of the race. They were a people knowing their rights, and knowing dared maintain, and prove that prior to 1776 they were in armed resistance to unjust taxation from the mother country. From Almanance to the finish at Yorktown which acknowledged their independence, their names are on muster rolls of every force engaged in fighting the foes of liberty. These rolls are many of them lost, but a few remain that have been rescued from oblivion. The Pedens, Mortons, Alexanders were scattered through this regiment, and fought under various leaders. A few of the captains of the companies have been obtained; a list of one company has the name of James Morton on the roll, Captain Wm. Smith. John Alexander was first lieutenant in one company. The names of some of the captains many interest the reader. Andrew Barry, John Caldwell, Edward Hampton, Shadrack Inman, Wm. Johnson, John Collins and others. The Majors were, Samuel McJunkin, Joseph Hughes, ___ Chronicle, Benj. Roebuck, Wade Hampton. The Colonel was John Thomas. They served under Daniel Morgan at the first, later under the partisan leaders of Upper South Carolina, taking part in the battles of the whole Revolutionary period.

John Peden, patriot, gave to the Revolutionary army himself and seven sons, James, Thomas, John, William, Samuel, Alexander and David; three sons-in-law, James Alexander, Sr., Samuel Morrow, William Gaston; grandsons, John, James, William and Thomas Alexander, John, James and David Morton, William, John, James and Thomas (?) Peden; about twenty-two in all. Some of these were mere boys, but it is a glorious record for one family. "It is not the names that shine brightest on history's pages that have done most for any land, it is the unnamed heroes that win the fields of glory. It is the fault of history to give too much prominence to officers and ignore the men, who fought and died to make them great, and in that way the truth is confounded."

History says, the "first men to respond to the call of the Continental Congress were the already organized companies gathered together by Daniel Morgan (who had suffered great outrages) from the 'over mountains' of Pennsylvania, Virginia and the Upper Carolinas. They were determined men, stern of mein, and very striking in their appearance. They wore coarse, fringed hunting shirts, belted with deer-skin bands, trousers of rough cloth, flax, wool or skin made by the industrious women in the cabins, raw-hide shoes of the roughest kind, woolen hats of cloth, also home-made; some three-cornered with springs of green for cockades; some like "Scotch bonnets;" many brimless crowns; they carried their blankets folded and strapped over their shoulders by thongs of deer-skin; pouches of the same held their day's supply of rock-a-hominy (Indian corn parched and pounded coarsely between two stones), a handful was eaten, then a cup of water was swallowed to moisten; this, and what wild game their rifles brought down had sustained them on the long march from the Tygers to Boston. Their arms consisted of their rifles, bits of lead, a powder horn, home-made, sometimes a cow's horn, sometimes a gourd, a hunting knife, and the "Spartan" soldier was ready for the fray."

John Peden was too old for active service, but made himself useful in many ways, but very reticent about any good he did. On one occasion he was asked if he did anything in the war by a favored grandchild, "Nothing much, nothing much." But in the silent watches of the night John Peden retired behind his wagon to pray, and in the hottest of the fight his hands swiftly loaded many a deadly shot into waiting rifles and handed them to less skilled hands, many savory messes met them on their return to camp from the depths of the "old Conestoga wagon, that went through the war."

At Valley Forge the Peden left his bloody foot-prints on the snow, and tradition tells that the feet of one brother were so injured that he never was able afterward to wear shoes in comfort (William). Three came home with coughs that lasted all their lives, not consumptive but bronchial (John, Samuel and Alexander). The barrels of their rifles made prints on their shoulders, often wore bare places through their clothing; these marks were plainly visible on the shoulders of one brother (John) when he was robed for the grave in 1810.

"The darkest hour comes just before daylight." (John Peden.) This was 1780, and the territory of South Carolina was completely subjugated by the British. After the defeat of Gen. Gates the people were crushed and inclined to submit to the powers that were for a period of rest, but their minds changed very quickly when they realized what the rest meant, and a ray of hope gleamed through the darkness, though many had taken protection. The Peden sternly refused to do this, "he had little worldly pelf, and a life of bondage was worse than death, he would hide in caves and dens until the calamity be past." (James Peden.) It goes down to history that the Peden never took protection, as the proudest record of this quiet race.

Such was the case in Upper South Carolina when a proclamation was issued requiring them to join the British army in order to keep their liberty (?), raised the mettle in their natures. While discontent had reigned as well as despair, and most of them believed the cause of freedom to be lost, and were for quietly submitting to their fate. Those active spirits, South Carolina's Immortal Trio, Marion, Sumter and Lee, with Roebuck, McJunkin and others, who had persistently defied royal authority were working among the Whigs. Thomas Peden was with Roebuck, also the Alexanders and Mortons, while the others were with McJunkin and Hughes. Their commands which had been reduced to mere handfuls of patriots soon began to swell, and were soon respectable in numbers. Hope revived, the people in small parties began to rendezvous and arm for resistance. Said they, "If we must resume our arms, let us rather fight for America and our friends than for England and strangers." So they flocked to the recruiting camps nearest them. Cedar Spring and Earle's Ford. Thomas Peden, having preferred outlawry to British protection, had gone to the North Carolina mountains, in Bedell County, with his wife and children, being a man of indomitable will and unconquerable spirit. His father, John Peden, would have gladly remained quietly at home, as would several of his sons, but the larger number sided with Thomas, so the father said, "I follow." Seeing his wife and numerous grandchildren safe in Chester, this old patriot, with the eagle eyes and lint white locks, again took up the line of march and battle cry of "Freedom!" They had been greatly troubled by the false report circulated by Tories, that the Continental Congress had abandoned South Carolina to her fate after Gates' defeat. Before the year which dawned so darkly (1780) ended, the following battles were fought and won: Cedar Spring, Thicketty, Wofford's Iron Works, Earle's Ford, Musgrove's Mill, King's Mountain and Cowpens. All of these partisan battles save King's Mountain are within the old boundaries of the Spartan district, where the Peden made his first home. To the world at large they seem insignificant, as compared with some of modern times, yet each one was a giant stride on the line of march to memorable Yorktown, on that historic peninsula where most if not all of America's greatest battles have been fought. Their work did not end with Yorktown. They came back to the Carolina hills to find the Tory in possession and their families scattered, to plunge again into brief but bloody partisan warfare.

While neither John Peden or his seven sons rose from rank and file to office, one grandson became a Major and another Captain. On many of the old grave-stones in the rock-walled God's acre at Fairview may yet be read this legend: "A soldier of the Revolution."

"They wrought better than they knew —
The guns they fired that famous day
Were heard around the world."

John Peden's was one of the train of wagons that did such service for the cause at King's Mountain so faithfully described by Draper. His sons, sons-in-law, grandsons, etc., were among Col. Williams' men in that memorable battle that paved the way to Yorktown. This is from Major McJunkin's Memoirs by Saye.

At Cowpens (the writer wishes it were possible to either copy, or place a copy of this great partisan battle in the hands of every Peden as depicted by Landrum in his History of Upper South Carolina) where, figuratively speaking, "they fought with halters around their necks," the three youngest brothers, Samuel, Alexander and David, were among the picked men of Pickens; men selected with the greatest care being brave and daring, all young unmarried men, they were culled from the whole of Morgan's army and stationed loosely, even carelessly, in the front line. Their names should have been preserved, but no record can be found. This front line or decoy were instructed to "mark the epaulette men." It was a favorite recital of David Peden to tell of this scene to his sons long winter nights, how they stood in very unmilitary positions waiting the charge, but the rustling of the wind, the fall of a dead twig, put them on the alert; how when they fell back in such perfect order as to throw the enemy into the arms of their army; how the color bearer tripped and fell; how he snatched the colors and ran on with them until his comrade recovered and took them back.

Then the last scene at Yorktown, when Washington reviewed his army, just before the battle, "when he and his staff neared Morgan's 'split-shirt men,' he dismounted from his charger, gave the reins to one of the officers, took off his three-cornered hat, removed his gauntlet from his right hand, held both hat and glove in his left, advanced the entire length of the line" shaking hands with all whom he could reach.

David Peden said, "That was the proudest moment of my life, to clasp the great general's hand, sufficient reward for all the hard marching." These last incidents are from David Peden's own lips, handed down to the writer by his youngest daughter. As a question arises as to where the other Peden brothers settled prior to the war of the Revolution, the writer, after much exhaustive correspondence with many different members of the race and strangers, evolved the following solution: John Peden, his wife and four youngest sons came direct from Pennsylvania, with their second son, Thomas. The landing took place in New York according to McDill testimony in 1770-1772. James Peden, the eldest son, came somewhat later from Chester, Penna., to Chester, S.C. The Alexander family came to Spartanburg just prior to the Revolution. They had large connections already settled in Penna., and also in Maryland. There are two versions as to the first home of the Morton's. First, that the husband of Jane Peden died from injuries received during the persecution in Ireland. (Reminiscences of her son, David Morton.) Second, that he was a brother of John Morton, one of the signers of the Declaration of Independence, "the pivot who turned the scale that memorable day and died the next;" after whose death, which occurred in Penna. about the same time of his brother's she, with her five Morton children, turned southward. Her marriage to Samuel Morrow taking place in South Carolina. The Morrows came from Penna. to South Carolina. As James Peden was a member of the Provincial Congress from Chester District, it is safe to presume that he settled there, and was 'a cord' to draw John and Peggy thither, as well as the McDill family. He went to Fairview about 1789. (This is from records sent direct from Chester by Dr. G. B. White, James Hemphill and others). It is safe therefore to assume that James Peden and his sons were not of the Spartan Regiments, but with those of Chester. All their patriotic hearts beat as one, and when the war ended the strong cords of brotherhood and clanship drew them together singly and in groups to old Fairview. Those chords are broken now and the Peden roams afar.

The following is a partial list of the officers of the Spartan Regiment, Battalion of the Tygers:

Generals — Dan Morgan, Nathaniel Green.

Colonels — John Thomas, Sr., John Thomas, Jr., Andrew Pickens, Wade Hampton, William Austin.

Majors — Benjamin Roebuck, Joseph Hughes, Samuel McJunkin, John Alexander.

Captains — John Barry, Andrew Barry, John Collins, Mathew Patton, William Smith.

These were not all in command at the same time, as will be understood.

John Morton's name appears on the roll of Capt. Smith's company, and John Alexander was first lieutenant, afterwards Major, of the "Tyger Irish."

The officers of the Chester Pedens, as far as known, were: Captains— John Hemphill, Berry Jeffries; and Major Joseph Hughes.

Most of. the old records are lost; fire, flood and winds have done their work, and "tradition becomes history." Even if the old swords are turned to rust, the old guns classed as rubbish, the powder horns playthings of the generations following, the clanking spurs creations of wonder to the eyes of today, a few remain at Fairview. The wheels that spun the flax and wool, the looms that wove the "hodden grey" homespun worn by the patriots, have been relegated to long forgotten garrets or became fuel long ago, this one grand fact remains, the Peden had a share, a very large share, in the founding of the glorious fifth power of the world, America!

Chapter Six - Migrations of the Peden

"Over the mountain's height
Like Ocean in its tided might
The living sea rolled onward."

It is the purpose of this volume to trace the Peden back into dim and misty realms beyond the sunrise sea, to the old home nest in Ayrshire, "in all Scotland," and in Ballymena, Ireland, and follow them up, step by step until they reach the throne of that long vanished king, Alexander, traditional founder of the house.

Their migrations, with the causes, are historic; their uprooting in Scotland in 1602-1609; their sojourn in Ireland, covers a period of nearly one century. Their banishment to the "emerald isle" along with the Hamilton, Montgomery and others under the High Sheriff of Ayre is no longer a mooted question, but historically proven. (Douglas Campbell.)

That they had some claim on the noble house of Hamilton no longer admits of doubt; but that house was never all Protestant, and was ever divided in its religious views, and its adherence to the Stuart the pages of history can prove. Robert the Bruce, of Norman descent, divided his patrimony in Ayre with Hamilton and Douglas on his accession to the Scottish throne, and the Peden went with the Hamilton ever after in his fortunes.

In 1630, to prevent the Scotch in Ulster from signing the covenant, Charles Stuart, tyrant, imposed the Black Oath, in which they swore allegiance to the king, promising never to rebel against him, never to protest against any of his commands, never to enter any covenant or oath without his authority. This spread consternation among them, and proving obstinate, the Lord Lieutenant of Ireland, Lord Wentworth, imposed heavy fines; this pouring gold into the king's treasury, made him a prime favorite and he was created Earl of Strafford. Then he decided to banish the contumacious Scotch to the new world and sell them into slavery, but "the Lord, who has been our dwelling place in all generations," interfered. He was sifting the golden grain for the last great planting in America.

The fates of Charles Stuart and the Earl of Strafford belong to English history. While the Peden and his compeers realized that Ireland was no longer a home for him and his — this was his first rude awakening from a dream of security.

The second came in 1700. The passing of the Test Act which completed the suppression of civil freedom.

It has been the earnest effort of the writer to settle the much disputed question as to the date and manner of the emigration to the New World, so, after much laborious and exhaustive correspondence, both within and without the clan, it is yet indefinitely proven. The best solution seems that given by the McDill annals; for they, unlike the Pedens, have kept their records dating back nearly three hundred years. This migration took place in 1770-1772. Though destined for the Carolinas they lingered for two years in Pennsylvania, "along the Jersey shore" in one of the three original counties, general opinion being Berks or Chester, preferably Chester.

"There were three shiploads of emigrants composed of the entire congregation of the church in Balleymena, consisting of about three hundred souls, with their pastor, whose name is not given but is supposed to have been one Alexander, left Belfast port on September 9th, 1768 or 1770. The names of these ships, one of them owned in part by the emigrants, named the "Eagle

Wing" which had attempted to cross thirty years before, but proved too heavy and was put back into port and remodeled, the "Morning Star," and the "Adventurer." The names of all the captains are lost to history save that of Captain Andrew Agnew, who is described as a kindly man and a Presbyterian. Of which ship he had charge and on which the Pedens came over is lost. The "Eagle Wing," 150 tons burden, was built in 1735, and attempted its first voyage in 1736, having on board one hundred and forty passengers, among them the following godly ministers, Revs. Chas, Campbell, Jno. Somerville, Hugh Brown and others." But, as stated before the ship was driven back. Nothing daunted the younger men made the voyage later, and it is a tradition that Hugh Brown came with the same company of the Pedens, that he went aboard one of the other ships leaving "godly Jno. Peden" to look after the spiritual welfare of part of his flock on the way over.

It is a well established fact that the heaviest emigration from Ulster took place from 1755-1768. Their destination being the "land of Penn." Yet many bore grants to the unopened lands of "Upper South Carolina." It is a curious, if not a providential fact, that this favored land of the Quaker Penn, ever open to the oppressed, received most of the Scotch emigrants from Ireland. It seemed as if they needed a brief respite from the buffetings and trials of the old world before encountering those of the new, so the land of Penn proved that haven of rest. It is also handed down by the families of White, Archer, Martin, Morrow, all of whom came to Penna. and settled in Chester County and formed a church called Fairview. The McDills also were of this congregation, and it has been alarmed to the writer by her maternal grandmother, Eleanor (Peden) Dunbar, that the Pedens of South Carolina named their church at Fairview for both the old church in Ballymena, Ireland, and the one in Chester County, Pennsylvania. The location of this latter church the writer has failed to find after much earnest effort, and is inclined to think it a mistake, though there are two Fairviews in Pennsylvania. West Fairview near Harrisburg and Fairview in the extreme northwestern portion. If there exists an East Fairview she has found no trace as yet.

Tradition tells that the wife of one of the brothers was a Friend or Quakeress; that she never lost the use of "thee and thou" all her life among the Pedens, as well as wore their garb, and while she attended faithfully the Presbyterian church at Fairview, her views never changed. "She was a tiny creature so sweet and demure" clad in her plain drab dress with white linen cap and kerchief (three cornered cape), and when she learned the secret of dying her peculiar color of drab, or dull grey, with an infusion of sweet-gum bark and a pinch of copperas, her delight was boundless.

The White family have recorded many reminiscences of their stay in Pennsylvania before coming to South Carolina, and as two of the seven brothers married aunts of Gen. Hugh Lawson White, and their nephew, David Morton, married the youngest sister of the same family it seems conclusive that they must have been co-resident. Elizabeth White was the wife of Thomas Peden, and Katherine of his brother Samuel. The first were married in Ireland and it was their infant (Mary) whom Peggy McDill brought ashore in her arms and "Mary was her darling all her days." Samuel and Katherine were married just prior to the journey southward, while tradition says that David Morton and Penelope were married in Chester, S.C., after the Revolution. These two crossed the seas together as children.

The Martin family also came from Pennsylvania and "Rebecca, wife of Alexander Peden, was the daughter of a neighbor in the mother country who came over with them." The family were undoubtedly from Pennsylvania.

The Morrows, to whom Jane Peden's second husband belonged, was a colonial family of Pennsylvania. They are very proud of their record and well they may be. The writer has seen some interesting relics of this house. The prevalence of the name Eleanor is as significant to the Morrows as to the Pedens descending from Eleanor Goodgion, wife of David, the seventh son.

Thomas Hughes, who settled in Chester, S.C., came direct from Pennsylvania and across the ocean with the same company and he always mentioned the McDills, Millers and others as being in the same colony with the Pedens. He shared their perilous voyage, and the statement comes from him that "under stress of weather the companion ships were driven apart at sea, and came together into the same port." He assisted Thomas McDill in quelling the mutiny on shipboard. He also gave the name of the ship in which he came over as the "Adventurer." This Thomas Hughes came to America, as he states, under a heavy cloud. He imparted his secret to John Peden alone, under pledge of secrecy, which pledge John Peden kept inviolate and was a good friend of Thomas Hughes as long as they both lived. Thomas Hughes married Annie Miller. Their history would make a vivid romance if ever written. Thomas Hughes also states that they (owing to the munity) did not reach the port for which they were bound (Charleston), but landed on the "Jersey shore," afterwards crossing over to Penna.

There are also traditions preserved by the James, Collins and Thompson families proving that the Pedens sojourned in Penna. some years ere coming southward. And the most conclusive of all, seems to the writer, the statement of her own ancestor, David Peden, that he was a boy of eight or ten when he crossed over. He was born in Ireland November 1, 1760. He was strangely silent regarding where the two or four intervening years were spent.

Howe's History of the Presbyterian Church in South Carolina in responsible for the statement that the Pedens landed in Charleston, S.C., and came direct to Spartanburg. His informants were men and women who came over on the voyage living at the time the book was written. This is accepted by Rev. R. H. Reid and also by a great many of the Pedens.

The shipping records of Charleston were mostly if not wholly destroyed during some of Charleston's many catastrophes. No trace is to be found there.

However they came, through whatever port they entered, "they came, they saw, they conquered." Accepting either version, John Peden came to America in 1768 to 1770, as the old royal grants show, as none were issued after that date for two reasons. George the Second died October 7, 1760, and "George the Third was king." The other reason is that Ireland was fast returning to "a howling wilderness" by the departure of the Scotch; a coast guard was placed and the "Press-law" enforced, so it is hardly supposable that a family of sons like John Peden's would be allowed to depart together and peaceably by a king like George the Third, under a royal grant.

The War of Independence found John Peden and his family in Spartanburg County, South Carolina. The family had already taken firm root in the new soil. "All seven followed their father through those trying days, and all came home together," is the statement of a daughter of David the youngest.

At the close of the war the next migration took place bringing the family to Fairview, in Greenville County. All lands were re-granted at this time and this country, recently wrested from the Indians, was opened to the settlers, so the pioneer Peden came among the very first. This may be considered the very cradle of the race, nay, the American house of Padan, Paden, Peden, in all its varied spelling. Every fact brought to light so far proves, with one exception, that all these trace their origin back to South Carolina. Here, with three exceptions, the older men and women of the ten original families spent their last years and sleep their last sleep. During the year 1803 the Louisiana purchase and acquisition of the "great northwest" began to stir the interest of these Pedens of the third generation. 1812 brought the excitement of war with England and many a stalwart young Peden mounted his horse, shouldered his gun and rode away to return with tidings of fair land farther on to the westward; Georgia, Mississippi and the great north were holding out hands to these brave, young pioneers to come help build up these waste places, occupy these lands. The call was resistless, they turned their faces toward the setting sun. Part of the second generation and most of the third leaving Fairview.

The story of some of these migrations as told by the venerable chronicler and clerk of the sessions, Anthony Savage, in the oldest church book now in existence, is as follows:

"April 4, 1815 — Jno. Peden's family and part of widow Peden's family moved to Kentucky; regularly dismissed."

"1815, Oct. 16 — Widow Peden and the rest of her family moved to Kentucky."

"1816 — Thomas Peden and family moved back to Chester, S. C, (Rev. Jno. Hemphill pastor at Hopewell church, Chester Co., S. C.)"

"18 1 7 — Robert Morrow, his two sons, Samuel and Thomas, with their families moved to Alabama territory."

"1820 — Maj. Jno. Alexander and family, Wm. Alexander and family, leave the State."

This ends the first manuscript book to be found, therefore a period of ten or more years and a number of dismissals or emigrations are also lost.

"1833 — Robert W. Peden, Dan and Alexander Peden (brothers), David S. Peden, with their families, regularly dismissed."

"1835 — Dismissed four of our families, Wm. Morrow, four in number, Jas. Morton, six in number, Wm. Armour, two in number, and Jas. McVickers."

"1836 — Dismissed, Linsay A. Baker and family, four in unmber, Samuel H. Baker and family, three in number."

"1837 — Jas. Peden's family, six in number. Alex. Alexander and family, six in number, Wm. Harrison and wife, Jas. Harrison and wife, Alexander Savage and his wife Rosanna" (Morton).

"1843 — Dismissed Andrew W. Peden, Rebecca Peden, Jno. M. Peden, Esther E. Peden, A. W. R. Baker, David C. Baker, Jno. W. Baker."

Here also is recorded so beautifully the death of Jenny Savage.

"1847 — The dismissal of Laurens F. Baker and his wife to Mississippi."

Here Anthony Savage lays aside the pen. The historian did not have time to follow these dismissals through the other books by James Dunbar, who took up the pen where Anthony Savage laid it down. He too, after "serving his generation according to the will of God, fell asleep." The pilgrim mantle and stafif then fell to the present clerk, Dr. David R. Anderson, worthy successor to these two saintly men. From these small beginnings began the "Westward ho!" of this now almost numberless race, scattered all over these fair United States and in other lands.

All Padans, Padens, Pedens in America have a common ancestry, as is proven by numbers of letters from almost every State telling the same legend, "my Peden ancestor was from South Carolina, his name was James, Thomas, William, Samuel, Alexander, David, or Mary Peden who married Jas. Alexander, or Jane Peden, who married first a Morton then a Morrow." They are in Tennessee, Missouri, Ohio, Indiana, Illinois, Iowa, Michigan, Minnesota, Nevada, Wyoming, Washington, Utah, California, Texas, Arkansas, Kansas, Louisiana, Mississippi, Alabama, Georgia, North and South Carolina, Oklahoma, New York, Massachusetts, as well as elsewhere. Some are combating the Papist in South America, one is in China, some are in the Philippines. All these do not bear the clan name of Peden (original spelling), but claim and prove their descent from John Peden and Peggy McDill.

It now becomes the duty of the historian to record in succession the nine houses of Peden as sent in by their own historians. Some are very meager. It is the sincere hope, that if this volume should ever reach the second edition all missing links will be found; that it may present to the world a perfect record.

In addition to this great house two brothers of John Peden, William and James, the former settling in Penna., the latter in Virginia, came over early in the past century, or about 1790. These brothers came down to the Carolinas but only lingered awhile as they "could not brook slavery in any form," retraced their steps back to the upper settlements, founding houses in Pennsylvania and some other western States. Two grandsons of John, the father, William and John, sons of James, migrated to Ohio, they had large families with whom the historian has utterly failed to come in touch. Other Pedens, who came over prior to the Revolutionary war, have only recently been traced by the writer, who has positive proof in a letter from J. S. Peden, New York city, that one Joseph Peden served honorably through the war of Independence, who was probably a brother of John Peden. His descendants are found in New York, Pennsylvania, Indiana and Missouri. In 1809 Alexander Peden, son of Mingo Peden, who was undoubtedly a brother of James Peden, father of John, came to Wilmington, N. C. He was the father of three sons, the eldest, Dr. Alexander D. Peden, whose biography appears elsewhere, being half brother to the two younger, who in time migrated to Kentucky, founding there the house of Padon. One of these brothers was for many years a member of the Kentucky legislature. Of Judge Peden once foreign minister under the administration of President Pierce, the writer has no trace. He seems to have been utterly alone, unless belonging to some of the missing links.

From time to time others of the name have come over from the old country and among those of recent date are, Jas. R. Peden, of Kansas City, Mo., and David S. Peden, of Anaconda, Mont.

Chapter Seven - Old Haunts and Homes

"Ancestral oaks!
Beneath your mighty shade,
They reared their altars, brothers hand in hand,
In shining order, there they stand,
Like a living hymn written in shining light."

In the fall of the year 1785 came the Peden brothers, John, Samuel, David, with their nephew, James Alexander, and their good friend, James Nesbit; their wives, little ones and the few possessions left by the fortunes of war, to the new and untried wilderness of what is now Fairview Township, Greenville County, South Carolina. Each holding a grant or deed from the new government to certain newly acquired lands. One of these old documents is still in the possession of Capt. D. D. Peden, Houston, Texas, showing the holding of David, his ancestor, to have been nine hundred and fifty acres. Another, kept by Mr. A. S. Peden, Fountain Inn, S.C., showing that of Alexander, who came a few months later, to have been six hundred and fifty acres. David's lands extended from Raeburn to Rocky creek. Alexander's lay westward toward Reedy river; John's (amount not known) reached the river, joining both Alexander, and the Alexanders, husband and son of Mary Peden; the lands of James Alexander, Sr., were nearest the center, and Fairview church is situated near where the lands of James Alexander, Sr., and David Peden met, at the church spring. It stands on land given by James Alexander, Sr., as the writer understands. James Peden, the eldest brother's possessions extended between those of John and Alexander Peden, and of William Gaston, husband of

Elizabeth Peden; William's joined David's, and both met Samuel's, while those of Samuel Morrow, husband of Jane (Peden-Morton), were further northward beyond the others, joining her sons David and John Morton and James Alexander, Jr. William for some reason, owned less land than his brothers, it is supposed that he preferred plying his trade — "blacksmithing" — to agriculture. Tradition says that he was "a giant of a man," while his wife, Mary Archer, was very small, and very pretty. The writer .had great difficulty in locating some of these old spots, and is still in doubt about those of Samuel, William and Jane.

However, to resume the narrative. The younger men, David Peden and James Alexander, Jr., acted as guides through the trackless woods, "blazing" a pathway for the others to follow. After leaving the old historic Blackstock road, and crossing the old boundary line on Enoree river, they followed an Indian trail for awhile, then struck boldly out westward! Night-fall found them foot-sore and weary beside a bold spring of ice-cold water, issuing from among the rocks and roots of "three" immense tulip, or poplar trees, and rushing swiftly away down a deep narrow valley, to join the waters of Raeburn creek. This natural fountain still remains a favorite resort of the present day; it has quenched the thirst of six or seven generations of Pedens; has been used in their baptisms for over a century, and furnished the water supply for the Peden camp during the great and memorable reunion (1899). Only one "big tree" remains, a silent sentinel.

Here in this green spot the tired guides kindled the first camp-fire to have "a cheery blaze" when the others should come "up the stream" Soon the whole little company appeared, and the little children ran merrily to the fire, their elders following more sedately. Before they allowed themselves to partake of food, or indulge in rest, "the brothers" retired apart on the "eastern hillside, beyond earshot," (on this spot they afterwards built their first rude "meetinghouse,") yet where they could over look the little company at the spring, joined their hands in solemn covenant with God, and each other. Then after a fervent prayer they repeated a psalm, and singing "Old Hundredth," they went down to the camp. These pioneers then pitched their tents, built boughs of pine into booths, while the women prepared a simple meal of Indian corn porridge known as "mush," this they all ate, drinking with it the new milk, which had been hastily drawn from the few cows and quickly cooled in "jugs" set in the limpid waters of the spring. Afterwards they had a prayer, sang a hymn and laid them down to sleep under the star studded canopy of heaven. With the Peden God was first, His worship more important than creature comfort; moreover, his faith was implicit. (For this scene the writer is indebted to her maternal grandfather, James Dunbar, son-in-law of David Peden, long years afterward, who had it told to him by his venerated father-in-law on the spot ,one quiet Sabbath day when there was "no preaching," as he, James Dunbar, of sainted memory, told the writer sitting beside him on the rock-curb of the spring in the sweet summer time of 1866.)

On the morrow after "worship" and a scanty breakfast work began in earnest. Winter was coming and homes were to be built. So after they made the little camp as secure as they could, they set out for the scene of the "first cabin home." The Indian and Tory were still a menace. Raeburn and his band still lingered near, but for some reason, God only knows, they did not molest the "hated Peden."

Soon the women at the camp, "Katie" White, wife of Samuel, Betsy Ann Baker, wife of John, and Eleanor Goodgion, wife of David, also Mary or "Polly" Miller, wife of James Alexander, Jr., the wife and children of James Nesbit, had their first callers, these were an Indian woman and her half-breed daughter named "Dagg" or Dagnall. The mother was skilled in "simples" and other woodlore which was gladly welcomed by these pioneer house wives, so they kindly made room for them around the camp-fire. While the Indian woman smoked and grunted over her pipe, the daughter made herself useful, and most acceptable help she soon became. To the children, however, she was a source of terror. "I'll call Sal Dagg to get you" was a direful threat, or "You're as mean as Sal Dagg" an epithet of keenest insult. This meanness consisted in concocting nauseous doses and pouring them down reluctant throats, for various childish maladies, this medicine they called "garbroth;" otherwise Sarah Dagg was a harmless, useful creature, despite her weird appearance, also she was a safe-guard against both Indian and Tory. Ere long both left the country in quiet possession of the Pedens, leaving only the name of Raeburn to the once turbulent, but now quiet, stream that flows through the lands once owned entirely by Pedens.

Soon the sound of the axe re-echoed through the forest, the trees felled, the rough hewn logs ready, the oaken boards riven. One of the brothers built a blacksmith's forge and made spikes of all the bits of iron attainable, and some old swords and gun barrels went that way. One was a stoneworker so they were independent, each one had a trade and they all worked together. The house of James Alexander was the first one built; the women assisted in drawing the logs by chains, and when the walls of the cabins were reared beyond reach the men mounted them and the women placed the chains around the logs so that they could be pulled up and placed by them. These colonial cabins were "twenty by twenty feet square," with huge chimneys in one end, these stand many of them and are beautiful specimens of stonecraft. There were no windows, only one door, this opened eastward for two reasons; first, a crack was left above it to show the coming dawn; the second, clocks were almost unknown and the sun marked the hours on the floor, what they did in cloudy weather is not handed down, but doubtless they had other signs as to how time was passing. The walls were smoothed, the crevices filled with clay, then white washed with this same white, blue or "pipe clay." The floors were of packed earth neatly sanded and swept into fantastic figures. In time however rude plank or "puncheons" covered them. These first homes were built exactly alike. All were built near some cool spring, and each had its sheltering black walnut tree, as Alexander Peden said, "The walnut gave both fruit, shade and also dye stuff."

The author remembers to have stood, a child of ten, upright in the great fire-place of the first chimney (Jas. Alexander, Jr.,), it was then part of "the kitchen," among the "pot-hooks" and "hangers," with its revolving "spit"; many were the great dinners it furnished forth, and the sable priestess of the everlasting fire informed her that the dinners were served when the sun came down the chimney and shone on the pots, exactly at noon. Alas, it is a ruin now, and a stranger owns the land. This old home stood on the "headwaters" of North Raebur4i creek, that is, the great spring was the source of this stream. Along the roadway stretched a line of tall cedars, and down to the creek an avenue of stately walnuts. These trees were all cut down and disposed of, for some strange reason, during the civil war, 1861-1865. Imagination brings back the ruddy faced, jovial gentleman, the stately dark-eyed dame, "Polly Miller," who spent her last days in a cripple's chair; gone are the tall and beautiful daughters, all so like the dear old mother, the sons all scattered like the leaves of the forest, leaving no trace.

In the greenest of green valleys stood the cabin of David, the seventh son, and it stands today erect, proud as in the day when David Peden first bowed his tall form to enter the door-way to hang up his rifle and welcome his young wife to her forest home, very bare it must have looked, but she was brave and true, she was very young; tradition tells us she was fair to look upon. Soon the home was furnished simply. It was a snug warm nest for the large brood it was to shelter. In front of the door stood a walnut tree too and its shadows fell athwart the floor when the sunshine played in. Around about it the everlasting hills in verdure clad, a sheltered spot, a safe retreat. Of the old land marks only the main house and chimney stands as of yore; gone the trees, the orchards; all save one hillside of primeval forest yet spared by the axe of civilization. Even the old spring has vanished. Hushed the voices of the children, who, with their descendants, found homes and graves in other States, while the old cradle home has passed, a silent monument, into other hands. It is now the property of L. Brownlee, going out of the family in the troublous days of 1864-1865.

Across the roadway toward the sunset, in another green valley, lay the home of William Peden, of which some traces may be found, but the most marked is the wonderful spring which seems never to fail, and which was the delight of these dear people. From out this home they went westward long, long ago, and it too went to the stranger in about 1820.

John Peden's home, too, nestled in a valley. The author saw it only once; then there were a few traces, the spring with its square stones, the walnut trees, the old house, now only a part of the old house remains. John dying in 1810, his family left the old nest and went westward; after passing through many hands it has come again into the hands of the Peden, Mrs. Ann Peden, whose husband was a lineal descendant of Alexander, the sixth son.

The home of Samuel, unlike the others, was on an eminence commanding a fine view. The old house is still standing, but has been added to and is well preserved. So far as can be ascertained it has always belonged to a Peden, not always of descent from Samuel. The present owner, Mrs. M.C. Templeton is descended from Alexander and Thomas, two of the original brothers.

The early home of James, the eldest brother, who came later to Fairview, stood on a hill-crest, at whose foot rushed a bold spring. Only a splendid walnut tree and pile of stone now marks the spot. It has never left the Pedens, and is now owned by Mrs. W. M. Stenhouse, a descendant of Alexander, the sixth son.

Alexander Peden's cabin home stood on a high hill, overlooking the surrounding country. Only a sunken spot marks the cellar. Like the others this home was of logs with a huge stone chimney facing the road, while a big walnut tree shaded the roof, whose charred stump now lies mouldering near where it once stood in towering beauty. The hill is now a vast field of cotton, or waving grain, the spring lies a pellucid pool at the foot of the hill, reflecting the stars at night, and heaven's own blue by day. Nearby are the rock foundations of the old barn, curious and skillful bits of stonemasonry of a past age. This old home place is now the property of Dr. H. B. Stewart, whose noble wife is a lineal descendant of the first owner, Alexander, the sixth son.

Between this and the land of James Peden there rushes a brave little stream known as the "Peden branch," it is fed by two or three Peden springs and comes merrily down among the ferns and mosses like Tennyson's brook:

"For men may come and men may go —
But I go on forever."

It rushes madly along over "cold grey stones" in gladsome whirls and eddys. Oft have the white feet of the Peden daughters been laved in its coolness in by-gone days. At one place it flows between two steep hills. An old roadway is still visible, though long disused and almost forgotten. Up and down these hills the Peden traveled wearily to and from market (Charleston or Augusta) before the days of railroads.

The homes of the Peden sisters were more pretentious than those of the brothers, for ere they came to Fairview wondrous strides had been made. David had acquired a sawmill, also one for grist "on the creek." The site is now to be seen, and part of the picturesque dam of black-gray rocks yet exists on the land of Hon. John R. Harrison, lineal descendant of James, the eldest son. There were several forges among the brothers, as each had some useful trade besides his farm. David Morton had brought his tools and was quite a good carpenter, having learned under his loved grandfather, John Peden.

Of these homes, that of Mary, or "Polly," wife of James Alexander, Sr., was by far the most attractive, being "a colonial mansion, a wonder in those days." It had, and has massive brick chimneys, and in the memory of the writer was a lovely old home, embowered in a grove of immense oaks and walnuts, a long vista of the later as far as eye could reach; down a steep hill at the back of the house was the loveliest spring and spring-house. It did not take much play of fancy to call up visions of the courteous old gentleman with snowy hair, knee buckles and ruffles, and the stately dame with the "keen, dark eyes," known as "Aunt Polly". The great doors stood wide open towards the high road. In that mansion where the old clock ticked against the wall there was freehearted hospitality — one hundred years ago. Today — it stands a tottering ruin, a monument to the past, the brave sons of Alexander, and the fair daughters also, have scattered far and wide, after passing those fair portals, while the dear old people rest in the rock walled God's acre over the hill at Fairview. James Alexander was the first magistrate at Fairview. He was as large-hearted and open handed a colonist as the old world ever furnished the new, but his nobleness must be left to his proper historian.

The second sister, Jane, the wife of Samuel Morrow, whom tradition says was a fair counterpart of her mother, "Peggy McDill," The spirit of the pioneer was strong within her. The house of Samuel Morrow was also colonial, and stood on a fair hill. Not a trace now remains, not a stick, tree or stone. It was a square house. "Pretty Jenny" liked to look abroad so there was not so many trees. The site is on the land of Edward Martin, whose wife is descended from both Thomas, the second son, and Alexander, the sixth son.

Elizabeth Peden, wife of Wm. Gaston, lived in a double house; her home was the favorite resort of her family. There seems to have been some wealth there, for it is said that Wm. Gaston, while only a silk-weaver in the old country, was of high lineage, that his guests were warmed with ruddy, old wine, surely not of colonial vintage, poured from flagons of silver bearing arms and crest; silver took the place of pewter in this house. Gone is the sweet warm-hearted hostess; gone the grand old host with the deep, blue eyes, the tall princely form, that bowed so gallantly to the ladies, yet so proudly borne in the face of foes. Lost the flagons, faded the fragrance of the wine. Out of the broken hearthstone there was growing some years ago a tall graceful sycamore tree. The very stones are gone, tradition says they were used to build the pillars of Pisgah church, which is nearby. The Gaston home is now owned by Mr. Louis Thomason. The Gastons were childless so their memory will live only on the memorial tablets of their tombs and unworthy pages of this humble volume.

Thomas Peden never came to live at Fairview. The following is from letters of his lineal descendant and family historian, Amzi Williford Gaston, who owns and resides on the lands of his fore-fathers:

"I cannot locate the exact spot where John Peden and Peggy McDill built their first cabin; but I can come within a few yards of it. There is not a tree or stone left; nothing but the bare hillside. The spring is still there, of course it is not much used, and is all grown over with bushes and briars. Thomas Peden, son of John and Peggy, is buried one mile from where I live, and I see his grave occasionally. He had a deed or grant for five hundred acres of land here on Ferguson's creek, where I live, from King George. The deed is lost, so that I cannot get the date, but recollect seeing it several years ago. The price paid was seventy-five cents per hundred acres, or three dollars and seventy-five cents for the whole five hundred acres, with the understanding that a certain portion was to be put in cultivation in the first year or two. My grandfather, Andrew Peden, inherited the plantation I now live on from his father, Thomas, so you see it is still in the family and has been ever since it was granted to Thomas Peden in 1770-1772. The house he, Thomas, built after the Revolution was a large, two-storied one, painted red with white doors, and was destroyed by fire in 1854."

Of the early home in Chester the writes has been utterly unable to obtain a trace, save that it was near old Catholic church, also located on lands adjoining the large possessions of the McDills, and probably after the death of John and Peggy, and the removal of their son, James, to Fairview, passed into their hands. The road thither being so intricate and difficult the writer shrank from making a personal tour of investigation.

Chapter Eight - Fairview and the Peden

"The base and foundation of the Church and Nation is the Family."

"Fairview stands with hills surrounded —
Fairview kept by power Divine."

The history of Fairview church and the history of the founders of the Peden race in America are literally one and inseparable.

The devout spirit coming down through long centuries — Culdee to Covenanter, Covenanter to Presbyterian; passing through the ordeals of blood, fire, death itself, to win the crown of martyrdom.

The following quotation is, in the main, from the centennial address of Rev. Marion C. Britt, lineal descendant of David, the seventh son, delivered at old Fairview to an immense congregation on the morning of September 25th, 1886, one hundredth anniversary of its organization:

"Fairview church was organized during the fall of 1786, by these five families, John Peden's, Samuel Peden's, David Peden's, James Alexander's, James Nesbit's, and was received April 10, 1787, under the care of South Carolina Presbytery. That the organization was effected in the year 1786 rests upon reliable and conclusive evidence. It was recorded by Mr. Anthony Savage, in his sketch of the church while some of the first members still lived and upon their statement. It is a matter of regret, however, that no record has been preserved, that can be found, of the month and day. There is ground for the presumption that it was near the close of the year. The fact that the church did not join Presbytery until the spring of the following year renders it probable that the organization took place subsequent to the fall meeting of that body. This opinion is also strengthened by the fact that the third Sabbath in December was selected for the semi-centennial celebration, at which time it is reasonable to suppose the exact date was still well known among the people. In 1787 three other families — those of James Alexander, Sr., William Peden, John Alexander and David Morton, a son of the second sister, Jane — came from Nazareth and united with the infant church. There were also other accessions to it, probably as early as the first year, from families living in Laurens County, Alexander Peden among them.

"It is worthy of record that a house of worship was built and the church organized the same year in which the new settlement was made. They came with no doubt limited means, to a territory but recently obtained from the Indians and therefore devoid of the comforts of civilized life. There were dense forests to be felled, fields prepared and cultivated and houses built. The rude temple which they erected for the worship of God under such circumstances becomes a grand testimony to their religious faith and zeal, and recalls the example of the patriarch of old who as he journeyed from place to place with his family, wherever he rested he built an altar unto the Lord, and called upon the name of the Lord.

"In the course of the next few years all the Pedens except the father and mother, who remained in Chester County, and Thomas who continued at Nazareth, had collected around Fairview with their families. They are all buried here, except Samuel and Jane. The former moved to Mississippi in 1832 and rests in Smyrna church-yard, Kemper County. Jane moved to North Alabama and rests near Somerville. Thomas lies in a family burying ground on his old homestead, near Nazareth church, which he helped to found, in Spartanburg County, South Carolina.

"The Rev. Samuel Edmondson preached the first sermon and organized the church; but this was the extent of his labors in connection with it. He was a Virginian, who came to this State soon after he was licensed by Hanover Presbytery in October, 1773, 'and spent a useful life.' The first ruling elders were John Peden, Samuel Peden, James Alexander, Sr., and his son, John Alexander. The first minister employed by the church was the Rev. John McCosh from the north of Ireland, who served one year as stated supply. It was during his ministry that the sacrament of the Lord's supper was administered for the first time. He was assisted by the Rev. Robert McClintock (who was related to the Peden family), and we are told that it was 'a. season of great interest and solemnity.' (Fairview kept up the custom of giving tokens of admission to the communion as late as 1840-1850. These were small bits of metal bearing the name of the church, and the candidate for admission had to answer some searching questions by the elders ere obtaining one.) These two ministers on account of their Pelagian views, were never recognized by South Carolina Presbytery, and it censured Thomas Peden of Nazareth for taking part in this communion as being disorderly. There was also a division in the church connected with the doctrine and practice of these ministers, but it was of short duration. From the time Rev. McCosh ceased to serve the church until 1794, Revs. J. Foster, J. Simpson and William Montgomery preached occasionally, but there was no regular supply. In 1794 Rev. James Templeton was called as stated supply for half of the time, and so continued for six years. During the year 1798 Revs. Wm. Williamson and James Gilliland are mentioned as supplying the church; but it is probable that they merely assisted Mr. Templeton, whose term of service embraced this year. From 1800 to 1802 the pulpit was again vacant, Revs, John Simpson, James Gilliland, Sr., and William Williamson were occasional supplies. In 1802 the church united with Nazareth to call as pastor the Rev. James Gilliland, Jr., each church for half of the time. (One of the Gillilands, father or son, was avowedly opposed to slavery and eventually went to the northwest territory carrying quite a number of Pedens with him.) Mr. Gilliland was licensed by the second South Carolina Presbytery April 8, 1802, and on April 7, 1803, was ordained and installed pastor of Nazareth and Fairview churches. He is described as 'a good scholar, a lively speaker, and popular in his manners.' He was the first pastor of the church, and it prospered under his ministry. His relation to the church continued until 1812 (date of the first emigration to the northwest territory). From 1812 to 1814 Revs. James Hillhouse, Thomas Archibald, Joseph Hillhouse and Alexander Kirkpatrick were occasional supplies appointed by Presbytery. In 1814 Rev. Hugh Dickson became stated supply for one-fourth of his time, and so remained until the spring of 1816, when he resigned and was succeeded by Rev. James Hillhouse, who only served the church until October of that year. From the fall of 1816 to the spring of 1817 Rev. Thos. Archibald supplied the pulpit, and from 1817 to 1818, Mr. Alexander Kirkpatrick, a licentiate of the Presbytery of Ballymena, Ireland, was stated supply. (This "fair, fat and rosy Irishman" was a great favorite with the younger portion of the congregation, while the elders did not consider him sufficiently sedate; to their reproofs he returned the reply, "only a Christian has a right to be happy.") From 1818 to 1820 Rev. Thos. Baird occupied the pulpit a portion of the time; but for the most part the church was dependent upon irregular supplies. It was however a period of activity in the church, as is shown by the records. Among other items of interest which they contain we find the following: August 11, 1818. 'About this time our new meeting-house is finished and dedicated by Rev. Mr. Carter. In the spring of 1820 Mr. Michael Dickson, who was at the same time hcensed by the Presbytery of South Carolina, began to supply the church under the direction of the Presbyterial Committee of Missions, and in the fall was called as pastor by the congregations of Nazareth and Fairview, each for half the time, and was ordained and installed as such April 5, 1821. His connection with Fairview ceased in 1827, and the church was again vacant until 1832, Messrs. Watson and Craig being appointed by Presbytery as occasional supplies. It is probable that this period embraced the ministry of Rev. Arthur Mooney, but as the church records covering this period are lost the information is not positive. (There is a blank of about ten years for some reason in the records, some of the old people now living say that the spirit of contention was abroad among the brethren.) In 1832 Rev. Jno. Boggs, of Virginia, took charge of the church, first as stated supply, then in the fall as pastor for half of the time. Rev. Boggs was pastor when Rev. David Humphrey was called as stated supply and continued so for three years (division the cause). He was succeeded by Rev. Wm. Carlisle in 1838, who was stated supply for six years. In the fall of 1845, the Rev. John McKitrick, who was stated supply during the previous six months, was installed pastor. He resigned in 1847 and was succeeded by Rev. Dr. E.T. Buist as stated supply, for six years. (This relation continued most pleasantly until Dr. Buist was called as pastor elsewhere, and Fairview gave him up most reluctantly.) Here we reach the ministry of Rev. C.B. Stewart, which extends over a period of thirty years, and embraces the era of greatest church enterprise and prosperity (moreover harmony). He began to serve as stated supply for eighteen years, when he consented to become pastor, and so remained for twelve years. In 1884 he felt it to be his duty to have the pastoral relation dissolved on account of the growing infirmities of age. He still residing in the midst of the people whom he had served so long and faithfully, held in the deepest veneration and love." Rev. M.C. Britt, his worthy successor, was installed pastor in the fall of 1885, having already had charge of the church since November, 1884, as stated supply. He being a son of Fairview, as lineally descended from David, the seventh son.

"There have been four church buildings. The first was built of logs and located, if tradition correctly marks the spot, not far from the church spring, on the east side. The second was also a log structure and situated near the spot on which the brick church afterwards stood." This long, low building had an earthen floor. Huge stone chimneys filled each end; the seats were of puncheons or slabs supported with pegs and placed against the walls. Light and air were admitted through openings near the roof, made by leaving out a few logs. The preacher occupied a rude pulpit in the middle of the space and preached all around. The third was a brick building which for some unaccountable reason, was razed nearly a half century ago, and is a source of keen regret. The writer with some assistance has outlined a rude sketch. The exterior presented the appearance of a huge brick barn, with a heavy square roof, without gables. Only a few years ago there could be found the remains of the gallery stairs, solidly built of brick, which ran up along the western side and opened into a wide gallery across one end and used for colored members. On the eastern or "sunny side" the older women gathered to smoke the friendly pipe, lighting them in summer by means of sun glasses, and to indulge in a bit of whispered gossip, generally harmless, during "intermission." To this sheltered side the mothers of babies stole out during service to quiet their crying so as not to disturb "meeting" and rest the tired little mortals, for Peden babies were expected at church when a few weeks old, and unlucky the small mite who went unbaptized past the sixth month of its existence. They grew upon the gospel, the catechism, and long sermons, these last were never delivered for less than one hour, oftener two, for in early days preaching was rare, therefore of great value. There was usually an intermission of a few hours at noon spent under the great trees in summer, around hospitable tables; in winter or inclement weather they gathered in the old log church or session house, a few rods away, where sometimes in very severe weather services were held as there was no way of heating the church building.

A very dim and vague picture of the interior is submitted as drawn from the reminiscences of a few of the dear old people yet at Fairview, but mostly from memories of the writer's own sainted mother, who delighted to talk of the dear old church of her own happy girlhood. The great doors at either end north and south were mullioned while those in the sides were small and bastioned. The windows were placed high in the walls and had shutters, no glass, and during the coldest weather stood open, consequently some shivering was done, although the early Pedens were a hardy race, and lung troubles almost unknown among them. The aged and the infirm had rocks heated in the fire-places of the session house and well wrapped in blankets or woolen coverlets to keep their feet warm during the long service. It was the good fortune of a few to possess soap-stones. To complain of being cold during "meeting" was considered a weakness bordering on crime as the sermons were supposed to keep the congregation warm.

The seats or pews were arranged in tiers or terraces of four then a step up or down as the case might be, that is, down from the doors towards the pulpit. Fairview church never countenanced the practice prevalent in most country places of worship of the men sitting on one side of the middle line the women on the other; their families were required to sit together under the eyes of their parents.

Above the pulpit hung the sounding board, this curious relic of a bygone age resembled an open umbrella or huge wooden toad-stool. The boxed up pulpit was so small, and so high with steps so steep and narrow that a visiting minister once gave great offense by remarking, "Satan must have planned this pulpit." About halfway down was a smaller box known as the "clerk's" place and from this perch he "lined out" the psalms and hymns for the congregation to follow his lead in singing. The last occupant was Moses T. Fowler, of the house of Thomas, the second son.

Supporting the huge roof through the wide middle aisle were large pillars, great trees hewn into shape, also down this space were placed the communion tables and benches. This beautiful custom is fast disappearing or falling into disuse. These tables were closely fitted together end to end across the entire building with benches placed alongside for solemn occasions. The long snowy linen cloths were of home manufacture, the flax having been grown, hackled, spun, woven and bleached, by Peden women; one of whom was regularly appointed by the session to take charge thereof and great was the honor conferred, as well as the pride and pleasure taken in keeping them beautifully laundried, and scented with thyme, cedar and lavender. They too prepared the unleavened bread for the communion. (The old Pedens would have lifted hands of holy horror at what is now used in the service. The writer was unable to ascertain the exact number of seats, but they were numbered like those of the present church, that is, all even numbers on one side, uneven on the other. For example, David Peden's family occupied number 12 and exactly opposite in number 13, against the east wall, sat his sister, Jane Morrow, and after her son David Morton, while James Dunbar took the seat left vacant at the death of David Peden. Nine of the first family had sittings in the old church, while most of the congregation were their descendants. It must also be borne in mind that a number of them emigrated as early as 1811-1814, and some had departed to the church above.

To resume. "The fourth and present edifice is a large commodious wooden structure. It was built principally by a legacy left by David Morton, aided also by general subscription. It was completed during March, 1858, and was dedicated by the saintly David Humphrey, assisted by Rev. Dr. E. T. Buist, on May 15th of that same year. This occasion was also a season of great spiritual blessing to the church and the membership was much revived.

"The congregation of Fairview has always been a homogeneous body. Those who first composed it and the pious households of godly men and women that have been added to it from time to time, belonged to a common ancestry. They had the same faith and customs. The history of Fairview, as a consequence, has not been a process of harmonizing conflicting elements with a composite result, as is true of so many churches and other institutions in this country'; on the contrary, the natural and almost uninterrupted growth of an unmixed Scotch-Presbyterian church, on American soil. This growth has been remarkably uniform in its nature. It has been a progress marked not by sudden expansions, but by a regular increase. It has the proud distinction of being the mother of Presbyterianism in Greenville County, and of many, many churches, in other States, colonists who have carried with them her faith and spirit. Several of her sons are in the ministry. An imperfect roll of communicants from the beginning to 1886 contains about twelve hundred names.

"The church has suffered greatly at times from emigration, and whenever there has been a decrease in membership it must be attributed to this cause and not to the loss of spiritual influence and life. It has now (1886) one hundred and forty-six communicants. The century of her existence has been rich in blessings and we can raise our Ebenezer today with thanksgiving and praise. She bears no marks of decay, and if her children are only faithful to their heritage, it can be said of her that she has but entered upon her divine mission of the 'gathering and perfecting of the saints.'"

A list of the various ministers and elders, as well as deacons, who have served Fairview is appended as of interest to the readers of this book.

Ministers. — Revs. Samuel Edmundson, John McCosh, John Foster, James Simpson, James Templeton, William Williamson, William Montgomery, James Gilliland, Sr., James Gilliland, Jr., Hugh Dickson, John Boggs, William Carlisle, John L. Kennedy, James Hillhouse, Thomas Archibald, Joseph Hillhouse, Alexander Kirkpatrick, Thomas D. Baird, Cater, Michael Dickson, David Humphries, Arthur Mooney, John McKittrick, Edward T. Buist, Clark B. Stewart, Marion C. Britt, William G. F. Wallace, Henry W. Burwell, David S. McAllister, W. W. Ruff.

Elders. — John Peden, Samuel Peden, James Alexander, Sr., John Alexander, Alexander Peden, William Peden, Robert Morrow, Anthony Savage, James Peden, T.W. Alexander, Lindsay A. Baker, David Morton, James Dunbar, James Alexander, Jr., Alex. Thompson, Adam Stenhouse, John M. Harrison, Austin Williams, James E. Savage, A. Wilson Peden, T.H. Stall, Wm. A. Harrison, T.L. Woodside, Wm. L. Hopkins, David R. Anderson, Robt. Wham, David Stoddard, J.W. Kennedy, H. Boardman Stewart, A.S. Peden and others whose names have not reached the writer.

Deacons. — John T. Stenhouse, Wm. Nesbit, Thos. L. Woodside, W.L. Hopkins, C.D. Nesbit, T.C. Peden, A.S. Peden, M. P. Nash, T. C. Harrison, D.R. Anderson, Thos. H. Stall, S.T. McKittrick, D.M. Peden, E.W. Nash, J.T. Peden, Jeff D. McKittrick and others since 1886. This office was not established until 1858.

The fair temple of today stands on an eminence facing northward toward the "everlasting hills." Southward the sunny fields and valleys. On the eastward slope lies the stone-walled God's acre where so many generations sleep awaiting the summons to awake. Its walls now enclose most of the site of the old brick church on whose "sunrise corner" stands the gleaming monument to the Peden race. This sacred enclosure is a silent, solemn epitome to man. On the western slope, at about the same distance, a few hundred yards, is the new session house, built with the present sanctuary. Both of these session houses have been used for schools, though the academy proper is some miles away, and belongs to the educational history of Fairview. The older Pedens were not indifferent to the education of their children, and at one time Fairview was a centre — drawing pupils from a distance. The first school was taught in humble fashion beneath the giant oaks that surround the present home of Mrs. Jane (Peden) McDowell, by a friend of the Mortons and Morrows, a Mr. Moffat. He was succeeded by others, names lost, until about 1820-1825, when the academy was established and became famous, who the teachers were is lost until the Rev. Boggs and his wife took charge, sometime in 1830-1840. They were followed by one Thomas Walker, and later Thomas Flannagan. Around the latter hangs a halo of romance, wrapped in mystery, it was hinted that he was one of the political exiles of France contemporary with the great Marshal Ney. Prior to these two there taught at Fairview, dates not given, Antony Savage and James Dunbar, the latter came to Fairview direct from Antrim, Ireland, in 1821. Married Eleanor G. Peden in 1824. Anthony Savage, described as a "clerkly" man, preceded James Dunbar a number of years. He was also direct from Ireland and married Jane (or as she was lovingly called "Aunt Jennie"), daughter of James Peden.

The later history of the Fairview schools is so varied and vague that the writer has almost no information to impart further than there has always been a school at Fairview. Some of the later teachers were, Revs. Hyde, C.B. Stewart, Austin, Kennedy and others, including not a few excellent women.

Fairview of today keeps even pace with the outside world; is no primitive pioneer station in the woods, "lost to fame and memory dear." The annual shows attract great crowds of visitors from all over the State. The hospitality of the Peden is proverbial wherever the name is found, and those of old Fairview are not lacking in this spirit.

Chapter Nine – Peden — Christian, Patriot, Soldier

It is the purpose of this chapter to bring into relief Peden characteristics; and will include several sketches and incidents.

As a fitting beginning two sketches of the island home of the traditional "Paidan" are copied from *The Christian Observer* and *The Houston* (Texas) *Post.*

Iona Cathedral, intimately associated with the early life and work of Presbyterianism in Scotland, form a part of the estate which for generations has been in the possession of the Argyll family. The present Duke, evidently contemplating the possibility of its alienation at some future day from Presbyterian keeping, has conveyed the site and ruins of the old cathedral to certain trustees to hold for the Church of Scotland. The cathedral is to be restored, and, in the event of Disestablishment, the Secretary for Scotland, the Lord Advocate and the Sheriff of Argyll are to determine what body the cathedral shall belong to.

The announcement that the Duke of Argyll has conveyed the ruins of Iona to a public trust in connection with the Established Church of Scotland is of more than passing interest, particularly as it is proposed to restore the venerable cathedral, which will thus, after the lapse of centuries, be used once more for public worship. Iona is indissolubly associated with the name of St. Columba, who had there established his base of operations long before St. Augustine came to convert the men of Kent to the Christian religion. The Scottish saint, a man of splendid physique, was in his forty-second year when he drove Druids from their ancient stronghold of Icohnkill in 563 A.D. It is interesting to note that at the time of this historic religious invasion the foundations of modern jurisprudence were being laid by the Emperor Justinian, and his great general, Belisarius was at the zenith of his fame. St. Columba and his twelve disciples built a monastery, which was a place of pilgrimage not only for the Picts and Scots, but even for the men of Strath, Clyde, and Northumbria, and till the end of the eighth century Iona was a veritable Scottish Mecca. In common with so many other great centers of religion it did not escape the ravages of the Northmen, who plundered and burnt it in 795, and again in 802. On several subsequent occasions the monks suffered martyrdom, and it is recorded that in 986 the ruthless barbarians paid a Christmas visit to the sacred island and slew the abbot and fifteen of his monks. St. Columba's monastery did not survive these devastations, but when John was King of England the cathedral of St. Mary was built, and survives to this day, though in ruins, with its choir and chapels, transepts, nave, and a central tower rising to a height of 75 feet, Iona has a further claim to the respect of antiquarians as the burying place of no less than 48 Scottish and four Irish and eight Norse kings. As all the world knows. Dr. Johnson was much impressed by his visit to this part of the Hebrides, and he described it reverently as "That illustrious island which was once the luminary of the Caledonian religions, whence savage clans and roving barbarians derived the benefits of knowledge and the blessings of religion."

This is followed by a sketch of the Prophet Peden, 1626-1686.

Alexander Peden — The Prophet

Charles I. succeeded his father, James VI. in 1625 and the year following Alexander Peden was born at Auchenloich in Sorn, Ayrshire, Scotland. He died in 1686, two years before the Revolution, and thus he lived through almost all the stormy time of Scotland's religious history, witnessing a good confession, and though hunted like a wild beast he escaped his persecutors and died at last in the house where he was born, on the Water of Ayr.

Dodd calls him the "Prophet of the Covenant," and says that "Peden in an age fertile in singular men and when the circumstances of the times brought out their qualities in the strongest relief, surpassed all in what may be termed romance of character. His memory has been overlaid by the doatingness of martyrology, by the very rankness and luxuriant foliage of tradition. Wonder tales crop and cluster, and twine all around him as the ivy does around some majestic, old tower. Love and awe, and primitive simplicity, working on an extraordinary subject, have well-nigh changed into a wizard this brave, wise, kindly old spirit, whose marvellous insight and intensity of feeling and expression were all taken for sorcery."

His father was a small proprietor, and it is believed he was the eldest son, for he is spoken of as having "a piece of heritage." He was intimate with the Boswells, of Auchenloch, an old and respected family in the neighborhood of his home. Nothing seems to be known of his early life, or of his university career. He first comes into notice as school master, precentor and session clerk to Mr. John Guthrie, minister of Tarbolton.

When about to enter the ministry a clamor was raised against him by a young woman, which was fully cleared up, proving him an innocent victim of a base plot. This circumstance, however, seemed to have in some degree tinged his whole after life.

A little before the Restoration he was ordained minister of New Luce, in Galloway, and for three years labored in this lovely spot, which the Luce watered as it wound by many a knoll, and clump of brush-wood, until lost in the sea; while around towered dark precipitous hills — those hills of Galloway which Mrs. Stewart Montieth has so beautifully apostrophized in her "Lays of the Kirk and Covenant."

What Peden's ministry was in this place, and how much he was beloved by his people we can have some idea of from their grief when, after three years, he was called to leave them and like Abraham of old, to go forth not knowing where he went. The reason of his ejectment from the place was his refusal to comply with the Act of Parliament, May, 1662, which required all ministers who had been inducted since 1649 to receive presentation from their respective patrons, and collation from the Bishop of the diocese in which they resided before the 20th of September, that year, under the penalty of deprivation. That he and many others refused to submit to these terms may readily be believed; recognizing no right of the civil power to break asunder so sacred a tie as that which existed between a minister and his people, they were therefore in not haste to desert their charges, when in October the Lords of the Privy Council passed another Act "prohibiting and discharging all ministers, who have contravened the foresaid act concerning the benefits and stipends to exercise any part of the functions of the ministry at their respective churches in time coming, which are hereby declared vacant and command and charge the said ministers to remove themselves and their families out of their parishes, betwixt this and the first day of November next to come, and not to reside within the bounds of their respective parishes."

In the face of this Peden and many others declining still to acknowledge the civil courts, forcible measures were taken for their ejection. On the 24th day of February, 1663, the Lords of the Privy Council ordered letters to be directed against him and twenty-five other ministers in Galloway, commanding them to remove themselves, wives and children and goods from their respective manses, and from the bounds of the Presbytery, where they now lived, before the 20th day of March following; forbidding them to exercise any part of their ministerial functions, and also charging them to appear before the Council on the 24th day of March." This order Peden durst no longer refuse to recognize so he had to prepare to leave his beloved and attached flock. When he preached his farewell sermon we are told "this was a weeping day in that kirk," the greater part could not contain themselves. He many times requested them to be silent; but they sorrowed most of all when he told them that they should never see his face in that pulpit again. So unwilling were minister and people to part that they continued together, he speaking to them and they listening, until compelled by darkness to stop, the night coming upon them." When descending from the pulpit he closed the door, and knocking three times upon it said, "I arrest thee in my Master's name, that none ever enter thee but such as come in by the door as I did," and it so happened that neither curate or indulged minister ever entered that pulpit during the persecution which followed. The church was completely deserted and desolate until after the Revolution, when a Presbyterian minister opened it. It has been said that his old pulpit was used in the church-yard afterwards at tent preachings on communion seasons. Though he never preached again in the church, he afterwards occasionally visited his old parishioners, for says Wodrow, "they were taxed and quartered upon for receiving him into their houses," and on "Martinmas, 1681, Claverhouse commissioned Sheriff of Galloway, brought two troops of horse on the said parish for baptizing of children with Mr. Peden."

In 1670 Peden passed his time sometimes in Scotland and sometimes in Ireland (whither his kin had been banished, 1601), in which country he seems to have visited Ulster (of which Antrim was a part), and preached to great multitudes there, thereby giving offense to some of the ministers who were annoyed that an ousted Scotch minister should come amongst them, and open his mouth, which was closed in his own country; but there was no law (then) forbidding full liberty of worship in Ireland. Returning again to Scotland, he was apprehended June, 1672, by Major Cockburn, in the house of Hugh Ferguson, of Knockdow, in Carrick, accordingly they were both, landlord and guest, carried prisoners to Edinburg. Ferguson was fined a thousand merkes "for visit, harbour, and converse with him." The Council ordered fifty-four pounds sterling to be paid to the Major out of the fine; and twenty-five pounds to be divided amongst the party who apprehended them. After examination, Peden was carried by a party of military to the prison of the Bass, to be delivered to the governor of the garrison there, who "is hereby ordered to keep him (Peden) a close prisoner until further orders." This Act was dated 26th June, 1673

> "Stone walls do not a prison make,
> Nor iron bars a cage,
> A spotless mind and innocent
> Calls that an hermitage."
>
> — Lovelace.

The Bass Rock is an islet in the Firth of Forth, three miles and a half distant from North Berwick, and is about seven acres in extent. It resembles in form the base of a sugar loaf. Precipitous on all sides, the only landing place is a little shelf of rock over-looked by the ramparts, where cannon were formerly placed to defend the entrance of the Firth. However calm the weather a strong surf is always seething round the Bass, and it is necessary to cling hard to iron rings, and clamps in the rock when parties land lest their boat should be dashed to pieces. The steep and slippery landing place is only a species of fissure, or chasm, and leads to a plateau of naked red rocks, always covered with dead gannets and Norwegian rabbits in all stages of decay. This sea-rock "the storm defying Bass, the giant fragment of a former world," has forty fathoms of water all around it, and is the haunt of myriads of gannets, or solar geese, and sea-gulls, which wheel in the sunshine and whiten its cliffs. The Bass Rock was purchased in 1671 by Lauderdale, in the name of the government, to become a state prison, and it was the last piece of British soil that surrendered to William of Orange. The castle of the Bass was never taken by storm, and it defied a blockade by sea and land for four years after the battle of Killiecrankie. In what was the soldier's garden there are still a few flowers, with a few pots herbs growing rank and wild; and in summer the Rock is covered with *Lavatera arbora,* or the tree mallow of the Bass, a rare plant in Britain, which grows there in great luxuriance to the height of six and eight feet.

When Alexander Peden was fifty-one years of age, we learn through the kind offices of the Governor, he was removed to the mainland; this was on the 9th day of October, 1677.

          (Signed) J. M. Ainslee Miller.

This sketch is closed with an incident showing the domestic side as well as prophetic nature of Alexander Peden. A prophecy literally fulfilled.

During those stormy times when pious Scotchmen were hunted like deer by Claverhouse and his dragoons, because they would not submit to the prelacy forced upon their churches by English tyranny, there lived, near Ayr, a lass named Isabel Weir. She had a pretty face, winsome manners, a lively disposition, and a very superior, well cultivated mind.

A young farmer, a widower, of fine character, much trusted by his neighbors, and greatly beloved tor his gentle ways by those who knew him best, often came to do business with Isabel's father. His name was John Brown, of Priesthill. Of course, he frequently saw the lass, talked with her, and, as was natural, loved her. She reciprocated his love. When he proposed to marry her, he very frankly said:

"The times are troublous, Isabel, and I have a foreboding that I shall one day be called to seal the Church's testimony with my blood."

This was, most assuredly, a very grave wooing, and a very unlikely method of winning a bride. But Isabel was no light-minded, frivolous girl. Like her lover, she was ready to suffer for old Scotland's religious freedom, and, instead of holding back her troth because of her wooer's ghastly foreboding, she nobly replied:

"If it should be so, John, through affliction and death I will be your comfort. The Lord has promised me grace, and he will give you glory."

These were not the words of a sentimental girl eager to secure a handsome husband, but of a true woman with a heroic soul, who fondly loved the man desiring to make her his wife.

A month or two later, in a secluded, romantic glen, Isabel gave her hand to the young farmer of Priesthill. Not in a church, but at Nature's altar, hidden from the eyes of persecuting priests, their vows were plighted and their hands joined by that distinguished Covenanter, Alexander Peden. A goodly company of godly people were there, of whom Mr. Peden said, addressing Isabel:

"These are to be witnesses of your vows. They are all friends, and have come at the risk of their lives to hear God's work and to countenance his ordinance of marriage."

At the close of the interesting service Peden took Isabel aside, and, looking into her face with paternal affection, said:

"Isabel, you have got a good husband; value him highly. Keep linen for a winding-sheet beside you, for in a day when you least expect it thy master will be taken from thy head. In him the image of our Lord and Saviour is too visible to pass unnoticed by those who drive the chariot wheels of persecution through the breadth and length of bleeding Scotland. But fear not; thou shalt be comforted."

A gloomy wedding benediction this; but though it, no doubt, chastened her gladness, it did not chill her heart. She respected Mr. Peden; knew, indeed, that he was esteemed a prophet; nevertheless, she would not believe that one so good and gentle as her beloved could be persecuted by any one, not even by prelatists.

In 1890 a new monument was reared to his memory instead of the single grave-stone, from which the following was copied by Mr. Ainslee Miller, and kindly furnished with his sketch:

<blockquote>
In Memory of Alexander Peden.
A Native of Sorn.
</blockquote>

That faithful minister of Christ, who for his unflinching adherence to the Covenanted Reformation in Scotland, was expelled by tyrant rulers from his parish of New Luce; imprisoned for years on the Bass Rock by his persecutors, and hunted for his life on the surrounding mountains and moors till his death on January 26, 1686, in the 60th year of his age, and here at last his dust reposes in peace awaiting the resurrection of the just.

"Such were the men these hills who trod,
"Strong in the love and fear of God,
"Defying through a long dark hour —
"Alike the craft, and rage of Power."

The inscription on the grave-stone is also furnished —

<blockquote>
Here Lies Mr. Alexander Peden,
Faithful Minister of the Gospel at Glenluce.
</blockquote>

Who departed this mortal life the 26th day of January, 1686, and was raised after six weeks out of the grave, and buried here out of contempt.

MEMENTO MORI.

JUDGE SAMUEL C. PEDEN.

In contrast to the preceding, and showing also the firm unyielding adherence to what they believe to be right in civil life, the character of Judge Samuel C. Peden stands out as boldly as did his predecessor, the "Prophet," for religious freedom. The Missouri Judge, while not a descendant of John Peden, shows remarkable similarity of character to many of them. He descends from Joseph Peden, also a brave soldier of the Revolution, and in all probability one of the long lost brothers of the founder of the Southern house of Peden. The letter, and incidents which follow show the strong points in Peden character.

The first clipping is from the Houston (Texas) Post, under the heading "Refuses to Accept Liberty On the Terms Offered by United States Judge:"

Kansas City, Mo., December 2. — Judge Samuel C. Peden, of the St. Clair County Court, one of the three County Judges who have been compelled to serve most of their terms of office in jail because they have disobeyed the order of the Federal Courts to vote railroad bonds which involve St. Clair County in great expense, today refused to accept his liberty upon the terms of Judge Phillip's decision rendered in the Federal Court Thursday, and decided to remain in jail.

The second is also from the same paper, of a later date:

One of the most unique cases in the civilized world is the St. Clair county bond case, which a dispatch from Kansas City announces is about to be compromised.

For years the Judges of St. Clair County, Missouri, have either been in jail for contempt of the Federal Court or fugitives from justice, holding court in the woods to avoid arrest.

In 1868 the County of St. Clair issued $200,000 worth of bonds to build a railroad across the county. In spite of the fact that the railroad was not built, the Federal Court rendered a judgment against the county in favor of the bondholders. The county officials refused to pay and the Federal Court committed the county judges to jail for contempt of court because they refused to order the county officials to levy the tax to pay the judgment. The debt, with principal and interest, now amounts to $1,500,000. For thirty-four years the county judges have patriotically refused to bankrupt the county by ordering the levy of the tax. It has been known that election to the office of county judge meant imprisonment or dodging arrest during the term of office. Yet men have never been wanting to serve their country in this arduous capacity, and St. Clair County has always had its judges, in jail or out of jail, resolutely standing between its people and the ruin threatened by the Federal Court. Of the three judges at the present time. Judge Thomas Nevitt is in jail at Maryville, where he has been a year, serving a sentence for contempt. Judge S.C. Peden is serving a similar sentence in Warrensburg jail. Judge Walker, it is reported, has lived in the brush since he was elected, and the United States deputies have not been able to capture him.

This remarkable state of affairs, which is humorous from one point of view and very serious from another, arises from our system of having Federal Courts besides State Courts. It is very questionable whether a Federal Court has the power to commit a State Judge for refusing to obey its mandate, and whether a Federal Court has the right to issue a mandate directed to a State Judge in his official capacity. It would seem as if the State Judge should be protected by the sovereignty of the State. Certainly when the constitution was adopted it was never contemplated that a situation like that in St. Clair county, Missouri, should ever arise.

Although the St. Clair County case is about to be settled by compromise, the law upon the subject should be made plain either by authoritative judicial decision of by legislation, that such an anomalous condition may not occur again.

The third is from the Atlanta (Ga.) Constitution:

St. Paul, Minn, August 28, 1902. — The United States Court of Appeals, in an opinion by Judge Seaborn, today denied the application for writs of habeas corpus or other relief in the cases of Thomas D. Nevitt and Samuel C. Peden, Judges of the County Court of St. Clair Country, Missouri, and sustains the right of a Federal Judge to carry out the mandates of a judgment by him.

This case, the like of which, it is said, has not come before the Courts since the early and unsettled days of the republic, dates back to a period shorty after the close of the civil war. St. Clair County, in aid of the construction of a railroad, issued a large amount of bonds and when these became due, the county sought to evade payment and to have the Courts invalidate them.

Judgments against the county aggregating more than $200,000, however, were issued in the United States Court. The county fought on, adopting every legal device to defeat the enforcement of the judgment until about two years ago, when United States Judge Phillips, at the instance of the judgment creditors, issued a writ of mandamus directing the County Court to levy a tax for the partial payment of the indebtedness. The judges refused to obey this mandate, holding that the bonds had been illegally issued. Then came the order of arrest and commitment for contempt of Court. The Judges evaded the Federal Court officers, who sought to serve the writs of commitment, hiding in the woods and other unknown places. Meanwhile the County Courts were not held, criminals went untried, civil cases could not be heard, the county roads and bridges fell into decay and other business commonly transacted by the County Court was wholly neglected.

Recently, however, the marshals discovered the hiding places of the fugitive judges and arrested them. Their counsel petitioned the Court of Appeals for their release on bail and for an order staying proceedings until an application could be made to President Roosevelt for a pardon.

In denying their application Judge Sanborn holds that a writ of habeas corpus cannot be made to perform the office of writ of error, as it is available only when a prisoner is illegally restrained by a Court without power to make an order for contempt.

The following letter will explain itself:

Maryville, Nodway, County, Mo., June 1st, 1902.

Mr. D. D. Peden, St., Houston, Texas.

Dear Sir: I will say that I have been shifted around some, and may have forgotten to answer your other letter. I live in St. Clair County and have a wife and six children, four girls and two boys. Am fifty years old. Have been in jail thirteen months at Bethany and Maryville. My father's name was Joseph Peden; he was born in Pennsylvania, and moved to Indiana, Clark County, but sold out in '68 and moved to Missouri.

I have been in the Bond Fight since '70. I would like to see my county and people free, and that is why I am in jail.

Yours truly,   (Signed) Samuel C. Peden.

David Morton

Among the strong, noble characters of a stern age, and of the race of Peden, there stands out in bold and beautiful relief, like some statue in marble that of David Morton, the third son of James, or David Morton and Jane Peden. Born in Antrim. Ireland, in 1760, he was brought to America when a boy of eight or ten by his grandfather, John Peden, along with his mother and her other children, as his father died while they were very young.

David Morton grew to man's estate under the guidance of his venerable grandfather, to whom he was peculiarly devoted. He, though a mere lad, took part in the War for Independence, serving in the Fairforest, or Spartan regiment a short while, then under the partisan leaders, Marion, Sumter and Pickens, at Cowpens and numerous local battles of upper South Carolina.

He was twice married, first to Penelope, a sister or daughter of Hugh L. White, who lived only a few years and died childless. He then married Mary or Mollie Jamison, also of prominent Whig parentage. She also died leaving him in his old age, blind, helpless and alone, save for the devotion of some excellent slaves, who deserve the enconium of "Semper Fidelis!" After the death of John Peden, he came to Fairview township and settled the place where he plied his trade and spent his long, useful life among kith and kin.

This old homestead is located on South Raeburn Creek, near its source. At the present time only the site of the old house remains, all traces of a once pretentious building are gone. The spring remains as he left it, but is disused. A forlorn apple tree, very decrepit, still stands in the old yard place. The once large plantation has been divided into several tracts and is owned by different parties, among them two brothers, James and John Putnam, lineal descendants of Thomas and Alexander, second and sixth sons of John Peden. There is a small tract donated to a negro church. Bethlehem.

Four of the former slaves still linger on the old home place, very old and poor. Their names are: Wilson, Alexander, Sallie and Jane. All bear the Morton name. Jane was house maid and her mistress chief assistant; Wilson was his master's boy, ministering to his wants in his blindness, caring carefully for him in his last illness, with faithful and unerring love, not uncommon among the well treated slaves of bygone days. Wilson has a few mementoes of his idolized master and friend that he resolutely refuses to part with even for bread, among them an old arm chair which David Morton made for his grandfather's comfort in his last days, meeting all overtures for its purchase with, "It was Mastah's chair. Misses died in it, and I can't sell it."

David Morton's trade was that of carpenter and cabinet maker, and most of the quaint old three-cornered cupboards, tables, benches, cradles to rock their infancy, and colons to bury the dead of the Pedens for three generations were made by the grand old man.

The history of the much coveted chair which is well preserved is as follows:

It was the first article made by David Morton in his shop in his new home. Thinking of his beloved grandfather, he made it and carried it across the country back to Chester, where he found John Peden very feeble. Abandoning everything else, gave his time and young manhood to nursing the aged saint to the end. From this chair he lifted John Peden to his last sleep, and from it he also was lifted by these slave friends to his own rest about fifty years later.

His was a character of great generosity and nobility, as well as deep piety. His mental attainments were very superior, despite educational disadvantages of pioneer times. He made friends of books, of which he had many, enabled by his ample means to procure those luxuries.

He was possessed of great physical strength and manly beauty, large and fair, with noble head and face, beaming blue eyes and a benevolent countenance.

David Morton came to his end beloved and honored. The present building of Fairview church is one of his monuments, and the record placed on his tomb is so true and faithful that it is copied here as a fitting tribute to one grand character of the second generation.

Sacred to the Memory of David Morton

Who departed this life on the 25th day of September, 1848, in the 88th year of his age.

He had been a Revolutionary soldier, and fought the battles of his country.

He was an elder in the church at this place, a worthy member of the session until the day of his death.

He was always liberal in its support, and at death left a handsome estate to be divided between this church and foreign missions.

He was a liberal soul and devised liberal things.

"And now abideth Faith, Hope and Charity, these three; but the greatest of these three is Charity." 1 Cor. 13:13.

Dr. Alexander Peden

Alexander David Peden, son of Alexander Peden, formerly a merchant of Wilmington, N. C, whose father was Mingo Peden merchant in Irvine Ayrshire, Scotland, whose father was Alexander Peden the "Prophet" whose grave is at Mauchline. (This is a mistake as far as Alexander the Prophet is concerned as he was unmarried and a sketch of him is in Capt. D.D. Peden's admirable sketch of the family at the Fairview reunion. Doubtless this Alexander Peden was a nephew of the Prophet.)

Alexander David Peden was born in Wilmington, but on the death of his mother was sent back to Scotland a small boy to the care of his grandfather and maiden aunt living in Edinburg. He was educated at Irvine, Ayreshire, graduating at Glasgow, as a physician, then went to sea out of London as surgeon's mate in employ of East Indian Company for twelve years, then for eight years roamed around the world. His daring to save the lives of a crew of American sailors "dubbed" him Com'd Perry, a name that clung to him on land and sea. He first settled in New Orleans where he married then moved to Galveston, Texas, but about that time the civil war between the states broke out. Two of his sons went into the Confederate service. "My father being an old man seeing things taken and destroyed, went to Mexico where he remained until the war ended." (Letter of Louis Peden.) When he went to the ill-fated town of Indianalo, where, during a cyclone and deluge (1875?) his wife and several children were drowned; also his ranch, houses, horses and cattle were swept away, all his earthly possessions, leaving him utterly without property, at the age of seventy-five. "My father died in 1881 — gone but not forgot. He was always a friend to the weak and helpless. Although he was one of the best physicians and surgeons in this country he did not make much money out of his practice for he refused to take money from the poor for his services. Therefore he never accumulated a vast fortune, as he could have done if he desired. While my father was not a rich man he was in good circumstances up to the great Indianola disaster, in which everything he possessed was destroyed. Afterwards (this terrible calamity) father gave up the practice of medicine; this world had no more attraction for him after the loss of his dear wife. Bowed down with grief, broken-hearted, he lived on very quietly until God called him home, where he claims his final reward in heaven with mother. (Extract from letter of his son, Louis Peden, with his permission, also the following letter from the pen of Alexander D. Peden, which brings out this beautiful character, a noble son of the house of Peden, the letter was never sent, but kindly loaned the writer for a copy here.)

"Excuse the freedom of an unknown stranger, one long lost to memory, and no doubt considered numbered among the dead. The Lord in His divine providence spared my life through many adversities by land and sea. Encountering gales of wind, cyclones, white squalls, and Borean blasts, with a restless sea and angry billows tossing our frail barques like chaff before the wind, leaving ourselves to the care of and mercy of an all-seeing eye.

"Now old age has crept upon me, seventy-five years old, feeble and worn-out, when anchored on a treacherous shore. God in His all-wise providence sent a cyclone with a deluge flood to sweep our ill-fated city from the face of the earth, (drowning) my wife and children and sweeping my ranch, houses, horses and cattle up into the prairies for the course of six miles. All I possessed in the world was on this ranch; myself being called away from home to serve on the jury of my country. If at home should not have troubled you with this epistle; should have died with and for my family being too much of a sea-dog to have lost all. But now left behind to mourn and bow to adversity.

People were hurried from sleep into eternity and up where rolls the boundless ocean of the stars. "Forever freed and unrestrained. Life's weary toil, forever o'er; which immortality is gained, "and pain and struggles are no more;" and all the joys that dying brings; submitting our fate to the Supreme Ruler of the universe, and short space of time allotted for man to live, deprived of youth to labor it seems hard to become a pauper; one sprung from the ancient family of Pedens in Scotia's isle. Having no friends here it struck me to address the sympathy of my kinsman to relieve me of the distress I am now suffering. If any doubt should arise in your mind that I am not the "Simon pure" A.D. Peden I refer you to your fellow townsman, Mr. Kidder, who had the pleasure of my company in Bagdad, Mexico, then on a voyage to Tisal, Yucatan, who can vouch for my credulity. (This kinsman was a halfbrother, William or James Peden, or both who went from Wilmington, N. C, to Virginia, and to Kentucky and Illinois; of these the writer has a trace, they were really a later emigration of the same line.) I am Alexander David Peden, son of Alexander, deceased, formerly merchant in Wilmington, N. C. My father's father was Mingo Peden, merchant in Irvine, Ayreshire, Scotland, where I was educated and graduated as a physician in Glasgow; then went out to sea out of London as surgeon's mate in East India Company for twelve years. Then for eight years roamed the world. That is my pedigree. Although American seamen are not entitled to their Christian names, being obliged to give shipping papers of their characters before entering upon another voyage; and all seamen avoid the law by false papers on every ship. My daring to save the life of a ship's crew of America they "dubbed" me Commodore Perry, a name which has hung to me on land and sea. If I was to write my life it would become volumes so I shall close, hoping your sympathy will be towards me.

(He here mentions a number of Pedens, James Peden, at Jonesborough, Tenn., who belonged to the 16th Alabama Regiment, and Charles Peden, at Atlanta, Ga., John and Thomas Peden, to ordinance train; this was during the civil war and they were with his son Louis, and expresses the wonder where and who they all were and where they came from.) "Although suffering now from want I will not commit suicide nor blast my good name, but will wander on until I can wander no more, so excuse a wanderer. Hoping to hear from you, I am, dear friends,

Alexander D. Peden.

(He seems trying to prove beyond doubt his identity, after long years of absence, to the members of his father's family, and the writer, as before stated, has letters from these Pedens, or as they spell the name Padon. One family lives in Kentucky (Carrsville), and copy here an extract from a letter by a devoted young doctor, who laid his young life down last year in Blackwell, O. T., W. H. Padon, M. D. "Our ancestry, grandfather's and father's families were all missionary Baptist, and have always been noted for their strict piety and great interest in Christianity."

Rev. Mitchell Peden.

Mitchell Peden was born in Spartanburg District, S.C., August 24, 1809.

He united with the church at Nazareth (Presbyterian), at the age of nineteen years. He had been a member of the Sabbath school for twelve years in Mr. Dickson's class. He was licensed to preach the Gospel by the Presbytery of Harmony in April, 1838, at the age of twenty-nine. The first year after being licensed he preached one hundred and six sermons, at thirty-three different places situated in Spartanburg, Greenville and Sumter Districts (counties), over two hundred miles distance.

He married Eliza Caldwell November 13, 1838, and settled at a place named Barrondale, near Longtown. He was ordained to the full work of the ministry at Mt. Olivet church, October, 1839, and served Aimwell and Mill Creek churches as pastor until 1844, when he removed to Pontotoc County, Miss., with a large following of kith and kin. Settled at Houston, Miss., in 1845, being elected principal of the Male Academy at that place.

In 1846 he was bereft of his wife and three children of scarlet fever. In 1847 he moved to Lowndes County, Miss., and took pastoral charge of Bethel and Mt. Zion churches. In 1847 (November 16) he married Mrs. Mary P. Ervine. In 1855 he removed to Winston County, Miss., and took charge of Bethsalem and Lebanon churches, where he continued to faithfully discharge his duties until God in His providence saw best to paralyze his physical powers in 1865. Although advised by his physicians to cease preaching, he would go to church and read his sermons, sitting in a chair, like John of old. He was very punctual in filling his appointments; there were very few meetings of Presbytery or Synod in which his seat was vacant. He was a member of the General Assembly a number of times, and was present at that notable meeting which saw the division of the Presbyterian Church North and South.

Mitchell Peden, like his race, was remarkably conscientious and faithful in his adherence to the principles and constitution of the Presbyterian church. In character he was kind, humble, fraternal in his feelings and intercourse with his brethren; zealous and affectionate in his manner of preaching and assiduous in his efforts to win souls for Christ, in which he was wonderfully blest.

He died August 31, 1868, of a final stroke of paralysis. A ripened sheaf of golden grain, garnered, and granted a place in the Master's Harvest Home.

Alexander Wilson Peden.
(By his son, Hugh L. Peden.)

Alexander Wilson Peden was born November 9, 1809; died February 8, 1868. He was a very pious man, one who was highly respected by the entire community. He was County Commissioner for the term of twenty-seven years, and at the time of his death Treasurer of the Board for Greenville County, S.C. He was bitterly opposed to secession though he took an active part in the Civil War did all he could for the country; gave it three sons and sent several negroes to work on the breast-works at Charleston. Was Commissioner of the Poor during this trying period and often said it was hard to please all who applied for assistance or pensions. (Extract from records of Fairview church, September 2, 1849.) "The Rev. E. T. Buist preached a sermon on the institution and qualifications of the eldership, and at the close of the sermon proceeded to the ordination of the elders elect, to wit: Austin Williams, John M. Harrison, James E. Savage and Alexander W. Peden, after the constitutional questions being proposed to the candidates and also to the congregation and they both had answered in the affirmative. Rev. Buist then proceeded to set apart by prayer the Elders elect to the office of Ruling Elders in this church."

He was a son of White Peden and Margaret Peden, grandson of Thomas Peden on the father's side, and of Alexander Peden on his mother's. Therefore springing from the Houses of Thomas and Alexander, second and sixth sons of John the father and founder.

John M. Peden.
(By his son Jas. B. Peden.)

I feel I must tell you of my father, but I know very little of the Pedens.

My father was left an orphan at the age of nine years. My grandfather, James Peden emigrated from Fairview, S. C, in 1824; died in this county; his wife followed very soon, both within five years of their arrival in Mississippi, consequently my father was left without educational advantages, and but little family history. He had three sisters and two brothers, Samuel and Frank.

Father was born in South Carolina September 14, 1819; died September 9, 1896. Served through the Civil War as a lieutenant in the 2nd Mississippi state troops, a brave and daring soldier.

In religious belief he was a Missionary Baptist. Held the office of deacon most of his life. He served his church faithfully, loved it dearly, and contributed freely to its needs, but all good men were his brethren. He lived upon, moved and acted on that broad plane that all Christians were of one family, regardless of creeds. He was also a Master Mason; was buried with Masonic honors.

He lived to just that period of life he so coveted, to see all his children grown up and educated to the very best extent he was able to give.

Rev. Andrew G. Peden.
(A Memorial — By Rev. Jas. Stacey, D. D.)

There is no death, the stars go down.
  To rise upon some fairer shore,
And bright in heaven's jeweled crown,
  They shine forever more. —

Rev. Andrew Gilliland Peden was born near Fairview church, Greenville County, S.C., October 28, 1811, and died at his home in Pike County, Ga., on Sabbath morning, January 19, 1896.

He was a son of David Peden and Margaret Hughes, his father, David Peden, being the youngest of ten children who, with their parents, John Peden and Margaret McDill, came to Spartanburg County, (then Spartan District), S. C, about the year 17681770, with a colony from Ulster, in the north of Ireland, from County Antrim. He (Rev. Andrew G. Peden) was the twelfth child of his father, and the second of his mother, she being the second wife; her predecessor leaving ten children. Out of this large family only one sister, Mrs. Eleanor G. Dunbar, now remains, she being his only own sister, and still resides in the old Carolina home. Mr. David Hamilton Peden, for years an efficient elder in the Griffin, Ga., church, and who died a few years ago being his youngest brother.

When about seventeen years of age Rev. Andrew G. Peden made a profession of faith in Christ. Soon after he entered the school of Dr. J. L. Kennedy in Spartanburg County, where he remained for three years, he then entered the Theological Seminary at Columbia, S. C, graduated in 1834, with the second class sent out from those venerated halls, and at the time of his death was the oldest surviving graduate of that institution.

He was licensed to preach November 28, 1834, by Harmony Presbytery, in company with Dr. R. S. Gladney, the sainted J. Henley Thornwell, and a number of names equally bright in the Southern Presbyterian Church. His first field was Indiantown church, to which he was called in January, 1835; on April 21, 1835, he was ordained and installed pastor of said church by the aforesaid Presbytery, where he remained until April 4, 1839, when this pastorate was regretfully dissolved, and he became pastor of the neighboring church of Williamsburgh or Kingstree, which he supplied twelve years, until towards the close of 1847, when he removed to Pike County, Ga., where he spent the remainder of his life, becoming the founder and pastor of Friendship church in April, 1848. He preached also at Greenville, Ga., for two years, 1854-1856, and at other places as the opportunity offered until the infirmities of years and failing sight laid him aside from the duties of the ministry.

Rev. A.G. Peden was a man of well-rounded character. Of fine physique, of handsome, pleasant countenance, in which could be seen depicted gentleness, coupled with great strength of character. He was a man of sympathy and neighborly feelings, kind, generous to a fault, of unbounded hospitality; a man of honor, unswerving in his devotion to principle, true as steel to his word, entirely free from double-dealing, with fine judgment, practical business sense, managing his own affairs with prudence and discretion; sound in his theological views, solid and practical in his preaching; a good presbyter and a man whose judgment might be safely trusted in all questions of Church and State. It is not a cause for wonder that such a man should enjoy as he did the confidence and esteem, of the entire community. As evidence of this confidence reposed in him, during and just after the Civil War, without any solicitation on his part, his neighbors and friends and fellow citizens nominated and elected him to represent them in the representative hall of the State of Georgia.

Though afflicted for several years with great physical weakness, and for sometime before his death with total blindness, yet he unmurmuringly submitted to the chastening hand of God, his Heavenly Father, and was frequently heard to speak of his unshaken trust in Him, and love to his fellowmen.

On his eighty-fourth birthday, a few months before his death, he asked his wife to send for a neighbor to come and pray with him. On being told that it was nearly midnight he said: "Hold me up on my knees, then." This was done, and there in the solemn stillness of that dark hour, upon his feeble, bended knees he poured out his soul in earnest prayer and supplication unto God.

After a lingering illness of three months this loved saint passed quietly away without struggle or groan, early on Sabbath morning, January 19, 1896, entering into his eternal rest.

"As fades the summer cloud away
   Or sinks the gale when storms are o'er."

His funeral services were held at Friendship church, where he had so long ministered in sacred things. They were conducted by his co-pastor and successor. Rev. R. N. Abrahams, the address being made by Rev. W. G. Woodbridge, of the Griffin, Ga., church, from Psalm 46:10. "Be still and know that I am God."

Rev. Andrew G. Peden was thrice married. His first wife was Miss Margaret Dantzler, of that union two of the five children survive, Capt. D. D. Peden, of Houston, Texas, and Mrs. J. Russell Tolbert, of Clarksville, Arkansas. His second wife was Miss Mary I. Britt, who lived but a few years and left no children. The devoted wife who remains was Miss Margaret C. Davis. Two daughters of the four children of this marriage survive, Mrs. J. W. Sullivan, Houston, Texas; Mrs. T. C. Sullivan, Pedenville, Ga.

This sketch is adapted from the Memorial prepared for Atlanta Presbytery at Riverdale, October 10, 1896, by his lifelong personal friend, Rev. James Stacey, D. D.

We leave him to rest, in hope of a joyful resurrection, beneath the somber shadows of the soughing Georgia pines, behind the pulpit he filled so long and so well, knowing that when the Lord descends we shall greet the quiet saint in his spiritual beauty, clad in the vigor of immortal youth, along with that youthful Andrew Peden, martyr, over whose bright curls closed the dark waters of Loch Mary, in Scotland, hundreds of years ago.

Captain D. D. Peden.

The parents of Capt. D. D. Peden were Rev. Andrew G. and Margaret Peden (nee Dantzler). He was born November 2nd, 1835, at the home of his grandparents, David and Elizabeth (nee Miller) Dantzler, in Spartanburg County, S.C. His father, Andrew G., was the twelfth child of David Peden, who was the youngest of the ten children of the venerable John and Margaret Peden, the founder of the South Carolina Pedens. His maternal grandfather, David Dantzler, was the son of Jacob, who, in turn, was the son of Harry Dantzler, who came from Germany prior to the Revolutionary war and settled in what is now Orangeburg County, S.C., many of whose descendants are still honored citizens of that section of the State.

His grandmother Dantzler, was the daughter of Michael and Nancy Miller, the latter was the daughter of Alexander Vernon and his wife, Margaret, nee Chesney. The descendants of Michael and Elizabeth Miller were quite numerous, and through this family Capt. Peden is related to very many of the best people in Spartanburg County, and other sections of the State and Western States.

Until about 12 or 13 years of age, he resided in Williamsburg County, where his father was pastor successively of the Indiantown and Williamsburg Presbyterian churches, the latter located near the village of Kingstree, the county seat of said county. His mother, his sister, Mary Crawford, and his brother, Anderson Vernon, are buried in the grave yard of this venerable church.

In the winter of 1848, his father (having married the second time), removed to Georgia, settling in Pike County. In the course of a few years he was sent to the "High School" at La Grange, Ga. About the years 1855 or 1856 he entered the "Georgia Military Institute" located at Marietta. He remained in this institute about two years. Being quite fond of the military feature of this institution, he became a good tactician. About the year 1857, his father purchased a plantation in Calhoun County, in the southwestern part of the State and he (D. D. Peden) was in charge of this farm when the Civil War between the States was declared, in 1861. He was among the first volunteers to enlist in his county. On account of his previous military training, he was soon put to work drilling the volunteers. At the organization of the "Calhoun Rifles," which was the first company to leave the county, many of his friends urged him to become a candidate for the captaincy. This he positively declined to do, saying, he could not think of commanding men, many of whom were by a number of years his seniors in age. He was, however, unanimously elected first lieutenant, which position he accepted. Soon after the organization of the company, he was detailed to go to Milledgeville, the then State Capital of Georgia. Arriving at Milledgeville, he found that Gov. Jos. E. Brown and staff had removed their headquarters to Atlanta. He proceeded to Atlanta and there tendered to the governor the services of the company. He was informed that the company would be listed, but would have to wait its regular "turn" to be mustered into the service and be organized into a regiment.

The prospect of delay and inaction was quite a disappointment. He returned home and reported results to the company. As many of the men had given up positions, some who were farmers having sold or otherwise disposed of their crops, and were consequently having to bear their own expenses, it was a sore disappointment to the men. Many of them threatened to leave us and join other organizations that had been previously mustered into service. About this time an opportunity presented itself which enabled them to make a direct tender of their services to the Confederate Government at Richmond. The regiment was organized and mustered into service there and was first known as the Third (3) Independent Georgia Regiment. Later it was known as the 12th Regiment Georgia Volunteers.

E. A. PEDEN.

D. D. PEDEN, JR.

ALLEN V. PEDEN.

EDWARD D. PEDEN.

The first regimental officers were, Colonel, Edward Johnson; Lieutenant Colonel, Z. T. Conner; Major, Smead; Adjutant, Edward Willis. The companies were. A., from Sumter County, Willis A. Hawkins, captain; B., from Jones County, Pitts, captain; C, from Macon County, Carson, captain; D., from Calhoun County, W. L. Furlow, captain, D. D. Peden, 1st lieut.; E., from Muscogee County, ___ Scott, captain; F., from Dooley County, ___ Brown, captain; G., from Putnam County, ___ Davis, captain; H., from Bibb County, Rodgers, captain; J., from Lowndes County, ___ Patterson, captain (?); K., from Marion County, Mark A. Blanford, captain.

Soon after organization was perfected, the regiment was ordered to Staunton, Va., by rail, thence to West Virginia on foot, over the Staunton and Parkersburg pikes to reinforce General Garnett. They were too late, however, General Garnett was killed and his troops retreated. For several months the regiment was encamped on Greenbrier river, between Allegheny and Cheat Mountains. Later they moved back and went into winter quarters on top of the Allegheny Mountain, one among the coldest spots this side of the north pole. This was the winter of 1861. The following spring they were started in the direction of Harper's Ferry. When the army reached McDowell, they were engaged in battle with the enemy, our troops being under command of General 'Stonewall" Jackson. In Dr. Dabney's life of General Jackson special mention is made of the gallantry of the 12th Georgia Regiment. The losses to the regiment were very heavy. Col. Ed. Johnson, afterwards promoted to Brigadier, and later to Major General, was severely wounded. Company D's losses were heavy, both in officers and men. Captain Wm. L. Furlow, the company's first captain, and junior 2nd Lieutenant, J. T. Woodward, were both killed in this engagement.

First lieutenant, D. D. Peden, then became captain and commanded the company until just before the Gettysburg campaign opened in the spring of 1863. Just prior to the opening of this campaign, he was assigned to duty on the staff of Major General R. E. Rodes as Inspector General of the Division. The appointment was quite a surprise to him as it was unexpected and unsolicited on his part, but very highly appreciated. The 12th Georgia Regiment was under General "Stonewall" Jackson in all of his brilliant battles and record breaking marches. Captain Peden was fortunate in never having been captured by the enemy. He was severely wounded, however, in the very last of the seven days battles around Richmond, and known as the battle of "Malvern Hill." His Division made the last charge that was made on General McClellan's stronghold on the above mentioned Malvern Hill. Captain Peden was leading his company at "double quick" when one of the enemy's shells exploded in front of him, completely destroying his right eye, besides lacerating his face and hands in a number of places. In a few minutes after he was wounded, it now being nearly dark, the seven days battles were ended. The friends of Captain Peden had small hope of his recovery, as it was in July, the weather very warm, and to make matters worse, erysipelas set in, which greatly aggravated the danger, besides adding additional pain to his suffering.

In about three or four months, however, he was sufficiently recovered to return to his command, which he rejoined at Bunker Hill, Va., soon after the battle of Sharpsburg, in Maryland, had been fought. Against the advice of a number of his friends, he resumed command of his company, and was with them in the battles of Fredericksburg and Chancellorsville. It was not long after the latter engagement when he was assigned to duty as Inspector General on Major General R. E. Rodes' staff. This position he held for quite a while, embracing the Pennsylvania campaign, including, of course, the battle of Gettysburg. General Rodes' Division was the advance guard of the famous 2nd Army Corps ("Stonewall" Jackson's) Army of North Virginia, and was the first of the Confederate Army to enter the town of Gettysburg. General Rodes' Division also acted as rear guard to the "Stonewall" Jackson Corps on the retreat from Gettysburg back in to Virginia. Some months afterwards, his health having been completely broken down, with the advice of both General Rodes and his chief surgeon. Dr. Mitchell, he reluctantly resigned the position of Inspector General and was later assigned to Post duty in his adopted State of Georgia. His headquarters were first at Griffin, near his father's home. Later on he was transferred to Savannah. The climate and water disagreeing with him he took a severe relapse, and by a competent board of surgeons he was placed on the retired list, a short while before General Sherman's famous march through Georgia, and on to Savannah.

He was in Calhoun County, Georgia, when the war closed, and in May, 1865, was married to Miss Fannie D. Plowden, a native of Sumter County, S.C. For about ten years after the war he was engaged in farming in Calhoun and Pike Counties, but on account of the difficulty of securing reliable labor for his farm he gave it up and moved to Griffin, where he successfully engaged in the cotton warehouse and fertilizer business. Later he was elected cashier of the Griffin Banking Company. Later still, at the organization of the Merchants and Planters Bank (in the same town), which he was largely instrumental in organizing, he was elected its first cashier.

His only two sons, Edward A. and D. D. Peden, Jr., meantime having moved to Houston, Texas, where they were engaged in business, Captain Peden and wife, in order that the little family could all be together, decided to move to Texas, which they did in 1891.

He and his two sons, under the firm name of Peden & Co., are successfully engaged in the iron business. They have four travelling salesmen who cover the greater part of Texas, reaching up in to the Indian Territory and into the southwestern portion of Louisiana. In their office and warehouse they employ on an average about fifteen men.

It goes without saying that he and family are all Presbyterians; he is an Elder of the First Presbyterian church, Houston, while his eldest son, Edward A., is a Deacon in the same church.

Mrs. J. R. Tolbert.

Mrs. Elizabeth Miller Tolbert, wife of J. R. Tolbert, was the daughter of Rev. A. G. Peden and his wife Margaret E,. Dantzler. She was born in South Carolina in 1838. After the death of her mother, at Kingstree, S. C, her father and family removed to Pike County, Georgia, about the year 1848. She graduated at the Synodical Female College, Griffin, Ga., in 1856.

In 1860 she married Mr. J. R. Tolbert, and was the mother of nine children, six of whom survive her.

On her father's side she was descended from John and Margaret Peden, founders of the Peden family in the South. On her mother's side she was descended from Alexander Vernon and his wife, Margaret Chesney, and is, therefore, related to many of the best people in South Carolina, specially in Spartanburg County.

Her only remaining brother is Capt. D. D. Peden, of Houston, Texas.

A good woman has gone to her reward was the unanimous expression used at her death, which occurred December 15, 1901. Her husband says truthfully: "Faith, love, charity, unselfishness and all the Christian virtues were highly personified in her daily walk and conduct. Indeed, her whole life was a striking illustration of the precepts and examples taught and practiced by Jesus when upon the earth. The high, the low, the rich and the poor were all regarded alike, and that great reHgious injunction, 'Love thy neighbor as thyself,' was exemplified through her whole life in a remarkable degree."

Let all, then, especially relatives and friends, strive to emulate her meek, gentle spirit, with the full assurance that if we live as we should we will meet her again in the "sweet by and bye."

Let us, as much as possible, emulate her faith, patience and perseverance, feeling and knowing as she did, that

"Heaven is not reached at a single bound:
But we build the ladder, by which we rise.
From the lowly earth to the vaulted skies.
And we mount to its summit round by round."

Mrs. E. M. Tolbert.   John S. Paden.

John Sanford Paden

"This son of the house of Peden has the honor of being fifth in line of descent, of the name John, was born in Cobb County, Georgia, February 11, 1842. Was son of John T. and Margaret (Foster) Paden. Was reared in Roswell, Ga. At the outbreak of the Civil War he entered at once the Confederate service, with company H, Seventh Georgia Infantry. Was in the first battle of Bull-Run, and in all the battles in and around Richmond, Va., and was with General Longstreet at Chickamauga, Tenn. Surrendered with Gen. R. E. Lee's army at Appomattox, Va.

"In 1867 he located at the new town of Gadsden, Ala., where he was very successful in business. Very active and influential in developing the resources of that now famous region, and becoming a familiar figure in the state history of Alabama. In 1874 (February 5th) he was married to Miss Anna Hollingsworth, who, with five children, survive him. His death took place on November 21, 1896."

A true Peden, useful citizen, faithful Christian, a brave soldier, a loyal son of the South, a model husband and father.

From an extract sent by his devoted wife.

(Signed) Anna D. Peden.

This letter from Rev. W. M. Paden will explain itself:

Salt Lake City, March 22, 1899.

D. D. Peden, Esq.:

Dear Sir: Your letter interests me very much, for I have heard a number of times concerning the Pedens of the South. At one time I had some correspondence with one by that name in North Carolina. I then concluded that my grandfather's relationship with the Southern family was not very close, and yet I do not think that there is any doubt but that the Pennsylvania family and the Carolina family have the same origin.

My grandfather came from the north of Ireland towards the end of the last century and settled in Pennsylvania. His name was William. His father's name was John. I am almost certain that none of my grandfather's descendants moved South, although I am not positive, not having traced the family very thoroughly. As seems to be the case with the Southern family my great grandfather's family were Presbyterians, and there are some five or six in the Presbyterian ministry, five or six Padens I mean. I do not know very much about the other branches of the family.

While my grandfather and great-grandfather spelled their name Peden, my father and all the grandchildren for perhaps the last forty years, have spelled their name Paden, it having been pronounced that way by the people.

I am sending the pamphlets to an old uncle of mine who knows more about our ancestry than any other man living, and I think it altogether likely that it will not be difficult to establish some remote relationship. The families seem to have had very much the same type of history and to be the same type of people.

W. M. Paden.

Col. Milton Peden.

The writer of the following account of part of the Northern family of Peden, Col. Milton Peden, was a brave, daring soldier during the recent war between the States, serving as Colonel of the 147th Indiana Regiment during the whole time; retiring to private life at the close of the civil war. He is now a hale, hearty old man of four score and is, in connection with Capt. D. D. Peden of the Southern family, planning a reunion of the entire Peden race as soon as practicable, at some central place:

"The following is something of the history of our branch of the Peden family as I obtained it from my old uncle, Daniel L. H. Peden, who died in 1873. I visited him some time prior to his death, at which time he gave me his best recollection of our family genealogy, to wit:

"Near the close of sixteenth century a Peden (given name not remembered), went from Glasgow, Scotland, to London as chief baker to royal family. The baker had a son, Joseph, who went to the north of Ireland, and his son, Samuel Peden, came to America about the year 1750, and settled in York County, Penna., where he married a Miss Potter, and they had born to them six children as follows: Obadiah Peden, Samuel Peden, Lydia Peden, Joseph Peden (my grandfather), Isaac Peden and Alexander Peden. Joseph Peden married Miss Rebecca Driver, of York County, Penna., an own cousin of Patrick Henry of Revolutionary fame. To them was born the following children, to wit: Margaret Peden, James Peden (my father), Jesse Peden, Elizabeth Peden, Joseph Peden, Daniel T.H. Peden, David Peden, Isaiah Peden, Samuel Peden and Abner Peden. The two eldest were born in York County and the others in Washington County, Penna. Grandfather Peden was a soldier in the Revolutionary War, and he being a gunsmith by trade was detailed to make guns for the army in the field. Grandfather died in Washington County, Penna., aged 94 years, and his father, Obadiah Peden, died in York County at the age of 100 years. These have all passed over to the great beyond long years ago. This ends Uncle Daniel's story.

"James Peden (my father), married Miss Margaret Love, of Sistersville, West Virginia. To them were born ten children, as follows: Elizabeth Peden, Rebecca Peden, James Peden, Joseph Peden, Jane L. Peden, David Peden Milton Peden, Reuben Peden, Hiram Peden and William Peden. All of whom have passed over to the better land, save Hiram and the writer hereof. My mother, Margaret Peden, died August 1st, 1855, and my father on August 19th, 1855, just nineteen days apart. Hiram Peden resides in Anderson, Madison County, Indiana; is 76 years of age, and in feeble health. I am 80 years of age and am quite rugged for that age."

"The Pedens were humble folk, good Christians and loyal citizens." — David H. Peden.

"The Pedens were never ambitious to shine, but in church and state were the staunch yeomanry." — David T. Peden.

"The Pedens were never politicians; all quiet farmers or mechanics, and always deeply religious people." — G. R. Paden.

"The Pedens are a quiet, home-loving race, have no taste for public life; farming is the favorite work of most of us." — J. Waddy T. Peden.

"The Pedens were, and are a quiet people, slow to wrath but 'Tak tent how ye meddle wi their rights.'" — A Kentucky Peden.

In reply to the question asked of a Missouri Paden as to whether any Pedens were in the Spanish-American war. 18971898, came the reply, 'The Padens have something better to do than be found idling time away around the campfires of useless warfare, .among the riff-raff of volunteer soldiery. When their country needs them to defend her liberties they are found in the front ranks."

One can fancy the spirit of old John Peden in the above. The Pedens were not triflers of old, neither are they today, this characteristic is the same in all ages. Ready to ,die for a principle but scorn a caprice. They are for "Liberty, civil, social and religious."

If the sons of Peden inherited the strongly marked traits of the father, John Peden, shorn of some of his enthusiastic faith, the daughters of Peden stand for all that is pure, true and sweet in woman, like the mother, Peggy McDill. She has always stood for the kingdom of home, always a homemaker. There were always some notable house-keepers or famous cooks among them, but as the wife, the mother, she shines brighter. The name has never figured in the civil courts as a "fair divorcee," nor has there ever been a divorced woman among them. To most of them the crown of maternity has descended and they wear it proudly, uncomplainingly. Into some lives there came and comes a minor chord that of widowhood. Now the Paden widow does not wrap her grief around her like a sable robe and sit inconsolable all her days. Second marriages were always rare. She lives for her children. There were many such during that dark period of 1861-65. Some left with large families of helpless little ones, but none of them ever gave up in despair and sent their children to some orphan home; they simply put their trust in God and struggled on. Verily they had their reward — in a generation of sturdy, independent men and useful women.

Spinsterhood is rare, but there were always one or two true "old maids" or household angels to step fearlessly into the lines when some devoted sister has fallen asleep to take up the tangled threads and smooth the way for the children's feet. There is in the writer's mind a picture sweet of Miss Jane Harrison, of precious memory, and Miss Elizabeth Peden, who has just bravely taken charge of a brood of eight or ten young nephews and nieces left orphans, this being the third or fourth time in her beautiful self-sacrificing life that she has placed herself in the desolate breach made by death. Also there is another, young in years but strong in spirit, Miss Irene Peden, who mothers a crowd of five motherless babes. These are only a few personally known to the writer, while from far off Mississippi she has just laid down a letter in which is this statement: "A Peden mother, a widow, laid five sons on the altar of the Southern Confederacy."

There is a tradition that Peggy McDill reappears once every generation in some female descendant, if so she must have doubled in the generation to which the writer belongs in Mrs. H. B. Stewart, Martha Eugenia Peden (line of Alexander), and Mrs. E. T. Jarvis, Eveline Peden (line of David). Both are notable housekeepers and model home-makers, both wear the crown maternal on fair unsullied brows, both have the sunny hair, the laughing blue eyes, both are divinely tall and fair, and each home is full of the merry laughter of happy childhood. Eugenia Stewart lives at Fairview, Eveline Jarvis dwells in Peden, Miss.

The Peden woman is little known outside her home. Its circle is wide enough for her happiness. She in not even "wrapt up in church work," which is quite frequently a sad misnomer for something else far less worthy. She cares little for the outside world. There are exceptions of course to this general rule, but they all stand firm, whatever their views, for "The peace, purity and perfect harmony of the home."

Julia Peden — A Peden Heroine

The young girl Julia Peden, of Montana, whose noble act or heroism copied from the Anaconda Standard, Anaconda, Montana, is inserted here as an example of the quick wit and ready resource peculiar to the Peden woman. She never hesitates in the hour of peril:

"It was on May 14 that Julia Peden, that brave and daring little rough rider woman of Eastern Montana, rode her race with the north coast limited train that has made her famous. Riding over the rolling prairie on her pet pony Kuter, she came upon a fire that was destroying a railroad bridge. The location was such that the fastest train in the Northwest, the north coast limited, due then in twenty minutes, could not see the fire in time to stop. Visions of the awful wreck that would ensue, the death and destruction that would result, flashed through the girl's mind. Her's was the duty, as she saw it, to ride to the station and stop the train before it had gained headway. Like the wind she sped away on the four-mile ride, covering the distance in fourteen minutes. And now the railway company has given her a testimonial of its appreciation. A Standard correspondent and photographer, who secured the photographs of the young lady posed especially for the Standard, that appear on this page, tells of his visit to her home.

"Miles City, June 11. — This morning just as the sun showed his red disk above old Signal Butte and gilded the metal and glass and rose-tinted the steam cloud of the eastbound 4:22 train, I put the little gray before the buggy and tried how quick he could cover the distance to Julia Peden's home. He's known hereabouts as a "fair good roadster," in Gray J. D., and I pushed him a little the last half, yet the four miles that Julia Peden rode at midday the 14th of May last, when she stopped the north coast train, took us 28 minutes. Julia did it in 14 minutes and had a good three-quarters further to cover that I had.

"Her father, Dave Peden, the well-known cowboy farmer, was in the stable yard when we rattled in to the narrow by lane among the young cottonwoods, and the little Scotch housewife and mother was already astir in the neat kitchen.

"'Yer takin' an early spin the morn,' says the Scotch farmer. 'Ye have the nag warmed up; he's fair too fat for the likes. Take out the bit, man, and tie to yon rack, where he'll get a mouthful of alfalfa while he cools, and we'll have a bit of breakfast shortly oursel's.'

"There's nothing quite like the sun and wind to blow the foolishness out of one. Joe — that's the farm name Julia has from her father — Joe's face shows she has plenty of contact with the sun and wind. 'Have ye the pigskin under the seat? Ye'll not let the mare go too fast, Joe? And ye'll be home against noontime?' were the father and mother's inquiries — not commands — as 14-year-old Julia, with her long, neat braid and her gauntlets and cowboy hat, stepped into the buggy at 6 A.M., and was off for the reservation course to put the aforesaid pigskin on Door Key and give him his regular work.

"'Door Key,' Julia had explained to me as we sat at the frugal breakfast of coffee, eggs, good, home-made bread and strawberry jam, 'is a dandy. He's getting his name from the range mark on the broad of his jaw. Indeed, yes. It would have been a different story if I had been up on that big bay lad instead of poor little Kuter. Kuter's a' right for a mongrel grasser, but the big bay, he'd no stop at ditches or fences — if I'd let him. Mack D. owns him. I am to work him every day. We will see what he can do at the race meeting on the Fourth.'

"Once Farmer Dave had gone to his work I sat for a few minutes with the mother, who talked in her quiet way about Julia, her brother, their's, her's and David's life since they came out from across the water to Michigan, then to New Mexico, where Julia was born.

"'She's 15 her next birthday. Her father says she's the licht, firm ha-a-nd that horses like. Yes, she's helpful, Julie is,' said the mother. 'She likes driving the mower for her father. Boys, ye know, have a way of losing their temper with young horses, jerkin' them about, but Julie always has patience and gets on well. No fear of her losing her head over a bit of notoriety. It's an education Julie — and the family — are wanting for her; not the taking of her to the wild west show.'

"'Yes,' went on Mrs. Peden, 'I think it was on the 14th of last month I gave Julia leave to take Kuter — the little bald-face pony — and go to the schoolhouse, just over near the bridge that burned. The teacher was having some doings and all the child's mates were riding there for a holiday.'

"And so it most fittingly happened that day that 'the little Peden maid who rides races' chanced to be astride a horse near the 85-foot bridge situated at the slough, a half mile east of her home — a pile and timber structure not unlike the one shown in the accompanying picture. Neighbor Leonard saw the bridge burning, saw Julia. It needed but a word to drive thoughts of holiday pleasures out of her mind and send her flying villageward. Faithful to the little mother, though, she took time to dash to the door as she passed.

"'Child! Child! Ye can't do it; the fast train must be due here in 20 minutes; but hurry, hurry; try it, try it.'

"Save for a couple of narrow gulches and one sharp turn the course lies true and straight along the railroad track to the town. The girl's training has been good, and it stood her in hand that day. She knew how and when to push a mount to his limit. Three miles up the trails ducks under a bridge so low one must 'scrooch a bit and take off one's hat, for they have started dumping gravel to fill it up, as the're doing all the pile bridges.'

"'Sell Kuter!' said Julia to me today. 'I think not! A while back we did want to sell him, but I think he's like to stay on with us now. Oh, no; he wasn't so beat, though, at the fast four miles, if he did shed lather from every strap the last burst, and there's many a 'grasser' that could't have headed us from the last crossing to the telegraph office.'

The Race to the Rescue

"She was in good time, the train was held. Neighbor Leonard piled ties east and west and kept a lookout until the work train arrived.

"President Mellen was out on the line at the time, and not much later Julia got a 'please call' card from the Northern Pacific Express Company. When she called there was tendered, as a testimony of the railway's appreciation, her choice of 'a pass for the year or a hundred dollars in cash.' It needed but one guess to tell which she would take. That hundred will soon be on time deposit along with the eighty-odd already there as a result of 'Joe's' getting several good horses under the wire first at last year's races.

"While the little maid in not in the least 'puffed' about the exploit and consequent complimentary notices, one thing is most pleasing to her and her family, and may be worth a great deal to them by bringing them in touch with their kinfolk scattered from the Atlantic to the Pacific. For instance, D. D. Peden, ironmaster, from somewhere South, writes: 'My Dear Little Cousin, etc.: I saw the article quoted in our daily paper. I am proud of you.' Then follow other letters telling of the reunion at the Fairview Presbyterian church, South Carolina, and the jolly time the 1,300 Pedens and their kinfolks had, and how John Peden and Margaret McDill came out before the Revolution, raised a family of ten, with never a bad one, etc.

"Here's to your success, thrifty Scotch lass. May your nag never put foot in a prairie-dog burrow, and here, finally, is my indorsement of the sentiments of one of your kin, a neighbor, who has long watched you 'sit straight' as you rode through the village, and said as he threw up his bonnet when you came ahead over the scratch: 'She's gude, the child is! She's no afraid at a pinch to put a mount's nose in where the're bunched and takin' a chance at findin' room for hersel' and the saddle gittin' through. Man, but the gerl sits like she was part of the horse!'" — L. A. Huffman, in the Anaconda Standard.

Chapter Ten - The Founders of a House

"The man who rules his spirit" —
Saith the voice that cannot err,
"Is greater than the man who takes a city."
—Hale.

"What is nobler for a woman than
To know, within her hands
Is the destiny if nations, and
The fate of many Lands."
— Bryant.

John Peden, father and founder of the American house of Peden, especially in the South and West, was born near Broughshane, in the Parish of Ballymena, County Antrim, Ireland, as nearly as can now be ascertained, about the year 1709. This statement is confirmed by his granddaughter, Eleanor (Peden) Dunbar, who claimed that he was born just one hundred years, to date, before she was. Her birth date being June 16, 1809. He was one of at least five brothers, family tradition says seven, and that David was "the seventh son of the seventh son," therefore supernaturally gifted. His father was named James, or Thomas, there is some dispute as to which. His mother, according to one testimony, was Mary Mills. His grandparents being James Peden and Agnes Miller. This James Peden was a younger brother of "The Prophet Peden." In this family there were three sons, Alexander, James and Mingo. Their mother was Isabella Robb, and the father was Hugh Peden, who suffered martyrdom; the grandfather being Alexander Peden, husband of one of the daughters of the "House of Hamilton, with whom he received a fair dower."

These statements are given as they reached the writer, but it is "a far cry" back to 1524, so there may be some mistakes. The father and brothers, as well as John Peden himself, were Ulstermen to the heart's core, having part in the long continued, bloody warfare that banished the Stuart forever from the throne. Of the "distaff side," mere mention calls up memories of covenanting names, glowing crimson on the annals of martyrology.

Only one of John Peden's brothers remained in Ireland. There is some uncertainty about his name, probably Robert or Samuel, and his descendants yet linger at the old home in Broughshane, while one or two others returned to Scotland, when the way was opened on the suppression of the woolen trade, and where their descendants are found in Ayreshire and other parts of Scotland. Tradition also state that two or three brothers preceded John Peden to America; another version states that they followed from time to time. Only very recently have traces been found of the descendants of these old brothers, and all families of Peden, who came to America prior to the Revolution of 1776-1783 trace their origin to one of these four brothers. The Pedens of Enon Valley, Penna., from whom the writer has been unable to elicit any replies to numerous inquiries, hold the same traditions as those held by the descendants of John Peden, founder of the Southern house.

John Peden grew to manhood in troublous days, which left an indelible impress on his character; an enthusiast in his faith, he inherited the fervid piety of long generations of saints and martyrs. He possessed a fair, almost liberal, education. "For be it remembered that the exiled Scots in Ireland were very careful to have good schools, and attended carefully to the education of their children, both secular and religious, therefore, they were not cast upon the shores of the new world a crowd of ignorant wretches." From Douglas Campbell's Puritans of the South.) He was therefore steady and industrious at his trade of wagon-maker; he also was skilled in other woodwork as well, and knew somewhat of "blacksmithing," which stood him good stead. He was a stern, silent man, of quiet temper and rigid self-control, ruling his own spirit, very humble in his own eyes, and reticent about his attainments which were many and varied, cheerful and content with his lot in life. His one pride and glory being in his descent from an ancestry which had never bowed the neck to Rome. Family tradition states that his grandfather, who bore the name of Andrew Hugh Peden, a young man, and the father of several young children, was shot by the orders of Claverhouse, while standing by St. Mary's Loch, in a lonely glen. He sprang forward in the death struggle into the black waters of the loch, which received his body and holds it in sacred trust until time shall be no more, and all will be revealed.

Scorning the intervention of the priest, which the Irish law required, John Peden was married by a Protestant minister to his neighbor's daughter, bonny "Peggy" or Margaret McDill. She always bore this name. [Note — For the history of "Peggy" or Margaret McDill the writer is indebted to several members of the McDill family, which family has kept its records intact for centuries.]

"Peggy" or Margaret was the eldest daughter of John McDill and Janet Leslie, his wife (what memories the Leslie name stirs). She was born during August, 1715, at Broughshane, Ballymena Parish, Antrim County, Ireland. "She was a winsome lassie, brimful of glee, buxom and rosy." She married John Peden after much coaxing on his part in the year 1730, being not quite sixteen years old at the time, therefore she was more like a sister than mother to her older children, while her staid husband acted for all. She is described as a sweet-faced, sunny-tempered woman, with deep blue, laughing eyes and golden hair, whose rebellious curl refused the restraint of cap or snood, and reveled in the winds." As to figure, she was not, as is generally supposed, a "little dimpled darling," to be cuddled and petted, but rather cast in heroic mould, "large and stately, with a spirit and mind of her own." Her supply of wit and humor was as great as that of her husband was lacking; his faith bordered on fanaticism, while hers took a very practical common sense form, and it is told that she rather delighted in "bringing her John to earth" sometimes, which he bore with great patience for the love-sake. Her personal energy was boundless, and while her household were not clad in purple and fine linen, her industrious hands kept them bountifully supplied. She was a famous housekeeper, and because her youngest daughter most resembled her in this respect, she at her death "willed to my beloved daughter Elizabeth my set of wedding china." While she loved work, she also delighted in "a little play." She maintained throughout life a strong devotion to her family, and always insisted on being called "Peggy'" McDill, and so well was she loved by them that there has always been in the American family of McDill a Margaret to bear her name, some of whom being marvellous reproductions.

Their children were all ten born in Ireland, and the parents were long past life's summer time when they came across the seas. Mary, the eldest, was born 1732, James 1734, Jane 17, Thomas 1743, William 1749, Elizabeth 1750, John 1752, Samuel 1754, Alexander 1756, David 1760. These all came to America with their parents. During that long and perilous voyage the Christian fortitude of the father shone out brightly through the darkest hours, though the mother sometimes murmured secretly for the "auld countree," she bore herself calmly, even cheerfully, all the way over. David her youngest was a "braw lad" of ten when they came over, and "Davie" idolized his fair mother, while he stood greatly in awe of his father, who wore a stern countenance. The numerous grandchildren, too, claimed the care of the mother, so she had little time to herself on that crowded emigrant ship. During the trying hours when crew and passengers were having that fearful struggle for the mastery, the spirit of "Peggy" McDill never once faltered. Her keen eyes were the first to sight the new shores, as they were the last to view the old, and when they came to anchor she stepped ashore with proud, firm tread, bearing, well wrapped in her shawl, one of the youngest grandchildren. Eminently fitted by nature for a pioneer's wife, she transmitted much of her strong character to her sons and daughters, while the father's piety and energy were splendid examples for his children, and they were faithfully followed. The mother's industry was tireless, and "whatever she put her hands to prospered," so when the Indians stole her "stuff" she forthwith made more. On one occasion when after much abuse and many threats, they set fire to her cabin during the absence of her husband and sons, she "outed the flames" with her own hands, having the children bring water from the spring in "piggins." In the hour of danger she was as ready with a musket as husband or sons; but she loved best the days of peace; to sing old-time ballads and psalms to the humming of her wheel.

When the call came for men to rise for the sacred cause of Freedom John Peden was too old for active service. He did not hesitate long. Peggy said "he must go with the boys" so she took from her "kist" of blankets, all the work of her hands, a goodly store, rolled and bound them with deer-skin thongs, packing in a few shirts, and woolen socks of her own knitting, then prepared the parched corn for their "rock-a-hominy," singing all the while to keep her "spirits up." John Peden made ready his wagon, while the sons, who were at home, the four youngest, burnished their guns, moulded bullets, filled their powder horns, and sharpened their hunting knives. It was the voice of this Spartan mother that sent them forth from that cabin home on the hillside. All together, husband and sons, to do or die for liberty, with the words, "Laddies be bra', dinna ye show white feather, remember ye mither, and God be wi ye." Then she stood shading her eyes with her hand until they were lost to sight, and "Davie" stole back a few steps to wave his bonnet "to mother." The father was very useful in many ways, a cheerful, though silent guide. Who knows but his "fervent, effectual prayers" brought them safely throvgh many hairbreadth escapes; many perils by flood and flame, back to the cabin door where Peggy welcomed them after Gate's defeat. The father, already old and much broken, found the Tory in possession, and his Peggy longing for a sight of her brother's family over in Chester, also deeming it a place of greater security, removed thither with the younger members of the family and several grandchildren, hoping to find rest, and here they (the old people) remained unto the end of their pilgrimage. [Note. — This removal is said by some to have taken place prior to the war, in 1774, but the majority lean to the date here given, 1780.] However the hope was vain, as is recorded elsewhere, and John Peden followed his sons to the grand finale at Yorktown; thence he came back to Chester to find a few more years of toil, an evening time of rest.

"Peggy" McDill was first to fall "on sleep," and lies among the green mounds of the McDills near Catholic church, Chester, S.C. She was about seventy-five years old, the date of her death is somewhat uncertain, but is supposed to have been 1788. John Peden survived her some years. It is handed down that he made a visit to his children at Fairview, passing about a year among them. When the longing came to be near his wife was no longer resistible, he was carried back by his sorrowing sons, James, the eldest remaining with him until his release came, which is said to have occurred in 1791-1792. This would, if the dates are correct have given him a long life of over four score years (1709-1791). The date of death is thus fixed, as it was during this year that David Morton was married and brought his first wife, Penelope White, to Fairview, and he had made it his duty to stay with his loved grandfather, and who records, that as he lifted him from his chair to his bed he uttered these words: "Lord thou hast been our dwelling place in all generations." They are recorded on his monument at Fairview church, S.C. But John Peden lies also in the beautifully kept burial place of the McDills, near Catholic church, in Chester. Not as is generally believed, in the church yard at Fairview.

The name of John Peden is not blazoned on his country's roll of fame; his good deeds are unwritten and unsung; his good name is borne by thousands of worthy sons scattered over all America's wide domains, so we inscribe proudly here: To the memory of our father, John Peden, Christian soldier of the American Revolution, 1776-1783.

The name "Peggy" McDill does not appear in Mrs. Ellet's book, *Women of the Revolution,* but we inscribe her here as the mother of a mighty race, who rise and call her blessed, among the Spartan dames of a glorious era.

Chapter Eleven - House of Mary

Mary, or as she was best known in her home and among her friends, "Pretty Polly," was the eldest daughter, as well as eldest child of John and Peggy Peden. Her birth place was near Broughshane, in Antrim County, Ireland. The best accepted date being 1730-1732. She is spoken of traditionally as being very lovely, both in character and person. She possessed the beautiful dark eyes inherited from the martyr Mill, or Mills; eyes that smile or glow as the soul within is stirred by varying emotions. She was a devout Christian, a model house-wife and true mother, yet withal full of the intrepid, pioneer spirit, utterly devoid of fear. Though the latter part of her life, covering many years, was spent in a cripple's chair, and though a great sufferer, she was uncomplaining, patient, and directed with great precision the domestic machinery of her large household. From its depths she was lovingly, tenderly, mournfully born "over the hill" by her stalwart sons to her last rest, in true Scottish fashion. She was married in Ireland to James Alexander, and was the mother of several children before the emigration took place.

The Alexander name needs no comment from the pen of the Peden historian, it shines, on Scotland's annals as far back as there are records. It is of Greek origin, the legend running thus: "The first Alexander, a Greek merchant, was driven ashore near Edinburg under stress of weather, meeting kindness at the hands of a Caledonian lassie, he forgot home and Greece," which is saying a great deal for a Greek. The name is peer to the oldest in the land, having its closest association with the fortunes of Stirling. Among the dissenting nobles, with the Cameronian leaders, with the long-roll of the Solemn League and Covenant, with the Scots exiles to Ireland. In both church and state in the old world and the new it glows with undiminished luster.

Of James Alexander, the husband of "Aunt Polly" the writer has only a few traditions. He was a master mind, and the pivot on which the settlement at Fairview turned. He was extremely liberal with his ample (for that day) means. He gave the land for church and school buildings. In a hollow dell between his old homestead and the church the bricks were moulded and burned for the old brick church and a few remains of the moulding and burning are yet to be seen there, 1900. He was noble of mein, inclined more to joviality than dignity; he was generous of heart and open of hand; his hospitality was boundless; his countenance was merry and ruddy. He lived to a great age, but no trace of his tomb was found by the writer after a long search. He, too, was actively engaged in the Revolutionary War, with several sons, among them his eldest, afterwards Maj. Jno. Alexander of the "Tyger Irish," in the famous Spartan Regiment.

Their children were in number thirteen; the sons are mentioned first and daughters last, not as they naturally came, and the writer simply follows the information given by their granddaughter, Mrs. C. A. Shannon.

I., John (1751); II., Joseph; III., James, Jr., (1760); IV., Thomas; V., William; VI., Alexander; VII., Samuel the last died young.

The daughters were: VIII., Katherine; IX., Margaret; X., Nency; XI., Mary; XII., Elizabeth; XIII., Jane.

I., John, the eldest son, was born in Ireland and was about fifteen or sixteen years of age when they came over. "During the Revolution, 1776, he commanded the 'Tyger Irish' in the great battle of King's Mountain. His grave is still visible in the church-yard of Fairview church, in Gwinnett County, Georgia, which church he and a number of Alexanders and Pedens really founded. The marble slab over his grave bears the inscription: 'Sacred to the memory of Maj. John Alexander, who departed this life May 29th, 1830, in the 75th year of his age. The Patriot, the Soldier, and the Christian.'"

The family to which his first wife belonged originally owned the land whereon now stands the flourishing city of Spartanburg. Landrum, in his Revolutionary and Colonial History of Upper South Carolina, makes the statement, "Where Spartanburg now stands was deeded for a court house by Thomas Williamson."

He was twice married, first to _____ Williamson. One record states that she was from Kentucky, but later investigation proves her from Spartanburg, S.C. She was mother of two sons, 1, Thomas W.; 2, James. After her death, he married a Mrs. Russell, of North Carolina. Her children were: 3, Elizabeth; 4, Newton; 5, Franklin; 6, Harvey; 7, Jane; 8, Amanda.

1. Thomas Williamson Alexander married ____ Walker, of Picken, S.C. Five sons and one daughter, Thomas W. Jr., William, Judge John R., Cicero, James P., Elizabeth. Of these the writer has scant record. Thomas W. Jr., married, ____ Hooper; their children, Hon. Hooper Alexander, Mrs. J. A. Rounsaville. Mrs. C. W. King, Mrs. S. P. Pegues. Hon. Hooper Alexander married ____ Word, a cousin on his mother's side. They have several children. He was one of the prominent figures of the Peden reunion, and holds a high position in the legal profession of his native State, Georgia. His sister, Mrs. Hallie Alexander Rounsaville, is president of the United Daughters of the Confederacy.

John R., now an octogenarian, was, in his prime, an eminent jurist and prominent both in church and state. Of his immediate family the writer has no records. As a man he is greatly loved and reverenced by all who know him. Owing to his great age and failing health, he failed to honor the reunion with his presence, or the address assigned him, and when asked to write his reminiscences, replied very courteously and regretfully that the fire fiend, which swept away his lovely home, had destroyed all his journals with his library, and he was unwilling at his age to trust his memory.

William. No records.

Cicero. No records.

James F. (The following is taken from the Atlanta Constitution; it appeared a few days before he went home):

"Dr. Jas. Franklin Alexander was born in Greenville County (then district), S.C., May 24, 1824. When a child his parents moved to Georgia and settled at Laurenceville, where he received the principle part of his early education at a school taught by Rev. James Patterson. He began the study of medicine in 1846, and graduated from the Medical College of Georgia, at Augusta, 1849 (two years after the graduation from the same college of the writer's father, 1847). The following account of the cause of his residence in Atlanta is given in the Memoirs of Georgia:

"In April, 1849, a man was attacked with smallpox, and Dr. Alexander, though he had just graduated, thought he saw an opportunity to establish himself in Atlanta. He immediately went there, thinking, as he says, that it was no worse to run the risk of smallpox than to have no practice. Arriving there he met Dr. E. C. Calhoun, a former classmate, who had come on the same errand, and who had secured the refusal of a room, the only one than to be had, that would serve as an office. Dr. Calhoun, however, decided that the rent for the little office (it was only $6.00 per month), was too great, and Dr. Alexander at once secured it. The smallpox patient was lying ill at the Thompson (the proprietor of this hostelry was Jos. Thompson, a brother of Alexander Thompson, who married first Elizabeth Alexander, then Eliza Peden, houses of Mary and Thomas, therefore connected by marriage), and stood where the Kimball House now stands, and was conducted as well as owned by Dr. Thompson, who soon after erected a small wooden structure outside the city to which the two patients, a man and woman, were removed. There Dr. Alexander took charge of them, and under his efficient care and treatment they recovered. This made Dr. Alexander's reputation at once and he entered upon a large practice which continued to increase until he retired from active work several years ago.

At the outbreak of the Civil War Dr. Alexander entered the Confederate army as surgeon of the Seventh Georgia Regiment (infantry), of which Col. L. J. Gastrell was the first Colonel. He served six months in the field then was detailed to hospital duty in Atlanta, in which he was actively engaged until the close of the war.

For ten years he was a member of the board of health of Atlanta, and its president for several terms. In 1896, during the yellow fever scare, he maintained, that the disease would not spread in Atlanta and as president of the board of health and against active opposition, he opened the doors of the city to fever refugees. One fever patient was brought and treated but without the disease spreading, thus proving Dr. Alexander's faith in the climate of Atlanta was not misplaced."

He was twice married and the author recalls vividly the often confusing resemblance of the first wife to her own sainted mother, and her own frequent mistakes regarding them, especially at church, which both attended as devoted members.

At that time there were Jennie, James F., (the writer supposes that Jennie is now Mrs. J. P. Stevens), Ada, whom she does not recall. The two families were separated to meet no more at the close of the civil war, they remaining in Atlanta, Ga., her father being transferred to Montgomery, Ala., in 1863.

Elizabeth was twice married, first to Dr. Gordon, who fell a victim to yellow fever during an epidemic in Savannah, Ga., nobly refusing to leave his post, and giving his life for suffering humanity. Their children were four, Alice, Albert, Thomas A., Florence.

Alice married ____ Cassells, mother of several children, and possibly grandchildren.

Albert gave his bright young life a sacrifice to the Confederate cause, dying in Mobile, Ala., in 18631864.

Thomas married in Virginia, and did not long survive his marriage. Whether they had any children or not the writer is in ignorance.

Florence, former schoolmate and playfellow of the writer, for a few brief months, married ____ Cassells, Has eleven children.

Elizabeth Alexander Gordon married the second time _ Lowry. No children.

2. James (son of Maj. John), married his cousin in the second degree, Margaret Peden, eldest daughter of David," the seventh son, therefore of the house of David. Their children were seven: 1, Eleanor; 2, Elizabeth; 3, Nancy; 4, Thomas; 5, John; 6, James; 7, Franklin.

1, Eleanor married William Knox.

2, Elizabeth married ____ Norton.

3, Nancy married Claiborne Brown. Of these no trace has been obtained.

4, Thomas married and moved to Texas. No further trace.

5, John died young.

6, James moved to North Alabama; later, 1866, to California.

7, Franklin. No trace.

This family moved from Fairview, S.C., to Gwinnett County, Georgia, either with Maj. Jno, Alexander or soon after his migration. The following, copied from the oldest church record in existence: "1820. Maj. John Alexander, his entire family and William Alexander (his brother), and his entire family leave the State for Georgia. Regularly dismissed. Anthony Savage, Clerk of Sessions."

These families went to occupy newly opened lands in Georgia, and settled in what is now Gwinnett County, founding together with a number of Pedens and others of the same family, the church of Fairview, in memory of the old home church, and many of them are sleeping in its church yard, especially the older members.

This completes the records of the two older sons of Maj. John Alexander and his first wife, ____ Williamson. Maj. Jno. Alexander and his second wife, Mrs. Russell,

1, Elizabeth married ____ Chatham. No children.

2, Newton married ____ Knox. Two daughters, names unknown.

3, Franklin married ____ Neal. Three children. Harriet, Mrs. M. A. Salmons, name of other child not given.

4, Harvey married. Wife's name not given. Four children. No trace.

5, Jane married. Name not given. Several children.

6, Amanda died young.

II. Joseph never married.

III. James Alexander, Jr., (1760-1761) married Mary or "Polly" Miller, of Spartanburg County (who also spent her last years a cripple), lived out his long, useful life at Fairview, S. C, where he sleeps his last sleep, among his race. There are two incidents in his life which show the spirit of this man. He was more daring as a soldier than prudent.

"In 1781 a certain Col. Greigson was shot at Augusta by an American militiaman, after having surrendered. It was claimed by the American authorities that no one knew who did the shooting. Col. Thos. Brown, the British officer in command of the captured garrison, afterward, in 1786, declared in a letter written from the Bahamas, that the shot was fired by a militiaman from Carolina under the command of Gen. Pickens, and that his name was James Alexander. Capt. Hugh McCall, of Savannah, states, in 1816, that the shot was fired by Samuel Alexander in revenge for great cruelties and indignities previously practiced by Brown and Greigson upon his father, Jas. Alexander, Sr. Now as Samuel was very young at the time and never in the army, the general belief in the clan is that the act of revenge was performed by James, Jr. The other incident is positively vouched for. He was so daring and reckless toward the British that he was in perpetual "hot water." He refused protection in the dark days and went home to see his mother; the enemy caught him, assured his mother that she should never behold him alive, they threw a halter round his neck intending to hang him.' They had not reckoned upon the spirit of Mary Peden. Alexander was rescued by his brothers and safely spirited away by them to another part of the country. His mother was kept posted as to his whereabouts, but none else knew. He did not return to South Carolina until the year after peace was declared. Then he joined his uncles, the Peden brothers, John, Samuel and David in the pioneer settlement of Fairview, S.C. Their children: 1, Rachel; 2, Elizabeth; 3, Nancy; 4, Harriet; 5, Jane Caroline; 6, James; 7, Robert.

1, Rachel never married, but spent a long, useful, beautiful home life, leaving a fragrant memory of good deeds well done and service lovingly rendered 2, Elizabeth married Alexander Thompson and settled near Fairview, S.C. Children': 1, Joseph; 2, James; 3, John; 4, William; 5, Jane; 6, Mary Ann.

1, Joseph married a daughter of Samuel Morrow, Jr.

2, James married Rebecca (Peden) Morton, daughter of Jno. Thos. Peden (house of Alexander), and widow of Montgomery Morton, who, with the wife of Joseph, above mentioned, were of the house of Jane. Their children were six: Alexander, John Thomas, Joseph, Mary, David, Jefferson.

3, "William married Hawk. No further trace of these three families, save they with the Mortons. Morrows and others located near Fayettville, Tenn., and Somerville, Ala.

4, Jane married A. W. Peden, son of M. White Peden (house of Thomas) where her record is to be found.

5, John married. Wife's name unknown, supposed to be Morrow.

6, Mary married ____ Moore. Four children; one son and three daughters. No further trace save they located near Somerville, Alabama.

3. Nancy married Jno. Anderson on the 4th day of October, 1825. Their children:

1, James Alexander was born on the 6th day of August, 1826; departed April 12, 1868, of consumption contracted in camp during the civil war on Confederate side.

2, Clarissa A. was born on the 14th day of November, 1828; departed on the 14th September, 1872.

3, Sara Elizabeth was born on the 4th day of May, 183 1; departed September 26, 1860. Never married.

4, Mary Jane was born on the 30th day of November, 1834; departed March 31, 1836; aged two years.

5, Martha A. was born on the 15th day of Feb., 1837.

6, William Denny was born on the 9th day of August, 1840; departed on Nov. i6th, 1863 amid the roar and carnage of one of the bloodiest battles of the civil war, in Tennessee, a brave, loyal heart as ever beat was stilled forever. He was one of the first to go and he never came home from the front even on a brief furlough or missed a battle of his command until he received his honorable discharge.

Of this family only two married.

1, Clarissa married Oliver P. Wood. Their children: 1, Augustus Reid; 2, Joe Wallace; 3, Boyd Durant; 4, William Anderson; 5, John Daniel; 6, Charles Isham. Of these no further records have reached the writer. Some are married some are dead.

2, Martha A. married Isham Robison. Their children: William James (1867), John Anderson (1869), Oliver Isham (1872), Samuel Henry Hamilton (1875), Edward Miller (1879), died an infant, Annie Weatra (1881).

1, William James married. No record.

2, John Anderson married. Name of wife unknown. Three sons; one daughter.

3, Isham Oliver married. No records.

4, Samuel H. H. also married. No records.

5, Edward M. died.

6, Annie Weatra married ____ Grosse. One child, a daughter.

The above records of the Anderson family were furnished by the sole survivor, Mrs. Martha A. Robison.

4. Harriet married J. Wilson Baker. Mother of three sons.

1, William L., who married Anne Hopkins. Their children: 1, James Alexander; 2, Pinckney Miller; 3, Harriet; 4, William L., Jr.; 5, John. Of these —

1, James Alexander died unmarried.

2, Pinckney Miller married ____ Woods. No record sent.

3, Harriet married a Kirby; died leaving a number of children. No further records.

4, William L. Jr., married twice; the first wife ____ was Cunningham; the second ____ Brockman. He has several children; names unknown.

5, John also married twice. The first wife was ____ McKnight. Name of second and number of children unknown.

2, James Harvey married Martha Caroline Young, youngest daughter of Colonel Young, of Greensboro, N. C, in 1852. Born to them six children: 1, John Washington; 2, Alice; 3, Sallie Lawrence; 4, Elliotte Sullivan; 5, Robert Vance; 6, Irene Electra.

1, John W. Baker married Emma C. Putnam, 1878. Born to them six children: George Putnam, John Harvey, Harold Harvey, Hazel May, Gertrude Irene, Eleanor, or as she is lovingly called, Nellie.

2, Sallie L. married John Cobb, of Greensboro, N. C. Born to them four children: Edsall Vance, Dorroh, Flora, Sallie, Carmie.

3, Elliotte S. married Samuel Dick, also of Greensboro, N.C. Born to them three children: Creighton, Martha, James Harvey.

4, Robert Vance Baker married Lillian Minor, of Denver, Col. Born to them three children, Hortense Adelaide, Merritt, Melvin.

3, Thomas P. married ____ Thompson. Two children, Beulah, Wade Hampton. The first is unmarried; the latter married in Mississippi. Name of wife unknown.

The Confederate cause had no braver or more loyal sons than these three Baker brothers; the two elder came out of the struggle wrecked physically, and died soon thereafter of the dread disease consumption, caused by exposure.

Their mother was a woman of noble mein and regal bearing. A strong, sweet character, thoroughly energetic and business-like in her dealings with her kind; honest to her heart's core she required the same honesty from others. A woman more feared than loved, save by those who knew her best, and who were admitted to the inner circle.

5, Jane Caroline "beautiful as an angel, a sweet saint," married Henry Merrit Cely. Their children, 1, Martha Ann Elizabeth; 1, Mary Ann Clarissa; 2, James Merrit; 3, Hamilton Wilson; 4, William Henry; 5, Jane Caroline; 6, Louisa Maria.

1, Martha A. E. married James P. Stewart. Their children are, 1, Dora Jane; 2, Robert H.; 3, James H.; 4, Wm. Franklin. 1, Dora Jane and 2, Robert H., unmarried. 3, James H. married Nannie Garrett. 4, Wm. F. unmarried.

1, Mary A. C. died an infant.

2, James Merrit died in boyhood.

3, Hamilton W. was twice married; first to Kate Lake. Their children, 1, Thomas Lake; 2, Hamilton; 3, Henry Merrit; 4, Mary Kate. The three youngest died in infancy. T. Lake is in business in New York city. Second to Sallie Lake. No children.

The war record of Hamilton W. Cely is brief but brave and bright. He was a member of Company E. Hampton's Legion, and was in the foremost of their brilliant dash during the First battle of Manassas, receiving a wound in the head that was nearly fatal and from which he has never fully recovered.

4, William Henry married Alice Means. Their children, Elanor, Charles Cunningham, Henry Means and Jane Caroline (twins), William Riley Jones, Arthur Hamilton.

Charles C, Henry M., J. Caroline, Arthur H. all died in infancy.

William H. Cely was a brave, daring member of Jenkins' Brigade, 1st S.C. Regiment, and fought through the whole war, spending about eight months a prisoner.

5, Jane C. married J. F. Fowler. Their children, William H., H. Pierce, Laurens D., Homer F., Annie L., Palmer C, Werner B. The two last died in infancy. William H. married ____ Park.

6, James married Esther Hanna, a daughter of the brave old Revolutionary patriot, and sister of Nancy, wife of Thomas Peden (house of David). Their children, James L., Elizabeth P., Katherine, Julia, Andrew, John Charles, Mary Esther.

1, James L. unmarried.

2, Elizabeth Palmer married W. S. Powell. One son, Alonzo Jerome.

3, Katherine was accidently drowned at the age of seven.

4, Julia died in infancy.

5, Andrew died in infancy.

6, J. Charles married Emma Reeder, of Louisiana. Three children. Ford, Mary Esther; name of youngest not known.

7, Mary E. Married M. W. Ford. One child, Caroline Griffin, who died in infancy.

James and his family moved to Cobb County, Georgia, about 1830.

7, Robert married Mary Brown Seaborn, a sister of Maj. George Seaborn, who was for many years editor of "The Farmer and Planter,', at Pendleton, S.C. They had three children, James, Matilda Caroline, George Seaborn, of these

I, James was burned to death in early childhood. 2, Matilda Caroline married Dr. Mark M.Johnson, of Greenville, S.C. Their children were nine, James Edwin, Mary Jane, Elizabeth Greenwood, William Henry, Caroline Melissa, Georgetta, Laura Henrietta, Celestia Adelaide, Kathleen Edins. Dr. Johnson died at Kingston, Ga., in 1854. His wife at the same place in 1874.

1, James Edwin Johnson, after graduating in dentistry, located at Anderson, Texas, where he married Sarah Parks. They left two sons, William and Joseph, in Texas.

2, Mary Jane Johnson married Benjamin Franklin Reynolds, of Greenwood, S.C. They had eight children, Mark J., Nannie, James B., Mary, Frank B., William T., Alexander E., Eva C.

1, Mark J. died at three years.

2, Nancy Reynolds married George R. Briggs, of Greenville, S.C. One child, a son, George Reynolds Briggs.

3, James B. married Mary Bellenger, of Barnwell, S.C. Four children, William Osborne, Mary Sue, Eleanor, Nannie.

4, Frank B. married Minnie Butler, of Eatonton, Ga. Two sons, Louis Butler, Samuel Fielder.

5, William T. married Carrie B. Owens, of Barnwell, S.C. Four children, Charles Telford, Marion Patterson, Kathleen Johnson, Lois Eloise.

6, Alexander E. died at nineteen months.

7, Mary unmarried.

8, Eva Caroline unmarried.

3, Elizabeth Greenwood Johnson married Joseph Dunlap, who was killed in the civil war. Their one son, Paul Dunlap, died unmarried. She married the second time Jewett Rogers, of Virginia. Two daughters, Carrie May, Lillian.

Carrie May married J. B. Bowen, of Atlanta, Ga. One son, DeWitte.

Lillian married J. E. Brown, of Bainbridge, Ga. One son, Hubert Earle.

4, William H. Johnson died at nineteen years, just as he entered Oglethrope College preparatory to entering the ministry of the Presbyterian Church. He was a young man of brilliant talent, but the Lord called him to higher work.

5, Caroline Melissa Johnson married Bertram Taylor, of Galveston, Texas. Three children, Lola, who married George Westmoreland, of Bainbridge, Ga.:

no children. Bertram, who died at eighteen, and Rollo, who married in San Antonio, Texas.

6, Georgetta Johnson marred H. H. Frear, of Tampa, Fla. Two children, who died in their infancy.

7, Laura Henrietta Johnson unmarried.

8, Celestia Adelaide Johnson married Homer W. Gilbert, of Brooklyn, L. L Three children, Fred, Benjamin, Laura Celeste.

9, Kathleen Edins Johnson married T. M. Dendy, of Troy, S.C.No children.

3, George Seaborn, third and youngest child of Robert and Mary Alexander married Celestia Adelaide Rogers, of Atlanta, Ga. They had no children. He died at the out break of the civil war.

This closes the records of the third son, James, Jr., and the historian is indebted for them to Messrs. H. W. Cely and J. W. Baker and Mesdame M. A. Robison and G. R. Briggs

IV., Thomas. No records.

V., William married Eleanor McCrea, of North Carolina. Six children were born to them.

1, Simpson, who married an Humphries. Had six children and died in Gainesville, Ga. Was brought home and hurried at Hebron church.

2, William Henry who died in Confederate service.

3, John M. who was twice married. His first wife was a Gunnells. They had seven sons and five daughters.

4, Mary Ann never married.

5, Catherine never married.

6, Cynthia A. married J. H. Shannon. Four sons and five daughters.

In the language of the devoted son of Mrs. C. A. Shannon, whom all who attended the Fairview reunion will recall with pleasure as a model son, whose devotion to her every want was beautiful. He says:

"Our dear mother left us on the 7th day of February, 1900, and we miss her so much; home does not appear like home now to us. She does not meet me at the door when I go; and the old rocker in the corner is not occupied; in fact it is no longer there."

Cynthia A. Shannon was the youngest child of William Alexander and his wife, Eleanor McCrea. Born in Franklin County, Ga., December 27, 1820, and died at her home in the same county February 7, 1900. She was said to have been the oldest one of the Peden relatives who attended the reunion of the house of Peden, 1899. She was a woman of strong intellect and had a well cultured mind. She was the wife of John H. Shannon, who preceded her to the grave only a few months. Was the mother of nine children, Emma E., Robert T., William A., John F., Mary A., Dicey L., Cornelia C, Frances L.

1, Emma E. married Thomas N. Neal. Children, Emma, Lula. Mother and children are dead.

2, Robert T. dead.

3, William A. married Frances Davis. Children, Floy Davis, Leith, Willard.

4, John F. married Eugenia Martin. Children, Hoy Fey, Claire, Mary Neal.

5, Mary A. married D. W. Hutcherson. Children, Jessie, Clara, Bermah, Leon, Rhodie, Eunice, Florence.

6, Dicey L. married Thomas Caruthers. Children, Harold, Horace, Charles.

7, Cornealia C. married Early C. Carson. Children, Ralph, Homer, Bernard, Lillian, Woodfin, Julia, Geraldine, Louise.

8, Frances L. married Thomas M. Patterson. Children, Carl Jewill, Wayne Maurice.

9, Died an infant.

For all records of this line the writer is indebted to Mrs. Cynthia Shannon and her noble son, Mr. Wm. A. Shannon.

VI., Alexander. No records. VII., Samuel. Died in boyhood. VIII., Katherine. IX., Mary. X., Margaret. XI., Nancy. XII., Jane. XIII., Elizabeth.

This closes the incomplete house of Mary. For information received the author is under many obligations to the following members of this family: H. W. Cely, H. Alexander, T. P. Baker, J. W. Baker, Cynthia A. Shannon, Mary E. Ford.

Chapter Twelve - House of James

"They were men of renown — like lions so bold,
Like lions undaunted, ne'er to be controlled;
They were bent on the game they hand in their eye.
Determined to take — to conquer or die."

The historian of this line is Hon. John R. Harrison, who will appear in his place among his family, as he seems quite unwilling to allow a sketch of his busy life inserted at the beginning of this chapter. His picture also appears among the committees of the reunion, over which assemblage he presided with easy, graceful dignity, as he has presided over legislative bodies he was quite at home in the chair. His noble head and face speak for his character and mental endowments of a high order. With this brief statement the writer is forced to be content.

On her own responsibility she introduces a traditional and historical account of the founder of this house, both from the reminiscences of her grandmother and letters of Dr. G. B. White, of Chester, S. C, who is well posted in the history of that county, and whose veracity needs no further vouchers than his word.

James Peden, eldest son of John Peden and "Peggy" McDill, was born, as all the other children of this couple, in Ireland, coming to America with his family about 1768-1770.

There seems to be a divided opinion as to the mother of this house, one statement is that her name was Mary Brown, another that she was a sister of the wife of John Hemphill, the founder of the Hemphill family, who was Mary Adair. This cannot be true as the writer has the Hemphill denial, also the statement that none of the Adair sisters married Pedens. The best solution offered is that she was a sister of John Hemphill. Her name was Mary. If, however, the theory of Mary Brown is correct there is connected with the life of the Scottish poet Robert Burns this fact: His mother, Agnes Brown, had a sister who went to Ireland with her brothers along with the Duke of Hamilton to his possessions there, and perhaps this was the wife of James Peden. Agnes Brown was born about 1740. The writer, for several reasons, inclines to the belief that she was Mary Hemphill.

James Peden was a member of the Provincial Congress from Chester District during the administration of the last Royal Governor of South Carolina (this is traditional). Also the following statement is from Dr. G.B. White and Mr. Jas. Hemphill, of Chester, S.C.:

"James Peden was a member of the South Carolina legislature which called the constitutional convention which ratified the United States Constitution. (The writer has heard that he objected to the lack of religion in this famous document.) There is a joke too on the earnest countryman. It seems that he, with others, went to call upon the then governor and seeing him arrayed in full dress, powder, ruffles and other gorgeous apparel, being a plain man and punctiliously neat, remarked to the governor, 'I see Your Excellency is of the same calling as myself (a miller), referring to the powder which had not been properly brushed from his dress. This created great merriment. Reading between lines, it was a reproof to the chief magistrate of a newly independent state. Anyway the powder went out of fashion very soon."

A regiment of Whigs was raised in Chester early in 1775, and there is no doubt that James Peden and at least two of his sons were among them. "Officers: Colonel, Daniel Smith; Captains, Thos. Hemphill, Robt. Patton, Thos. Lytle, John McDowell, Jos. White, and others." — Draper's King's Mountain.

James Peden did not come to Fairview for some time after the War of Revolution. He is among the early eldership of that church and with Mary, his wife, rests in the rock-walled God's acre at Fairview. He is the founder of the Chester Pedens. With a few clippings from letters from other members, the historian is strictly followed,

James Peden migrated from Chester; buried at Fairview church; son of John Peden and "Peggy" McDill. James Peden's wife was named Mary. Their children were: I. William; II., John; III., Jennie; IV., James; V., Thomas; VI., Mary.

I., William Peden married and emigrated to the State of Illinois about 1830 (on account of their views of slavery). We have no further information in regard to him. It is supposed that his family are there still.

II., John Peden married and also went to Illinois at the same time. Information is that he had a very large family. We have had no communication with these families since the Civil war.

III., Jennie Peden, the eldest daughter, married Anthony Savage. Anthony Savage came to South Carolina a young man, from County Antrim Ireland, as a school-teacher. He taught for some time. He married Jennie Peden then turned his attention to farming. Became an elder in Fairview church (Presbyterian). Was recognized as a good business man. Consulted on business matters by the community. He settled near the church and lived to be old. His wife Jennie lived to be ____ years old. She died in 1848. (He laid aside the clerk's pen, and laid his mantle on the shoulders of James Dunbar, 1848, as clerk of the session of Fairview church.) They had four children, Alexander, James, Eleanor, Margaret.

Alexander Savage married Rosa Morton (granddaughter of Jane Morton-Morrow). Settled near Fairview and remained here for a number of years. They left South Carolina about 1830, and when the State of Mississippi was opened up for settlers he, with his entire family went to Tishomingo County, where he settled and lived for a number of years. Died and left a large family. When the civil war broke out we know that two of his sons were in 22nd Mississippi Regiment, Adams' Brigade, Loring's Division. John Savage, the eldest of the two, survived the war and passed through here on his way home after the surrender. Robert Savage was a lieutenant in the 22nd Mississippi Regiment. Passed through the entire war unhurt until the battle of Smithfield, N. C, a few days before Johnson's surrender, when he was killed and buried on the field. Other members of the family were residing in or near Corinth, Miss., when last heard from.

Eleanor Savage married John McDowell Harrison. Their children were: William Alexander, James Anthony, Pinckney McDowell, Jane T., Mary E., Maggie I., John Ramsey, Sarah.

John McDowell Harrison, my father, settled on Raeburn Creek, near Fairview church.

William A. Harrison married Elizabeth Bryson Campbell. Settled near Fairview and practiced medicine there thirteen years. Is a graduate of the University of Pennsylvania. Moved from Fairview to Reidville, in Spartanburg County, and is still practicing medicine. William Harrison's children are, William Campbell, Edward Bryson, John Hunter, James Wade, Elizabeth, Nora.

William Campbell Harrison married Emma Waldrop, and their children are, Maggie, William Sloan, Norman Alexander, Lloyd Bratton, John Ramsey. Settled near Reidville, S.C.

Edward Bryson Harrison married Hannah Amanda Smith. Live in Reidville, S.C. Their children are, Eugene Scott, Robert Perry, Mary Elizabeth, William Herbert, Edward Campbell, Annie Nora.

John Hunter Harrison married Sidney Gwinn. Settled on North Saluda river, near Marietta, S.C. Their children are, Gerard, Ralph.

James Wade Harrison married Linnie Smith, of Rockton, Fairfield County, S.C. Lived there a number of years then moved to Columbia, S.C. Their children are, William Alexander Smith, Elizabeth, James Wade.

Elizabeth Harrison died when twenty-three years of age. Never married.

Nora Harrison died when about eight years old.

James Anthony Harrison was a civil engineer, but did not practice his profession. He entered the mercantile business when quite a young man in Augusta, Ga., where he remained a short, while. From there he went to Charleston, S. C, where he continued in the mercantile business until driven away by an epidemic of yellow fever, when he located at Laurens, S. C, and engaged with Pinckney McD. Harrison, his brother, in the mercantile business. They were thus engaged when the war between the States commenced. He entered the Confederate army as a member of Company A., 3rd South Carolina Volunteers (State Guards name of Co.). Remained in that company fifteen months when he was transferred to the Pedee Light Artillery, attached to McGowan's Brigade. He was killed at Fredericksburg, Va., at a point on the battlefield known as Hamilton's Crossing, on the 13th Dec, 1862. His death was caused by the concussion of a shell passing so near the heart as to result in death almost instantly; the skin was not broken; he bled slightly at the nose and ears and died on the field.

Pinckney McDowell Harrison resided on the old homestead, near Fairview, until his brother, James, entered the mercantile business at Laurens, when he went to that place and entered business with him. He was thus engaged when the war came on; volunteered in the service of the Confederate States in Company A., 3rd South Carolina Volunteers (States Guard Co. name) in which company he remained for about fifteen months, when he was transferred to the Pedee Light Artillery and was killed at the battle of Fredericksburg, Va., at a point on the field of battle known as Hamilton's Crossing, on the 13th of Dec. 1862. His right leg having been shot off near the hip-joint by a cannon ball. He lived about five hours after he was shot. Was carried to the field hospital off the scene of battle before death.

James A. and Pinckney McD. Harrison were neither married. They were in business together; entered the service of their country together; during their term of service they each received a furlough of fifteen days which they spent at the old homestead together in the spring of 1862. They were engaged in all of the battles in which their commands participated in Virginia. They were never wounded until the fatal day, Dec. 13, 1862, when both gave up their lives for the cause of the Confederacy. Their bodies were brought home and buried in one grave in Fairview church cemetery, where they now repose beneath the shade of a magnolia planted by affectionate hands.

Jane T. Harrison, the eldest daughter, was never married. She lived a life of unselfish usefulness and died respected by all who knew her. Her death occurred Sept. 2, 1899, and she is buried in Fairview cemetery.

Mary E. Harrison married Wm. Thos. Austin. They settled near Fairview. Wm. Thos. Austin volunteered in Hampton's Legion in the late war. She left no children. Both husband and wife are buried at Fairview.

Margaret I. Harrison married John C. Bailey, of Greenville, S.C. She lived in Greenville city. Mother of three sons, John C. Bailey, Jr., William Price, James Pinckney (twins). She died May 7, 1873, and is buried in Fairview cemetery.

John C. Bailey, Jr., was educated at the South Carolina Military Academy, in Charleston, S. C, and afterwards in the Theological Seminary at Princeton, New Jersey. He entered the ministry of the Presbyterian church and is now pastor of Summerton and Wedgefield churches. In 1900 he was married to Mabel Cantey. One son.

William Price and James Pinckney Bailey died soon after their mother and are buried by her side at Fairview.

John R. Harrison was born January 1st, 1845. He left school to enter the Confederate army. Was a member of Company H., Palmetto Battalion of Light Artillery where he served for more than one year. Thence he was transferred to Company I., 16th South Carolina Volunteers, Gist's Brigade, Army of Tennessee. He was made a sergeant in his company and surrendered with it at Greensboro, N. C. Gen. Joseph E. Johnson being in command. After this he returned to Fairview and engaged in farming. Elected to the legislature from Greenville County, S. C, in 1880 and served six years, having been elected three times. He was then elected to the Senate from Greenville County where he served for four years. During that time was elected and served as President pro tem. of the Senate and presided over that body in the absence of the Lieutenant Governor. In 1896 he was candidate for Governor, but was defeated by W. H. Ellerbee. Since that time he has not served in any public office. Was presiding officer at the Peden Reunion at Fairview, S.C. John R. Harrison and Lillie Helen Adams were married in November, 1869, and lived near Fairview, on the old homestead. His wife died May 20, 1872. He has never married again. Has two children, Mary E., born August 29, 1870, and Lillie H., born May 10, 1872.

Mary Ellen Harrison married Angus McQueen Martin, of Marion County, S.C., October 24, 1894. She has three children, Mary Helen, born October 22, 1895; John Harrison, born November 10, 1897; Janie, born March 21, 1901.

Lillian Helen Harrison is not married and is living with her father.

James E. Savage lived near Fairview church (old Alexander place). Married Malinda Baker. Two children were born to them, John Lindsay Savage, Ana J. James E. Savage and his wife lived to an old age. She having lived to see all her dear ones laid away and for a very brief time was alone in the world as the last representative of her immediate family. He was an eminent Christian, a useful citizen, an elder in Fairview church for many years. Both are buried in Fairview cemetery.

John L. Savage engaged in mercantile business at Greenville when quite young. Afterwards at Fork Shoals, Pelzer, Piedmont and Williamston, where he died in 1897. He was twice married. First to Mattie Anderson, who died shortly afterwards. Then to Jeannette Root, of Anderson, S.C., who is still living and resides in Anderson, S.C.

Ana J. Savage was never married. Died at Williamston, 1896, and is buried with her parents at Fairview.

Margaret F. Savage was never married. She lived all her life on the old homestead and died at a ripe old age. Is also buried at Fairview. The Savage line in Greenville, S. C., is extinct.

IV., James Peden married Margaret Alexander, and lived near Fairview, on headwaters of Raeburn Creek, where they resided for a number of years. Had three daughters born there: Eveline, Teresa, Elizabeth. Moved from Fairview, S.C., to Decatur, Ga., where they died. Teresa and Elizabeth never married. Both died of fever. Eveline remained with the family until the old folks died then married a Gordon, of Bartow County, Ga. Became the mother of nine children. After the civil war they moved to Texas. No further information of her.

V., Thomas Peden, of Chester County, married Sarah McCalla. Settled and lived near Old Catholic church, in Chester County. Children five, Mary, Peggy, David, Ginnie, Catherine. His wife died and he married his first cousin, Isabella Peden (house of William). Four children, William A., Sarah B., Belle T., Emily Teresa.

Mary Peden married James Harbison, Esq. He only lived about one year. She then married John Brown, of York County, S.C. No children were born to them.

Peggy Peden married William Hood and moved to Alabama. She had one daughter, Sarah. All of this family died before 1861.

David McCalla Peden married Margaret Hood. Lived on Rocky Creek, near the old home. He died April 17, 1894, aged seventy-eight years, and is buried at Catholic. Their children are, Thomas, Elizabeth, Andrew.

Thomas Peden married Sallie McCreary. Children five, Martha B., Judson McCreary, Margaret H., David McCalla, Wm. H. Martha died when about two years old. His wife died and he then married her sister, Irene McCreary.

Elizabeth died October 31, 1866. Is buried at Catholic.

Andrew Peden, the second son never married and lives with his mother at the old homestead, near Catholic church, Chester County, S.C.

Ginnie Peden married Wm. Storment and lived also near Catholic church. Her children were, Sallie, Thomas, Mary. They moved to Mississippi and died. The children are now living at Burnt Mills, Miss.

Catherine married Turner McCrory, of Fairfield. No children.

William Alexander Peden never married. Was a talented musician. Went into the Confederate service in the First South Carolina Calvalry. Was promoted to captain. Made commissary, serving in that capacity until the close of the war. He was chairman of the Board of Commissioners of Chester County at the time of his death, 1874.

Sarah Brown Peden married Rev. David Pressly, of the Associate Reform Church. Went to Starkville, Miss., and died January 17, 1883, leaving five children, Thomas Peden, Elizabeth Hearst, William Cornelius, Isabella Teresa, Sunie Montgomery.

Rev. Thomas P. Pressly, Troy Tenn. Now living with his second wife. Has five children.

Elizabeth H. (Pressly) Young, wife of W.A. Young, Atoka, Tenn. Five children.

William C. Pressly, M.D., has a wife and four children.

Isabella Teresa Pressly. Unmarried. Home with Rev. Thos. P. Pressly.

Sunie M. (Pressly) Smith, wife of W. A. Smith, Troy, Tenn. Two children.

Isabella T. Peden married Wm. Douglas. Had one child named Janie Brice. Fairfield County, S.C.

Emily T. Peden married J. W. Blake. Moved to Prescott, Arkansas. Mother of five children.

VI. Mary Peden, youngest child of James Peden, married John Stennis, of Fairview. Died childless and sleeps at Fairview after a long pilgrimage.

Chapter Thirteen - House of Jane

"Such was this daughter of the Emerald isle,
 Herself a billow in her energies
 To bear the bark of others' happiness,
 Nor feel a sorrow 'til their joy grew less."

There has been little of romance in these annals of a race proverbial for plain, practical common-sense, even in their love affairs, until one wonders if they did any love-making at all. Possibly they did not tell the younger generations of these episodes in their lives, regarding them with the sober eyes of middle-age as too frivolous for young ears. Yet the historian would like occasionally to record a romance like that one in Chester, of the young emigrant who, when he heard that his beloved Mary had arrived from the old world and was nearing him left his oxen attached to the plow, standing among the corn, tossed away his Scotch bonnet of homespun and ran miles under a burning Southern sun to meet and greet the dear lass after the long years of toil and waiting. They were happy ever after, as the story goes, and well they deserved to be. However, this is not Peden history.

The writer cannot repress the desire to chronicle the first love story of bonny Jennie Peden, as she heard it in the long ago from dear lips now dumb. Turn back the leaves of Scotland's history to the days of chivalry and daring; recall mediaeval knights and stately ladies, and none shine with brighter luster than the illustrious house of Morton, staunch adherents of country and king through all the early battles royal of that bloody land against Saxon, Norman, Dane. The house of Morton furnished brave knights as leaders, lances and archers to swell Scottish armies; bold crusaders with the Bruce, Douglass, Dunbar, Mar, Murray, Hamilton and others. The last Earl died on the scaffold in 1575-1580.

The title became extinct but not the family. During the next two or three centuries their fortunes varied. They were divided in religion, Papist and Protestant. About 1760, for political reasons the eldest son of Morton became desirous of getting rid of his younger brothers, and the plan of banishing them to the West Indies and selling them into slavery occurred to him, so he proceeded to carry this atrocious plot into execution, but was foiled by the escape of the boys. At the same time a similar scheme was brewing in the house of Dunbar, the younger brother being Protestant.

One dark, stormy night the three met on the rocky coast by appointment, there they found faithful Sandy McRee, husband of the old housekeeper of the Dunbars, who had warned the lads that morning that -the ship which was to bear them away was at anchor not far away. These lads, the Mortons, John and James or David, both tall and slenderly built, while James Dunbar was stout and broad shouldered, all were wrapped in shepherd plaids and wore no insignia of birth, their tracks had been covered by the softly falling snow, but a new danger threatened, for the coast guard hailed them, the lads were slow to speak so old Sandy replied, "They be shepherd laddies to my Lord of Hamilton that I am fetching over 'til him the night." The guard made, some remarks on the weather and time of night, but Sandy was quick of wit. "Shepherd lads dinna min' a skip like this, and my Lord is in haste lest the sheep get lost in the snaw." So he walked on and they were suffered to depart with the parting thrust, "My Lord of Hamilton methinks is choice in the build of his shepherds, soldier lads belike." Sandy rowed slowly until out of earshot then seeing some commotion on the coast gave each lad an oar and they rowed with speed toward Ireland. A swift boat followed and as it neared Sandy's the boys threw off their plaids and swam ashore, so old Sandy was alone and was so deaf to all questions that he was left to himself to follow the lads, but they never met on earth. After wandering all night in the cold and dark they took refuge in one of those treacherous peat-bogs. John Peden found them, took them to his humble home warmed and fed them, but the younger Morton "fell ill of a lung fever" and "Peggy" McDill nursed him with her homely skill. The natural sequence was he had fallen in love with bonny "Jennie Peden" so he learned the trade of weaving along with the sons of Peden, and cast all his high-born pride away, wooed and won the Scotch-Irish lassie in truly noble fashion.

The Morton records are very incomplete. The four sons were all, except William perhaps, in the Revolutionary army. John was with Capt. Samuel McJunkin at the beginning of the war. With other leaders later. He was a daring soldier all through. James was with Capt. Wm. Smith, of the Spartan Regiment, while David was with Capt. Roebuck. Both Captains McJunkin and Roebuck became majors.

The birth dates of these children were I., John, 1756; II., James, 1758; III., David, 1760: IV., William, 1762; V., Mary, 1764. Whether Jane had married her second husband, Samuel Morrow, before the emigration or not history is silent. It is also a disputed question whether her first husband was named James or David, and opinion is divided. The writer is under the impression that James is correct. As the Morton records have not reached her can give detached notes wherever attainable.

I., John Morton. All trace is lost and it is presumed that he left Fairview about 1825-1833. There are no records to be found of this period and there was some bitterness among the clan on the question of slavery, which led to several Pedens seeking homes in the Northwest territory and perhaps he went with them. There is no tradition as to whom he married. All is lost.

II., James Morton married Mary Montgomery of Spartanburg County. The Montgomerys are a proud old family, tracing their ancestry back to the old Norman days "before the coming of Rolfe." French history is full of their knightly deeds, and in Scotland the Morton and Montgomery were brothers-at-arms.

III., David Morton was twice married. First to Penelope White, who did not live long. She had no children. He then married Mary Jamison. No children were born to them. A memorial to David Morton appears elsewhere as one of the rare characters of a rude age.

IV., William Morton, too, is lost and no trace has been found. They all lived at Fairview several years then emigrated.

V., Mary Morton, the only daughter of this family, is also lost even to tradition, and only her name remains, and there are those who say she never existed at all.

From the oldest church book at Fairview is taken the following: "Nov. 1835. Dismissed regularly four families, Wm. Morrow, four in number; James Morton, six in number; Wm. Armour, two in number; Jas. McVickers, two in number. Anthony Savage, clerk session."

"The Peden who married the Morton (James or David) was my great-grandmother. Her son, James Morton, was my grandfather. Of the families of her other sons I know nothing

"My father was Dr. Josiah Wilson, Morton, the youngest of nine children, all of whom are dead. The living children of those nine are few. Wilson Morton, of Mississippi; Mrs. Mary Turner, of Texas; children of John Washington Morton. Dr. J. W. Morton, of Somerville, Alabama, son of Montgomery Morton who married Rebecca Peden, daughter of John Thomas Peden, son of Alexander, the six son of John, the father. Their daughter Rosa married Alexander Savage, of the house of James. J. D. Morton, Cameron, Texas, son of Harvey. Mrs. Jane Wright, Brownwood, Texas, and Miss Mary Savage daughter of Mrs. Rosa Morton Savage, and five of us, Mrs. E. M. Wise, Waxahachie, Texas; Mrs. C. M. Lyon, Lancaster, Texas; A. H. Morton, Prairieville, Texas; Mrs. John W. George, Oak Cliffe, Texas; Miss Emma Morton, Lancaster, Texas. (The inference is that five of the children of James Morton were, John Washington, Robert Montgomery, Harvey, Rosana, Josiah Wilson. They were all born in Greenville County, S. C.)

"My father, Josiah Wilson Morton, was born near Fairview, Greenville County, S.C. Left there for Tennessee when nine years old. Married Jane Alexander in 1847, and afterwards moved to Mississippi. Came to Texas in 1856 and died February 17, 1898.

(Signed) "Emma Morton."

The date of Jane Morton's marriage with Samuel Motvow is unknown. There were five Morrow children: L, Samuel; IL, Robert; IIL, William; IV., Thomas; V., Janet. The last named died at nineteen years and sleeps at Fairview, S.C. There is some discrepancy in names of the Mortons and Morrows;

the names William and David occur in each (on one record) and some of the Morrow family say that it was Robert, not Maj. Samuel Morrow, who married Jane Peden Morton. Maj. Samuel Morrow was born in Baltimore County, Maryland, 1760; his father was also named Samuel, and as Jane Peden was born about 1738-1742, their ages are too different. Was Maj. Samuel Morrow her son? The Morrow records have not yet arrived; perhaps the historian will explain, but in case he does not send in records in time will copy from the old church book:

"Robert Morrow and his two sons, Samuel and Thomas, and their families moved to Mississippi (Alabama). Regularly dismissed March 18, 1817.

"1833. Wm. Morrow is mentioned as one of a committee to raise the pastor's salary.

"1835. James Morrow unites with the church; also the dismissal of Wm. Morrow and his family, three in number."

"My father was the oldest of ten brothers. He was born near Fairview church September 22, 1799. The entire family came to Alabama in 1818. At or about the same time three brothers of my grandfather (Robert Morrow), Samuel, David, William or Laurens, came from South Carolina and settled near Sommerville, Tenn. Thomas, the other son, who went to Texas in 18561857, came too.

"Jane Peden and her husband, Samuel Morrow, are buried in North Alabama, near Somerville. They lived with my grandfather until they died.

"The war record of the Morrows is splendid. There were twenty Morrows, all first cousins, on the Confederate side, besides a daughter's son named Harris.

(Signed)   "R. B. Morrow."

I., Samuel Morrow married his first cousin, Katie Peden, (house of Samuel).

Chapter Fourteen - House of Thomas

The question of the time and manner of Peden emigration has never been fully settled. The tradition in the house of Thomas differs from that coming down through the other houses. Which one is true will only be revealed "when the leaves of the judgment books unroll," when this immense clan gathers before the great white throne in a solemn and endless reunion of joy.

Thomas Peden, the founder of this line seems to have been a man of great force of character; firm, unyielding in principle, willing to do, to dare, to die, for what he believed to be right. He was free from sectarian or creed prejudices as is proven in Howe's History of the Presbyterian Church in South Carolina. As a soldier, patriot, citizen he was brave, loyal and strictly law abiding, yet never following blindly the leading of any man; always his own master. In religion a devout Presbyterian; in politics an ardent Whig.

His place on the family roll is ten years later than his brother James. If other children, save his sister Jane, came between they must have died young.

Thomas Peden was among the pioneers of what is now Spartanburg County, S.C., preceding his father and brothers some years. This county was part of the 96th district, and in 1774 was called the "Spartan" by Wm. Drayton, who exclaimed with enthusiastic admiration: "Truly a Spartan people!"

The historian of this house, Mr. Amzi W. Gaston, lives on the tract of land granted first by King George, 1772, and later regranted by the new government to the then incumbent, whose record as a Whig soldier does not admit of question. As before stated, the exact location of the first cabin home is lost, for there is not a tree, or stone left, nothing but the hillside and overgrown spring. It will be pleasant for the clan to know that this sacred spot has never left the possession of the race planted there.

John Peden, his wife, with their son Thomas and four youngest sons, and Morton grandsons, all of whom were mere lads, came together to the Tyger settlements, whether from Pennsylvania or Charlestown tradition is silent. They settled near Nazareth church; while it is now believed that James and his sisters, with their families found their first homes in the land of the Quaker, Thomas came direct to South Carolina.

Thomas married Elizabeth White, and his nephew, David Morton, of blessed memory, married her youngest sister, Penelope. "These wives were of the staunch old Revolutionary Whig stock." Around the name of White clusters memories of many a brave, daring deed; it shines on the fame-roll of Upper South Carolina with deathless luster. Hon. Hugh Lawson White, of Tennessee, was a nephew of these sisters.

Thomas Peden and his old father were driven off by Tories and Indians in the dark days of 1780-1781. Thomas took his family to North Carolina for safety, to Iredell County, while John, the father, took his wife and a number of grandchildren over to Chester. Both then resumed their places in the Revolutionary army. In the meantime the youngest sons, William, Samuel, Alexander and David were with their respective leaders among rocks, mountain dens and impenetrable swamps. It was a proud boast of the Pedens that they had "little to lose therefore had no need of British protection." Among the grandchildren was little Peggy, second child of Thomas, who remained with them as long as they lived, and among her special treasures she held dear a silver coin, of about the size of a ten-cent piece, presumably English, and she kept it during her eighty years sojourn on the earth. She gave the historian of this house, A. W. Gaston, many incidents of early frontier life; among others of how their wheat was harvested with reap-hooks, or sickles, showing him how the hooks were held while the reapers tied the bundles. After things were quieted down they returned from North Carolina and settled again within half a mile of their former home, or rather its ruins, and reared their large family of children, of whom four were sons and seven were daughters.

This family is not given in order of birth, the names of the sons are given first: I., Andrew; II., M. White; III., James; IV., John. The daughters: V., Mary;

VI., Margaret; VII., Eleanor; VII., Elizabeth; IX., Sarah; X., Jane; XI., Nancy.

I., Andrew, the eldest son, married Jane McConnell. Their children:

1., Rev. Mitchell Peden, a Presbyterian minister. He married Mary Jennings and spent most of his life in Mississippi. A full sketch of his life work is to be found in a previous chapter. Pie was the father of twelve children, only two of whom are now living. Several sons died for the Confederate cause. One of whom, Joseph Caldwell, fills a hero's grave. The surviving son is Rev. W. P. Peden, Baptist minister, who married M. J. Hanson. No record of children. The daughter is Mrs. E. S. Lee, of whose family the writer has no trace.

2., Rufus, who married Margaret Narcissa Peden, of the same house. Was killed in the civil war, leaving two young sons: John M., Rufus, Jr. These appear elsewhere.

3.. Elizabeth, who married Rev. Arthur Mooney, was the mother of a large family. Moved to Mississippi where she died. No records save that one son, Church, died bravely for the South, 1861.

4, Jane, who married Amzi W. Gaston. Only one child, a son (historian of this house), named for his father Amzi Williford; he however, has been blessed with many sons. He says: "My mother was the second daughter of Andrew, the eldest son of Thomas Peden. She had only one brother in the civil war, Rufus, who gave his life to the cause, leaving a young wife and two small sons. Her other brother, Rev. Mitchell Peden also lost a son. I have neither brother or sister, and I fought for our beloved South for three long years. If I have any regrets they are that I did not fight harder; but I now sincerely believe it is for the best that we did not succeed."

[Amzie Gaston, like his great grandfather, Thomas Peden, stands for purity of church and state, clean politics, good citizenship, and is an avowed opponent of the so-called reform in South Carolina. In appearance he is a tall, commanding figure, a typical Norman Gaston, with the steelest, bluest, truest eyes of the fearless race.]

Moreover, he is the father of eight goodly sons and two fair daughters. Sons — 1, John Williford; 2, Robert White; 3, Amzi Cason; 4, James Gordon; 5, Thomas Craig; 6, "Jeb" Stuart; 7, Baird Lamar; 8, Palmer DeWitt (died in infancy); 9, Morton Reid; 10, David Holder. Daughters — 1, Fitz Hampton, named for the mother of South Carolina's "knightliest leader of them all," Gen. Wade Hampton; 2, Mary Elizabeth.

II., Moses White married his first cousin, Margaret, eldest daughter of Alexander, therefore of the house of Alexander, Their children were: 1, Eliza E.; 2, A. Wilson; 3, Rebecca E.;

4, T. Jefferson; 5, James M.; 6. Munro; 7, Andrew W.; 8, Robert M.; 9, Mary A.; 10, David M.; 11, Hugh L. W.

1, Eliza E. married Alexander Thompson, who was a member of that Thompson family famous in South Carolina history from colonial days. Its men have been found in the arena of war and the forum of politics. He was twice married, his first wife having been Elizabeth Alexander (house of Mary), which includes the elder line; while the younger belongs to that of

Thomas, as both came from the "distaff side," or through the mother. The children were: 1. White; 2, Drayton; 3, Lawson; 4, Thomas; 5, Elizabeth; 6, Margaret; 7, Rachel 1. White served brevely through the entire civil war, so also did Drayton. At its close or just before these two brave young brothers were brought home to die of consumption. Both were members of Company E., Hampton Legion. White died on the 22nd day of January, 1865.

2, Drayton followed him on the 24th day of February, 1865. Neither were married.

3, Lawson came home safely. Married Lou Farmer. Their children: L. Grace, Margaret E., Leila White.

4, Thomas married ____ Earle. No records sent.

5, Elizabeth married Thomas Babb. Their children: 1, Drayton; 2, Homer; 3, Chalmers; 4, Lawson; 5, Paul; 6, Eliza; 7, Eva.

1, Drayton Babb married ____ Tribble. No children.

2, Eliza Babb married Robert Thompson. No children.

3, Homer Babb married Lidie McKelvey. Two children: Annie R., H. Thomas.

4, Chalmers Babb unmarried.

5, Lawson Babb married Sue Spencer. One child.

6, Paul Babb unmarried.

7, Eva Babb unmarried.;

6, Margaret unmarried.

7, Rachel died young, August 26, 1868.

2, A. Wilson married Jane Thompson, daughter of Alexander Thompson, and his first wife, Elizabeth Alexander (house of Mary), showing a mixed relationship that will puzzle their numerous descendants. Their children were ten in number: 1, Elizabeth H.; 2, Margaret; 3, Hugh Lawson White; 4, Alexander Thompson; 5, James F.; 6, Mary E.; 7, William Buist; 8, John Pickens; 9, Welthy Ann; 10, Roxanna.

1, Elizabeth H. never married. She lives at the old home near Fairview. Hers has been one of those long and beautiful livies. A pure, noble, unselfish character, of generous self-sacrifice; one whose very name deserves to be written in living letters of gold.

2, Margaret, who died unmarried in young womanhood.

3, Hugh L. W. married Mary McKnight. He was born and educated in Greenville County, S.C. Volunteered in 1861, in Company E., Hampton Legion. Served four years. Their children are:

1, Ellie J., who married ____ Edwards. Mother of three children: Willie, Hugh, Sara.

2, Carrie P. unmarried.

3, Elizabeth H., who married ____ Mitchell, of New York. One child, named Albert S.

4, Wilson McKnight.

5, Margaret E. who married ____ Harris. One child, Genevieve.

6, Hugh L. W. Jr.

4, Alexander Thompson, who died leaving a wife and three children, who did not long survive him. He was a brave, heroic member of Company E., 6th S, C Cavalry, serving through the entire war.

5, James F. married Ella Mosely. Three children: Margaret, Joseph Thompson (who died young), Lee.

6, Mary E. died young.

7, William Buist died.

8, John Pickens married Emma V. Cunningham. Eight children: Janie, Eva H., Cora, Roxanna, Edgar, Eliza, Jessie, the last not named.

9, Wealthy Ann married J. L. Haynes, Three children: Annie, Norman, Guy.

10, Roxanna married Olin B. Talley. One child Eliza N.

3, Rebecca Elvira married Silas M. Mooney. Eight children: 1, Alexander; 2, John William; 3, Margaret Ann; 4, Sarah Jane; 5, Mary Eliza; 6, Nancy Elizabeth; 7, James Arthur; 8, David M.

1, Alexander Mooney laid down his life for the "lost cause." Unmarried.

2, John W. Mooney married Martha Cousar (house of David). Their children are: 1, Oliver, of whom there is no trace. 2, Alice who married ____ Brady. Four children; names not given.

3, Margaret A. Mooney married Henry Arrington. Their children: 1, William Thomas; 2, Jane; 3, David; 4, Arthur.

4, Sarah J. Mooney married J. W. T. Peden, a son of M. W. Peden, of Chickasaw County, Miss., (houses of Alexander and David).

5, Mary E. Mooney married C. N. McArthur. Their children: 1, John; 2, Minnie; 3, James; 4, Jessie; 5, Benjamin; 6, Eugene; 7, Henry; 8, Lillian; 9, Mary.

1, John married ____ Grube. Four children; names unknown.

2, Minnie married Stephen Palmer. Seven children; names unknown.

No records of 6, Nancy E.; 7, Jas. Arthur; 8, David M. 4, Thomas Jefferson, second son of M. White Peden, married Elizabeth Gray, of Laurens County, S.C. Their children: 1, Moses White; 2, Charlotte Eliza; 3, Mary Ann; 4, Margaret Jane; 5 and 6 (twins) Sarah Emma and Nancy Caroline; 7, Martha Rebecca; 8, Thomas William.

1, Moses White married Olive Wilder, of Newton County, Miss. No children.

2; Charlotte Eliza married Walker Nash, of Greenville County, S.C. No children.

3, Mary Ann married Wm. K. Stennis (house of Alexander and are partly recorded there). Their children: 1, John Knox

2, Anna Elizabeth; 3, Margaret Jane; 4, Rose Ella; 5, Thomas Dudley, and 6, Jas. Henry (twins); 7, Cora Emma; 8, Carrie May.

1, John Knox Stennis married Margaret McNiell (house of Samuel). No children.

2, Anna Elizabeth Stennis married T. W. Adams. Their children, three daughters: 1, Cornelia; 2, Rosa Stennis; 3, Mary Anna.

3, Margaret Jane Stennis married A. A. Overstreet. Their children: 1, Carlyle; 2,DeBerri; 3, Mary.

4, Rosa Ella Stennis married John D. McNiell (house of Samuel). Their children: 1, Lillian; 2, Henry Grady; 3, Myrtle.

5, Dr. Thomas Dudley Stennis married Daisie Hampton. No children.

6, Dr. James Henry Stennis married Regina Davis. No children. These twin brothers are prominent physicians in the State of Mississippi.

7, Cora Emma Stennis married John Little. One child, Hampton Stennis.

8, Carrie May Stennis. Unmarried.

5, Sara Emma, one of the twin daughters of Thos. Jefferson Peden, married S. J. Peden of the house of Samuel and Alexander. Their children: 1, James Thomas; 2, William Thaddeus; 3, Dougal Jefferson; 4, Marion Wilson; 5, Archibald; 6, John Harrison; 7, Margaret Elizabeth; 8, Alexander.

1, James Thomas. No record.

2, William Thaddeus married Ella Heath. One child, Lydia.

6, Nancy Caroline, twin to the above, married James Hugh Peden. Same house. Their children: 1, Dr. Thomas White; 2, Mary; 3, Hugh Coiett.

7, Martha Rebecca. No record, presumably dead or unmarried.

8, Thomas William, the youngest of Thomas Jefferson Peden's children, and writer of these records, married Nannie Arlette Cook, of Noxubee County, Mississippi. They have no children.

5, James M., the third son of M. White Peden. never married.

6, John Munro, the fourth son of M. White Peden, married Esther Baker (house of David). Their children: 1, Eleanor Narcissa; 2, Whitner; 3, Moses White; 4, James Hugh.

I, Eleanor Narcissa married Rufus Peden and in this marriage were united the houses of Thomas, Alexander and David, Rufus being a son of Andrew, the eldest son of this house, this family should be properly recorded under Andrew, but instead are placed here. Their children, two sons: 1, John Munro; 2, Rufus, Jr.

1, John Munro married Mary J. Kimmel. Their children: 1, James Rufus; 2, Joseph Whitner; 3, Eleanor Esther; 4, Ora May; 5, Mary Anna; 6, Hugh B.; 7, Corrie M. (Since the reunion he lost his wife, and has married a second time. Wife's name unknown).

2, Rufus, Jr., died an infant.

2, Whitner died for the Confederacy.

3, Moses White married Eliza Carr. Their children: 1, Anna; 2, Walter; 3, Guy Hugh; 4, Effie Belle; 5, Julia.

1, Anna married Trino Lambeth, of Tennessee, two children: Laverne, Milton.

2, Walter married Estelle Waldrop. One child, Walter.

4, James Hugh married his first cousin, Nancy Caroline, already recorded with the family of Thos. Jefferson Peden. One of the twin daughters.

7, Andrew W., the fifth son of M. White Peden, married Margaret Knox, of Alabama. Their children: 1, James Knox; 2, Margaret Jane; 3, Catherine Alabama; 4, Moses White; 5, William Asbel.

1, Jas. Knox married Elizabeth Lyle. Their children: 1, Catherine; 2, Emma, who married a Bradshaw. Mother of three children; names unknown.

2, Margaret Jane married Leroy Campbell. One child, Waldo Emerson.

3, Catherine Alabama married Joseph Huickle, of Panola County, Miss. Two children: 1, Margaret; 2, Jodie.

4, Moses White married Emma Spears. Five children; names unknown.

5, William Asbel married Annie McNiell (house of Samuel). No further record.

8, Robert M. Peden, sixth son of Moses White Peden, married Rebecca T. Fowler (same house). Their children:

1, Margaret A., married J. P. Rogers. Four children.

2, Nancy, who never married.

3, James O. A. married Martha A. Rogers. Six children.

4, John W. married Margaret C. Baker (house of David), has six children.

5, David J. married Margaret P. Bostick. Five children.

6, Ada V. married Felix Helms. One child.

7, Alexander B. married Sara Richardson. Ten children,

8, Cornelia E. married John W. Kyle. Three children.

9, Rebecca M. married John C. Ray. Eight children.

10, Robert M. unmarried.

(The names of the children were not sent to the regret of the historian. The writer is John W. Peden, the fourth child.)

9, Mary Ann, the third daughter of M. White Peden, married James Thompson, eldest line (house of Mary), where they are recorded.

10, David M., seventh son of M. White Peden, married Mary Griffin. Their children: 1, Richard; 2, Margaret; 3, Nancy; 4, David M., Jr.

I, Richard married, but the name of his wife is unknown, and all trace of this family is entirely lost.

11, Hugh Lawson White, eighth son M. White Peden, lost in the civil war.

All of the sons of M. White Peden who emigrated to Mississippi, and several grandsons, served in the Confederate army, making brave soldiers. Those giving their lives for the lost cause were: from South Carolina, White and Drayton Thompson, sons of Eliza E., eldest daughter, and A. Thompson Peden, son of A. Wilson Peden, eldest son; from Mississippi, Alexander Mooney, John W., Moses W. (sons of T. Jefferson Peden), John Knox, a grandson. None of the other grandsons were old enough, or else they would have been in their places in that cruel war. The names of the sons who fought through: T. Jefferson, Jno. Munro, James M., Andrew W., Robert M., David M., Hugh L. W. A. Wilson was too old, but aided efficiently. Most of the line of M. White Peden are of the Presbyterian creed, while there are a few Baptists and Methodists among them. They dwell as brethren should in peace and love.

(Signed)   Thomas William Peden.

III., John Peden, my father, married Nicey Fowler in 1820, settled one mile north of grandfather's place (in Spartanburg County, S.C.,); mother died Oct.

11, 1830; father Oct. 14, 1832, leaving five children, three boys and two girls, who were kept together and raised by Aunt Margaret Paden (his sister).

My oldest sister, Margaret Paden, married Andrew Johnson; settled near Cashville, S. C, then moved to Chattooga County, Ga., and died May 30, 1848, leaving four children, who, with their father, moved to Arkansas.

My oldest brother, Moses White Paden, moved to DeKabb County, Ga.; taught school a few years, then moved to Cherokee County, Ga., and married Rosannah Delaney; had two children, boy and girl. In 1857 he went on a visit to South Carolina. Died in Spartanburg County, August 16, 1857. Was buried in the family grave yard on the old home place. His wife and children moved to Mississippi. No further trace.

Thomas Paden, my next brother, married Elizabeth Johnson and moved to Cherokee County, Ga., and died April 6, 1846; not having lived but a few months in Georgia, leaving one child, who, with her mother, moved to Arkansas. No further trace.

My youngest sister, Rebecca Paden, married James R. Westmoreland. They lived together in Spartanburg County, S.C. over fifty years. I had the pleasure of attending their golden wedding.

Rebecca Esque Peden was born Sept. 22nd, 1827. She married James R. Westmoreland on November 23, 1842. Rebecca was, at the time of marriage, sixteen years and one month old. James R. Westmoreland was, at the time of marriage, twenty years and four months old. We were a very young couple and had great opposition. Her aunt, who raised her, was greatly opposed to our marriage and consequently it was for a long time that she would not allow me in her house. However, the dear old aunt soon became reconciled and in her old age we cared for her until she died. In our courtship I might note a lot of amusing experiences, however I shall omit them on account of their failing to apply to history. We were poor but able to work, and we went to work with a fixed purpose. That purpose was to make a living, and I am thankful that we were so blessed as to be able to accomplish our purpose and not only that, but to raise a family of eight children, some of whom grew to maturity and married. One died at thirteen years, two in infancy, which made ten in all.

My oldest son. Dr. Jno. Andy Westmoreland, was born Aug. 29th, 1843. Married Margaret Ann Barbara Rush, Aug. 31, 1874. Dr. Jno. died very suddenly, on Oct. 31, 1895, leaving a widow and five children, two boys and three girls.

James Ripley Westmoreland, born Oct. 8, 1876.
Frederick Stroble Westmoreland born Dec. 27, 1877.
Nannie Peden Westmoreland, born Feb. 14, 1880.
Goldie Luellen Westmoreland, born Nov. 12, 1882.
Bettie Barbara Westmoreland, born Dec. 5, 1886.

My second son, James White Westmoreland, was born Aug. 8, 1845. Married Juhan Leonard Dec. 28, 1876. He has had five children, but of this number only three are living. His children are as follows: Coke Fenner, born Jan.

14, 1881. John Peter, died in infancy. Duncan, died in infancy. Margaret Rebecca, born July 23, 1890. James Walter, born Oct. 13, 1898.

My third son, Thomas Peden Westmoreland, born Sept. 22, 1847, and died at the age of thirteen years.

My oldest daughter, Nicey Temperance Westmoreland, born Aug 16, 1849. Married John Warren Martin April 24, 1879, and died, after a very short illness, July 11, 1890, leaving a husband and four children, three girls and one boy. Mattie Maude Martin, born April 30, 1880. Freddie Ellora Martin, born Oct. 3, 1882. Lena Temperance Martin, born Aug. 3, 1885. John Laurens Martin, born Feb. 22, 1890.

My second daughter, Margaret Westmoreland, born May 31, 185 1. Married Frank Buist Woodruff Nov. 16, 1875. He has had eight children and of this number four are living. William Anderson Woodruff, born Aug. 18, 1876. Mary Amelia, born May 8, 1878; died May 18, 1878. Lillie Lee, born March 2, 1880; died May 2, 1890. Nellie Westmoreland, born Feb 12, 1882. Vallie Vance, born July 7, 1884. Furman Frank, born June 4, 1887; died May 27, 1888. Maggie Cyrina, born May 27, 1889; died June 15, 1895. Paden Esque, born May 14, 1892.

My third daughter, Mary Jane Westmoreland, born Feb. 6, 1854. Married Henry Hardin Arnold on Dec. 20, 1877. They have had ten children, all of whom are living, except two. They are as follows: Orlando Peden Arnold, born Dec. 23, 1878. Walter Hardin, born May 5, 1880. Maggie May, born Dec. 14, 1881. Roy Othello, born Dec. 31, 1885. Bruce Kirkland, born Oct. 6, 1885. Frances Folsom. born Oct. 4, 1887. Bessie Ruth, born Feb. 25. 1890; died in infancy. Temperance Annie Belle, born Oct. 11, 1891. James Ralph, born Jan. 18, 1894. John Andy, born Jan. 14, 1896; died in infancy.

My fourth daughter, Lola Esque Lee Westmoreland, was born Dec. 23, 1863. Married John Warren Snoddy May 17, 1881 and died, after a long illness, March 25, 1892, leaving a husband and four boys. Oliver Patrick Snoddy, born Feb. 18, 1884. James Richard, born Aug. 31, 1885. John Martin, born June 13, 1887. Warren McCord, born March 17, 1889.

My fourth son, William Wilks Booth Westmoreland, was born May 14, 1870, and married Minnie Elizabeth Woodruff, Jan. 3, 1892. They have had five children, but have been very unfortunate; only one of this number is now living, Mary Rebecca Westmoreland, born March 12, 1896.

At the beginning I did not state how Rebecca Esque Peden Westmoreland died. On July 25, 1895, she went to Spartanburg to attend to some business (and right here I will state that she was a very energetic and also a very fine business lady, doing a very extensive dry goods and millinery business at Woodruft, S.C.), and while talking to Mr. R. T. Beason, in front of J. W. Allen's store, she was stricken with apoplexy and died very suddenly.

War record of myself and two sons, John Andy and James White Westmoreland.

I (James R. Westmoreland) went into service Jan. 1, 1862, with a company made up from this place (Woodruff, S. C), with Wm. T. Roebuck captain. The company joined the Holcomb Legion. I served in this company for eighteen months; my health failed and was transferred to the cavalry, company "E." (Capt. James Knight), Col. Aiken's Regiment, Gen. M. C. Butler's Brigade and Gen. Wade Hampton's Corps. I served here until March 9, 1865, when I was captured near Fayetteville, N. C. I was sent to prison at Hart Island, N. Y., for three and a half months. When first captured my coat, hat and shoes were taken off and burned. I was not given anything to eat for five days and made to walk eighteen or twenty miles each day, notwithstanding my blistered feet. While in New York city it sleeted and I was out in this weather from 12 o'clock m. until 12 o'clock at night. Came so near freezing that I could not walk without help for three weeks. For such treatment my religion has not been good enough to prompt me to forgive. I was in fourteen fights while in service and was so fortunate as not to receive but one wound. I was knocked down by a piece of shell.

Myself and two sons fought the war through and by the prayers of a wife and mother the good God shielded us from the thousands of bullets that were hurled at us. Not one of us was seriously hurt, but all received slight wounds.

John A. Westmoreland went out in the spring of 1861. L. White Westmoreland in the fall of 1861. They belonged to Company "E.," (Capt. H. P. Griffith), 14th Regiment, Col. Joseph Brown, McGowan's Brigade and "Stonewall" Jackson's Corps. They were in all the battles that the regiment was in: among some of the most important Chancellorsville, Gettysburg, Second Manassas, Wilderness and Horse Shoe, at Spotsylvania. Jno. A. Westmoreland was captured near Reames Station, Va., and sent to Point Lookout, where he was imprisoned for two months. Afterwards he was exchanged and given a furlough. While on his way back to duty Lee surrendered. J. White Westmoreland was never captured and surrendered with Lee at Appomattox C. H.

Very sincerely,
J. R. Westmoreland.

I, (Mark Simpson Paden), now an octogenarian, have been married three times. My first wife, Elvira, was a daughter of Mark Fowler. She died Sept. 10, 1856, leaving me two children, Margaret and James.

My second wife was a sister of my first, Emma Fowler. She died July 17, 1878, leaving me two children, Alice and Willie (W. D. Paden, of Atlanta, Ga.).

Margaret, my eldest daughter, married Osborne Nicholls and died March 30, 1878, leaving two children, Ella and Willie.

James, my eldest son, married first a Benson, who died some years ago he then married the widow Wilson. No children. They live in Woodstock, Ga.

Alice, my second daughter, married Dr. Samuel Parsons. She is the mother of seven children, one of whom died in infancy. Their names are on the Peden Register. Lucy, Sam, Jr., Lillie, Bruce, Grover Cleveland (two are missing). They live at Woodruffs, S.C.

Willie (W. D.,), my second son, married Maggie Carter, a niece of Ex-Governor Northen, of Georgia. They live in Atlanta, Ga., and have three children. Dean, Ruth, Carter.

My granddaughter, Ella Nicholls, married Oscar Benson. Has five children. They live in Cobb County, Ga.

My grandson, Willie Nicholls, married Bertha Holland. They have no children, and live in Atlanta, Ga.

My third wife was Eliza Maroney. There are no children to this marriage.

May God bless you all is the prayer of this one of the numerous Peden descendants.

(Signed)   Mark Simpson Paden.

This prayer falls like a benediction from the venerable writer, who was a familiar and revered figure at the Peden reunion in 1899.

IV., James married Lettie McCrey, or McCrary, in North Carolina, then moved to Decatur, Ga. They had five children, three sons and two daughters, all of whom except the eldest daughter, who married a Chandler and went to Texas at the close of the civil war, settled around their father. Jane, the other daughter, married a Guess and lives at the old homestead. Nothing more could be learned of this line though every effort was made by the Peden historian. All letters to Pedens in and around Atlanta, except W. D. Paden, already recorded, met with absolute silence.

V., Mary or Mollie.

VI., Margaret, or Peggy.

VII., Eleanor, or Ella.

These three were the eldest children of Thomas. The two first lived past four-score years of useful spinsterhood, beloved and cherished by their family circle. The last died in early womanhood.

VIII., Elizabeth married her first cousin, John or "Jackie" Peden (house of Samuel), where full records are given. This family moved to Kemper County, Miss., in 1832, along with the venerable Samuel Peden and a large number of Peden pioneers.

IX., Sarah married Anthony Pearson and lived out her long, useful life near Nazareth church, in Spartanburg County, S.C. Her sons were seven, her daughters three. Sons: 1, James; 2, Jackson; 3, Jefferson; 4. Wilson; 5, Thomas; 6, David; 7, William F. Of the last named only has any record reached the writer. He was a Presbyterian minister greatly loved by all who knew him. A powerful man physically and menially. It is a source of keen regret that no sketch of his useful life and pious example was prepared for this volume. A noble man, nobly planned. He rests from his labors and his works do follow him, having gone to his reward a few years ago. The wife, Mrs. E. E. Pearson, and the following children survive: 1, J. T.; 2, M. M.; 3, A. A.; 4, W. G.; 5, Paul C.

1, J. T. unmarried.

2, M. M. married S. L. Wilson, a Presbyterian minister. Their children are: Frank Pearson, Parks T.

The daughters of Sarah Peden Pearson were 1, Ella who married John Snoddy, of a prominent Spartanburg family from early colonial days. A sketch of the Snoddy family appears in Landrum's History of Spartanburg County.

2, Elizabeth, who married Sampson Bobo, of Mississippi, who attained great legal prominence in that State.

3, Mary, who married John Haddon, who gave his life for the lost cause.

X., Jane married her first cousin, Robert Peden (house of Alexander). They were best known as Robin and Jennie, a model couple. Their records are fully given in the house to which they belong.

XI., Nancy, the youngest, married John Fowler. "Like the leaves of the forest, when autumn has blown," this large family are scattered abroad. Few traces have been found. Most of their names are lost even to memory.

Alexander, the eldest son, went to Florida. Married there. No trace of his family.

Three of the daughters married Pedens thereby drifting back in to the ancestral name.

The Fowler line belongs so mutually to the two houses of Thomas and Alexander it was difficult to place impartially either way, coming as it does on the "spindle side" of both houses.

Moses T. Fowler, second son, was twice married, first to his cousin, Elizabeth Ann Peden, daughter of Robert and Jane (houses Thomas and Alexander). He served nine months in the S.C. Militia during the civil war, three months as first lieutenant, then six as captain of his company; was transferred to Company E., Hampton Legion. (This company of this famous legion was composed of at least two-thirds Peden descendants. Its history is immortal in the South and, like the Light Brigade at Balaklava, the memory of its brilliant charges and daring leader grows brighter, not dimmer, as the years roll on bearing the legend of heroism. The writer has tried in vain to obtain the roster or muster roll of this company for insertion but it seems irrevocably lost.) To resume, Moses T. Fowler was wounded in the left shoulder at Riddle's Shop, Va., and surrendered with Lee, passing through the entire time bravely. As history repeats itself, he, like John Peden, the father, gave his sons, four in number, to the Confederate cause, laying two on the altar of his country. He and his wife raised seven children: 1, Robert A.; 2, John T.; 3, J. Wilson; 4, M. White; 5, D. Simpson; 6, Mary Jane; 7, E. Nancy.

1, Robert A. volunteered in Company E., Hampton Legion. Served as corporal. Was killed at Seven Pines, Va., May 31, 1862.

2, John T., being in Tennessee at that time volunteered in the Second Louisiana Regiment, Jackson's Corps. Was in several hard battles in Virginia, receiving a slight wound in the left hand at the Second Battle of Manasses; never flinched; had it tied up and on with the fight. Also a severe wound nearly shattering right elbow during the fatal Chancellorville, which was "Stonewall" Jackson's last. May 3, 1868, and the star of the Confederacy began to sink. After he recovered use of his arm was transferred to Company E., Hampton Legion. Losing his horses was sent home for one; while on the way back the war ended and he did not have the pleasure (?) of surrendering with Lee He went to Mississippi and there met and married a kinswoman. Serena Baker, daughter of Rebecca (Martin) Baker, [her husband being Franklin Baker, son of Penelope (Peden) Baker, daughter of David Peden, seventh son of John, the father], daughter of Janet (Peden) Martin, daughter of Alexander, the sixth son of John, the father, thus we see the union of three houses, Thomas, Alexander, David. Two of their children died young, eight are living: R. Elizabeth, T. Franklin, Robert W., Moses M., Nancy R., John S., Harris L., Albert T. Of these two are married. R. Elizabeth married Samuel A. Snead. Two children: John R., Laura E. T. Franklin Fowler married Delpha Pass. All in Texas.

3, J. Wilson Fowler was only sixteen years old at the outbreak of the civil war, but volunteered in Company E., Hampton Legion. Was highly praised for heroism by his commanding officers. Was the first man to mount the enemies breastworks at the First Battle of Manasses, and placed in line of promotion, but died of pneumonia at camp Wigfall on the Potomac River, Dec. 28, 1861.

4, M. White Fowler was serving in Company A., 1st S.C. Militia at the close of the war. Married Oasa Garrett. Only one child, a daughter, Elizabeth Ann, who married Augustus Pollard and is mother of six children: Fred H., Martha A., Geneva N., Ethel E., Zelemma, Sarah B. All living near Simpsonville, S.C.

5, D. Simpson Fowler married Eliza Gray. One son died young, ten children living: Harriet E., Martha J., J. Thos., Effie T., David E., George A., Stewart A., Nancy L., H. Grady. Of these four are married: Harriet E. married Wm. P. Garrett. Three children died young, two are living: W. Crayton, Anna R. Martha J. married Olin B. Talley. One child dead; one living, Mary T. Wm. R. Fowler married Dora Nash. Two children: Ethel M., Robert S. Effie T. married Carlton Boyd.

6, Mary J. Fowler married Florence L. Garrett, of Mississippi. Has five children: Henry H., Waddy L., Rosa E., Nancy B., Florence T.

7, Nancy E. Fowler married Anthony Wayne R. Baker, brother of John T. Fowler's wife, a son of Franklin Baker (house of David), and his wife, Rebecca (Martin) Baker (house of Alexander) [union of the three houses, Thomas, Alexander, David]. One of their children died young. There are five living: Beulah M., John Thomas, Samuel R., Wm. P., Jesse J. Living near Springtown, Texas.

Moses T. Fowler's second marriage was to Amanda Richards. Ten children: Alice A., Martha C, Wm. P., W. Richard, Callie D., Eula L., Jesse L., Walter A., Maggie L., Lora B.

Alice A. married Edward B. Martin. Nine children: James L., C. Ellen, Jennie W., E. Luther, Wm. T., Elger B., Alice, Mary B., Nannie. Living near Simpsonville, owners of the old Morrow homestead.

Martha C. married Humphrey K. Ezell. Seven children: Hettie L., Boyce, Kinsey J., Paul, Nina. Living near Winnsboro, S.C.

Wm. P. Fowler married Minnie Parsons. Three eldest children died in infancy. Living: Moses T., Grover C, Wells W. Living near Cashville, S.C.

W Richard Fowler married Maggie L. Harris. Four children: Casper, John, Myrtle, Bessie. Home near Fountain Inn S.C.

Callie D. Fowler married Sloan D. Gibson. One child died young, Wm. M. Three living: Grace T., J. Earl Lila.

Eula L. Fowler married Howard Y. Boyd. Three children: Fowler R., Pearl E., Ivey. Living near Fairview, S.C.

Jessie L. Fowler married John B. Boyd. Three children: Margaret S., Mary, Annis. Living near Simpsonville, S.C.

Descendants of Moses T. Fowler: Living, 86; died 16. Total, 102.

(Signed)   M. White Fowler.

Chapter Fifteen - House of William

William is generally accepted as the third son of the house of Peden. The exact date of his birth is unknown, but the date of his death and age at the time places it about 1749. He followed his brothers John and James and preceded David and their sister Elizabeth. Like all of the first family he was born in Ireland, coming with his father to America, according to the best authorities in 1768-1770. He was a brave, daring Revolutionary soldier. A tradition still held at Fairview says he was a "large, portly man, fair of countenance like his mother." For some reason he preferred to follow his trade, that of blacksmithing, instead of extensive farming, so did not possess as many acres as his brothers. A few years ago the remains of his forge were visible.

His niece, Eleanor Dunbar, stated that he was much shattered by exposure and hard living during the war, 1776-1783, and contracted a bronchial trouble which was never cured. She remembered him quite plainly and recalled the conversations of the four brothers, her father and uncles, in which they indulged during the Saturday nights they always spent under the roofs of each other alternately. She also described his wife, "Aunt Mollie," as a thoroughly domestic body, always busy, a famous butter maker and housewife.

William was with Dan Morgan during the entire war, but which his company, or who his captain was, is lost. Tradition says he was with Captain Andrew Barry, of the "Tyger Irish" in the famous "Spartan Regiment," in which company his nephew, John Alexander, was first lieutenant, afterwards Major. The brothers were not all together in the same company, some were with Capt. Benjamin Roebuck. It is safe to assume, however, that the five younger brothers were together as they were inseparable in peace and war, and not apart from each other more than six days of the week, until death entered their circle and claimed John in 1810. William was among the first elders of Fairview church.

The threads of his line were furnished by his grandson, Wm. D. Paden, and granddaughter, Mrs. Mary P. Aughey, and great-grandson, Guilford R. Paden, and great-granddaughter, Bettie Williams.

My grandfather, William Peden, was one of the seven sons of John Peden, the emigrant father. He married Mary Archer, of Pennsylvania. Died near Fairview, S.C., where he rests under the shadow of the Peden monument. On his grave-stone these words are inscribed: "Sacred to the memory of William Peden, who departed this life Dec. 23, 1817. Aged 68 years."

My grandmother moved with my father to Fayette County, Tenn., in 1833, and died at my father's house about 1846. (This emigration is corroborated by the following from the oldest church book now in existence at Fairview: "1833. Robert W. Peden, Dan Peden, David S. Peden (a brother-in-law), and Alexander Peden, with their families, regularly dismissed. (Signed) Anthony Savage, C. S.")

Their eldest son was, I., Robert W. Peden, who died in Tishomingo County, Miss., about 1860. He married Elizabeth McCalla and left three sons and two daughters namely: William Paden, David McCalla Paden, and James M. Paden; the two first named died in Missouri. James M. now (1900) lives at Burnt Mills, Miss. Mary, their eldest daughter, married William T. Settle. Both died some years ago leaving one child, Bettie, who married John Williams and now lives in Iuka. Miss. Martha, their other daughter, married Elijah McCalla. Both dead. No children.

II., The second son of William, Dan, married Kate McCalla. Both are dead, also all their children, save Robert W. Paden. These two wives, Bettie and Katie, were daughters of Samuel McCalla, of Chester County, S.C.

III., The third son, Alexander, was my father. He married Sarah Gardner McCalla, a daughter of David McCalla, of Chester, S.C. They left three sons and one daughter: 1, William D. Paden; 2, David Ramsey Paden, who died in Iuka, Miss., leaving a wife and three children; 3, Dr. Thomas G. Paden, who now lives at Burnt Mills, Miss.; 4, Mary J., the only daughter, married Rev. John H. Aughey.

William D. Paden (the writer) married Sallie Frierson, and has now living two daughters and one son. The daughters are, Mrs. Lizzie Cross and Mrs. Kate McLane; the son, William F. Paden, all of whom live in Cameron, Tex.

The three daughters of William Peden, my grandfather:

IV., Isabella, or "Ibbie," who married Thomas Peden, of Chester, S. C, her first cousin (house of James). I know very little of their family, only William A. and his sister, Belle. (Recorded in house of James.)

V., Margaret or "Peggy," married her first cousin, David S. Peden, (house of Samuel), where her family is placed.

VI., Mary married George Tankersley and died in Tishomingo County, Miss., about the close of civil war.

(Signed)   William Drayton Paden.

Mary J., the only daughter of Alexander, third son of William, the third son of John, the father, was married in Iuka, Miss., to Rev. John H. Aughey, a Presbyterian minister, Jan. 22, 1857. Her daughter, Kate A., born Sept. 3, 1858, married Dr. James Walter Ferguson, of West Salem, Wayne County, Ohio,

Sept. 25, 1884. She died Nov. 23, 1890, leaving one child, Mary Aughey Ferguson, born Feb. 22, 1890.

John Knox Aughey was born in Amsterdam, Ohio, August 20, 1862; graduated from the medical department of Wooster University, Cleveland, Ohio, with the highest honors of his class in 1883. He died May 19, 1886.

The third child, Gertrude Evangeline, was born in Livonia, Washington County, Ind., Feb. 12, 1867. She married Dr. John H. Stanton, in Chariton, Iowa, June 30, 1894. Her daughter, Sarah McCalla Stanton, was born in Chariton, Iowa, April 4, 1897. Second child, Jessie Mary, was born in Chariton, Iowa, March 3, 1900.

Rev. John H. Aughey, husband of Mary J. Paden, was licensed by Chickasaw Presbytery, Mississippi, Oct. 4, 1856. Was born May 8, 1828, so is now seventy-five years of age. Has been actively engaged in the Master's service for nearly fifty years and can preach regularly every Sunday. Now has charge of a congregation in the city of Leavenworth, Kansas.

(Signed)   Mary Paden Aughey.

Robert W. Peden, eldest son of William, married Elizabeth or "Bettie," McCalla. Their children were five: 1, William; 2, James M.; 3, David M.; 4, Mary; 5, Martha.

The records of the third son, David M., sent by Guilford R. Paden, his son, are as follows:

David M. Paden was born March 10, 1820; died June 3, 1868. Moved to Missouri in 1857, and left eight children, who were born to him and his wife, Susan E. Settle: 1, Mary I.; 2, Guilford R.; 3, J. Frank; 4, Robert M.; 5, James P.; 6, Bettie Mc.; 7, Sarah Jane; 8, Mattie S.

1, Mary E. married James McKibben. Their children: Robert G., William F., James M., Mary J., Emmet B.

2, Guilford R. married Nora Payson. Their children: Frank, Nannie, Bessie, Willie.

3, J. Frank unmarried.

4, Robert M. married Amanda Farr. Their children: David, Etta, Nora, Eunice, Erma, Naomi.

5, James P. married Belle Caldwell. Their children: Martha, Lizzie, Zella, Walter.

6, Bettie Mc. No record.

7, Sarah J. No record.

8, Mattie S. No record.

David M. Paden was a ruling elder in Augusta church, also his sons James P. and Guilford R., and his son-in-law, James McKibbon. I never knew any of the race to go to law. As far back as I can remember my kin they were leaders in the church. There are at least twenty families of Paden in and around Shamrock, Mo., and all possess a high grade of morality, and are a truly religious people.

(Signed)   Guilford R. Paden.

Mrs. Bettie Williams furnishes the following: My great-grandfather was William Peden and his wife was Mary Archer. Their children were (my grandfather) Robert W., Margaret, Dan, Isabella, Alexander, Mary.

I. .Wife of Robert was Elizabeth McCalla. Their children: Mary (my mother), William, David, Josiah, Martha, James.

II., Margaret married a relative whose name was David Peden (house of Samuel). Their children were: Porter, Isabelle, Catherine, Jennie, Rosa.

III. Isabelle married Thomas Peden (house of James). Their children: William, Emily, Isabelle.

IV., Dan married Katie McCalla. Their children: William, Nixon, Leroy, Robert, Mary, Martha, Jane.

V. Alexander's wife Sarah McCalla. Children: William, Ramsey, Eliza, Mary, Thomas.

VI. Mary married George Tankersley. Children: Wm., Elizabeth, Perry, James D., Margaret.

I., Robert and Elizabeth (McCalla) Peden. Their descendants:

1, Mary married Wm. Settle. One child, Bettie, who married John Williams.

2, William married Jane McCalla. Six children: John, Laurens, Baxter, Jeannette, Adolphus, Belle.

3, David married Susan Settle. Children given elsewhere.

4, James married Amanda McDougal. Children: David, Genevieve, Baker.

II., Margaret and David Paden. Descendants:

1, Porter married Jane Reneau. Children: Ella, Luke, Kate.

2, Isabelle married Wylie. One child, Nixon.

3, Rosa married McRae. One child, Wallace.

III., Dan and Katie (McCalla) Paden. Their descendants: I, Nixon married Mary McDougal. Children: Leroy, Sophia.

IV., Alexander and Sarah (McCalla) Peden. Their descendants:

1, William married Sallie Frierson. Children: Lizzie, Alice, Katie, Willie.

2, Ramsey married Mrs. Mitchell. Children: Mary, Lyman, Lizzie.

3, Mary married Rev. John H. Aughey. Children: Kate, John K., Gertrude.

4, Thomas married Sibbie Thompson. Children: Ward, Sallie, Charles, John.

V., Mary and George Tankersley. Their descendants:

1, William married a Mrs. Wise. Children; One, Emma.

2, Elizabeth married Ed. McGeehee. Children: George, Callie, Benjamin.

3, Perry married Miss Harrison. Children: Dick, Jack, Jim, Mary.

4, Margaret married a Campbell. Two children: Willie, Johnnie.

(Signed) Bettie Williams.

Chapter Sixteen - Elizabeth Gaston

Mother of no house, yet loved and reverenced by all of the houses of Peden; the guiding spirit of all. Youngest and fairest of the Peden sisters.

Born on Christmas Eve, 1750, in Ireland, she was, therefore, about eighteen years old at the time of emigration, and had been the wife of William Gaston nearly two years. He was many years her senior, the son of an exiled Huguenot, of the noble house of Orleans, which dates back to the ninth century. With this long and noble lineage behind him, he was content to follow the humble occupation of a silk weaver.

His father was an officer in the army of William of Orange, and fell in one of the battles of that leader in Ulster.

William Gaston is described as of tall, soldierly bearing, with the manner of "a courtier masquerading as a peasant." When the bugle blast of freedom sounded William Gaston donned the garb of the continental soldier, found his place in their ranks and fought bravely for the independence of these United States. Among all the shining names on the roll of Upper South Carolina's Revolutionary heroes, in rank and file, none are fairer than that of Gaston.

Such was the soldier husband of sweet Elizabeth Peden. He survived the war of 17761783 long enough to leave her comfortably placed among her people, and far above want. She was a woman nobly planned. "Divinely tall and most divinely fair." With sweet, winning ways, ready tact and boundless, loving sympathy, ever ready to lend a helping hand to her brothers and sisters, and their overflowing households. It seems strange that to women, in whom the instinct maternal is so strongly developed, that the crown of maternity is denied; Elizabeth Gaston realized this, yet it did not embitter her nature, she simply adopted the numerous crew. Her soft, warm hands welcomed the shivering morsels as they came into the world, with a soft, little chuckle she cuddled them into their first robes an4 for baptism, and sometimes, not often, bathed their tiny faces with hot tears, as she laid them in rude caskets for burial. These same hands arrayed the brides in their homespun linen bridal dresses, her china and silver decked all the wedding feasts.

When love affairs did not run smoothly it was to that quiet place, Aunt Elizabeth's, the troubled young hearts went for comfort and advice, which was never lacking. She smoothed the tangles away. It is recorded that she never broke a confidence however trivial it seemed. Many a simple trousseau did her skillful fingers evolve; many a household treasure found its way from her always well filled "kists" to humbler homes and young couples just "nesting." Hers was the authority on dress, manners, and etiquette, for her numerous nephews and nieces; the court of appeal for brothers and sisters. For some unaccountable reason her educational advantages had been far better than the others. It is presumed that she was teachable and her husband had lifted her to his own intellectual plane.

In the house of darkness, sickness and death, the beauty of her character glowed with peculiar luster. She was always first to respond to the call of sickness with her bag of "simples" culled from nature's stores. If the balances were for life she welcomed the patient back so gladly, preparing nourishing food and drinks no others knew their secret. If, on the other hand, death claimed the patient, her soft hands closed the weary eyes and folded the tired hands over the snowy glen shrouds that she alone knew how to fold so deftly. It is said that she shed no tears over the sainted dead; her faith was so bright and strong that death held no terrors for her; she ever looked beyond, cheering the bereft wonderfully by her cheerful views of the great transition.

Her memory is one of the sweetest of Peden traditions, and as far back as the race goes and down to this generation, there were, and are, stately Elizabeths, sweet Betties, dainty Bessies, and fair Lizzies to keep her "memory green."

Elizabeth (Peden) Gaston rests in the rock-walled church yard at Fairview, beside her noble husband, with only a simple stone to mark her resting place. Her old home, now in ruins, is in the hands of the stranger. Her rare and precious china and silver have, too, gone out of the Peden race, which is a source of keen regret as it passed by her will to her favorite niece, Mary Peden Stennis, from whom, she being childless, it passed to her favorite niece, Margaret Savage, who never married, and who in turn gave it to her favorite niece. Ana Savage, who died in young womanhood, leaving it to her brother's wife, a childless widow.

Chapter Seventeen - House of John

"His life was gentle and the elements
So mixed in him that nature might stand up
And say to the world, 'This was a man.' "

— Shakespere.

After years of searching, months of waiting, at the ninth hour as it were, the writer of this book found trace of the lost house of John, fourth son of John, the father. He was a gentle soul. No stone marks his resting place at Fairview, S. C, of which church he was the first elder. According to tradition his death broke the devoted band of brothers in 1810. His birth date is 1752. As a Revolutionary soldier his record stands high for courage and endurance. Never very strong physically, the hardships told on his health, and he tramped home with his brothers much broken in health, but not in spirit.

He was one of the three pioneer brothers to Fairview. Tradition says he was a skillful stone mason and the wonderful old chimneys of the first habitations yet standing attest that skill. The writer, as a child, has stood on the great square stone and drank from the rock-basin of the spring he kept with such care. She is not sure, but thinks that on its face was chiseled the initials and date, "J.P., 1785." This is a misty memory of 1861, so it not given as authentic. Most of these wonderful old springs are fallen into disuse long ago, as change of roadway and other conveniences caused abandonment of most of the old homesteads. There is also a memory of a stone-walled garden falling into decay where a dear old saint dreamed the sweet summer days away among the old time flowers, the red and white roses, the pinks, thyme, lavender and numerous other old favorites, beneath the wide spreading branches of a giant black walnut, or gnarled apple tree. Such is the picture of this old stead.

In the search for this lost house the writer has had many amusing conjectures. There has been great diversity of opinion, and some will be given to show the necessity of record keeping in families.

To begin, at Fairview there are no very early church records. Fire destroyed the home of Anthony Savage, the first clerk of the session, and with it the records. Afterwards, in 1815, he resumed writing a few from memory and the first trace is thus: "1815, April 4th. John Peden's family, with part of widow Peden's family, moved to Kentucky. Regularly dismissed. In October of the same year, widow Peden and rest of her family moved to Kentucky." This led the writer a wild goose chase all over Kentucky; letters and advertisements all in vain. The few responses received proved the writers as belonging to other houses. To whom the copied paragraphs refer the writer has not discovered to this day, and is now under the impression that the mistake is in the date. The family of John Peden did not leave for the West earlier than 1825, as the land transfers to Wilson Baker show.

One letter states very positively, "John Peden never married, but made his home among his brothers and sisters, mostly with Polly Alexander." The Alexanders did not corroborate this statement. Another, "John Peden married, but had no children." Still another, "Uncle John was father of two daughters, both of whom married out of the kin and went to Pickens, S.C. One was Mrs. Hamilton, the other married a Warnock." Neither the Hamilton family or Warnocks had ever heard of this, so no proofs. These are sufficient to show some of the difficulties the writer has encountred. So at the ninth hour comes the following from indisputable authority, one of his descendants, to the effect: John Peden married Elizabeth Ann Baker rather late in life, being a number of years her senior, she therefore survived him quite a number of years. Tradition states that she was a large, fair woman of boundless spirit and energy, industrious and persevering, a striking contrast to her rather quiet, easy going husband, who inherited the fervid faith of his father, dwelling much in the "border-land." Their children were: I., Cynthia; II., Melinda or "Linnie"; III., Amanda; IV., Rachel; V., Jane; VI.., John; VII., Samuel

I., Cynthia married her first cousin, William Peden (house of David), she therefore becomes identified with that house.

II, Melinda, or "Linnie," married her first cousin, Samuel Peden (house of David), and also is merged into that house. These two brothers, having married these two sisters, reduce considerably the size of the house of John.

III, Amanda married John Corley. Their children were: 1, Samuel; 2, John; 3, William; 4, Mary.

1, Samuel married two sisters named Walker, both bore him a goodly number of children. All trace lost.

2, John married ____ Payne, of Atlanta. There were only two children, but their names and whereabouts are unknown.

3, William was, married three times, but only had two children. All trace lost.

4, Mary married Ben Parr. Their children: Amanda, Lula, Sallie, William. These all married but the names are unknown, also their children.

IV., Rachel married David Wardlaw. Their children: Robert, Amanda, Julia, Laura, Emory, John, Paden, William. No further records.

V., Jane married ____ Lewis. No trace. They went westward after the civil war.

VI., John married twice; the first time Margaret Foster. Their children: 1, Robert; 2, Alice; 3, Ada; 4, Clifford; 5, John Sanford; 6, James; 7, Jemima; 8, Edward. The second time Elizabeth Samples. One child, Susan.

1, Robert married Cymantha ____. Children: 1, Maggie, who married Newton Cane. Their children: Robert, Ernest, Newton. 2, Claude; 3, Ethel; 4, Alice; 5, May.

2, Alice married Ralph McDunov. Children three, Oliver and two others names not known.

3, Ada married Dr. Augustus Lyons. Children three: Paden and names of other two not given.

4, Clifford married ____ Upshaw. Two children, names unknown.

5, John Sanford married Anna D. Hollingsworth. Their children are in Gadsden, Ala.; names: William Clifford, John Sanford, Jr., Joseph Perry, who died aged six years, Anna Josephine, Alice Maude.

6, James died during the civil war on the Confederate side in Virginia; unmarried.

7, Jemima married Gustave Gunter. Their children: 1, Lara; 2, Barton; 3, Robert; 4, Lizzie.

1, Lara Gunter married Thomas Rodgers. Two children.

2, Barton Gunter married Lou Powers. Number and names of children unknown.

3, Robert Gunter married Lizzie Webb. Number and names of children unknown.

4, Lizzie Gunter married Bascombe Ball. Two children.

5, Edward. No record.

9, Susan married Nat Sherman. Their children: 1, Mamie; 2, Minnie; 3, John; 4, Elijah; 5, Emma; 6, Rino.

1, Mamie Sherman married Forrest Crowley. No children.

2, Minnie Sherman married Ralph McDermot. Four children.

3, John Sherman married. Wife's name unknown. Two children: Frank, Eva.

4, Elijah Sherman married Adelaide Bellhouse. Their children: Lulu, who married Oliver Pharr; Clifford, who married Earle Saunders, two children; John, who is unmarried.

5, Emma Sherman married J. Fowler. Three children, names unknown.

6, Rino Sherman; unmarried.

VII., Samuel married a Massey; names and number of their children are unknown.

Chapter Eighteen - House of Samuel

"For doubtless unto him was given
A life that bears immortal fruit."

Samuel, the fifth son of the house of Peden, was born in Ireland in the year 1754. He was therefore one of the four younger sons who came with their parents to Spartanburg, S.C., and remained with them in their homes on the Tyger until the bugle blast of freedom called them forth to do or die for the independence of the land of their adoption. Samuel, like his brothers, was a brave soldier, a true patriot. At the close of the war he married Katherine, or as she was best known, Katie White. Her memory lingers yet around Fairview as a sweet incense, and her tomb is there while that of her husband is afar. He, like a true pioneer, took up the line of march westward along with his children, and, like a true American, sleeps far away from his fathers.

He left Fairview, S. C, in 1832, along with many of his kith and kin, and most of his own numerous family. Died December 26, 1835; aged eighty-one years.

Samuel Peden was one of the founders of Smyrna Presbyterian church, in Kemper County, Miss., and is buried in its church yard, his being the first grave dug in the virgin soil. There is a rock monument with a marble slab to his memory.

The children of Samuel Peden and Katie White: I., John or "Jackie"; II., William Thomas; III., James; IV., David S.; v., Sallie; VI., Dillie; VII., Ellen; VIII., Senie; IX., Penelope; X., Katie.

I., John or "Jackie" Married his first cousin, Elizabeth Peden (house of Thomas), grandparents of the writer, Mrs. Leanna Peden McNiell. Their children: 1, Thomas White; 2, Mintie; 3, Katie; 4, Givens; 5, Lawson Perry; 6, James; 7, Samuel Robertson; 8, Bettie; 9, John; 10, Andrew.

1, Thomas White. No record.

2, Mintie married a Davis. No record.

3, Katie married a Buchanan. No record.

4, Givens married. Wife's name not given. Their children: Laura Ann married J. D. Peden. No further record. Ruth Elizabeth married a Smith. No further record. Leanna married McNiell. No further record, save of one daughter, who married a first cousin named McNiell. The mother of one son, name not given.

Andrew Simpson died in 1860.

Mary L. married a McDougal. No further record.

John Jasper died in 1863; aged nineteen,

Sallie Wilson married a Phillips. No further record.

Aaron Ellis Samuel died in 1864; aged fourteen.

Givens. No record,

Margaret Jane also married a Phillips. No further record.

5, Lawson Perry. No record.

6, James. No record.

7, Samuel Robertson. No record.

8, Bettie died in childhood.

9, John. No record.

10, Andrew accidently shot himself and died; aged fourteen. John or "Jackie" Peden came to Kemper County, Miss., in the winter of 1836, from North Alabama. He lived to be eighty-four years old, and is buried in Smyrna church yard where his father Samuel lies.

II., William Thomas married his first cousin, Mary Peden (house of William). Their children:

1, Rebecca married a Dees. No record.

2, Katie married a Kavanagh. No record.

3, Alexander died at nineteen years,

4, Margaret Martin; unmarried,

5, Nancy; unmarried,

6, David W. No record.

7, Mary Jane; unmarried.

All of these have been dead many years.

Children of William Thomas Peden and his second wife, Mary ____:

8, Sallie Wilson Harrison married a Myatt.

9, Archie Mc. No record.

10, James Samuel married and moved to Texas.

11, Isabella Barbara married a Knox and moved to Texas. William Thomas lived to be very old, over ninety, and is buried with Samuel, his father, and the greater number of his own children in Smyrna church yard, Kemper County, Miss.

III., James, whose records were furnished by his grandson. Dr. W. F. Moore, will follow instead of precede the next brothers, so as to avoid breaking the narrative of Mrs. McNiell.

IV., David S. married his first cousin, Margaret (house of William). Their children: i. Porter. No record; 2, Isabella. No record; 3, Katherine. No record; 4, Rosa married Kenneth McRae; 5, Jennie married Daniel McRae. This family settled near Highlands, Tishomingo County, Miss., where their descendants are yet living.

For more than sixty-five years Smyrna church yard has been the burying place of the Pedens and many of their connection.

The Peden descendants in Mississippi alone would fill a large volume, therefore are too numerous to count or try to mention in fuller detail. It has been a notable fact, too, that the children of the seven brothers intermarried extensively.

The pioneer Pedens who settled in Kemper County, Miss., were: Samuel, with his sons John or "Jackie, William, Thomas and their families, also John, James and Alexander, sons of David, the seventh son of John; also Moses White, son of Thomas, the second son of John. All the wives of these Pedens, except those of James and Alexander, were first cousins of their husbands.

The Pedens who went to Mississippi settled in the following counties: Adams, Benton, Calhoun, Chickasaw, Choctaw, Covington, Hancock, Holmes, Jackson, Jasper, Lauderdale, Lowndes, Montgomery, Neshoba, Noxubee, Oktibbeha, Pontotoc, Tallahatchie, Tate, Tishomingo, Winston and probably others, are descendants of this remarkable couple of Scotch-Irish emigrants, John Peden and his wife Margaret McDill.

          (Signed)   Leanna McNiell.

 III., James married Frances Brockman, in Spartanburg County, S.C. After the birth of several children my grand parents (the above), removed to Alabama, thence to Mississippi, where he and grandmother died within eleven days of each other. She went first, he followed, as the doctor said, without organic disease, just heart-broken. They left the following children: 1, John M.; 2, Samuel H.; 3, Frank B.; 4, Clarinda; 5, Elizabeth; 6, Marinda; 7, Susan; 8, Frances. All of whom are dead except Frank B., who lives in Western Texas.

 1, John M. Paden died in Chickasaw County, Miss., near Sparta, leaving several children there. He married a Miss Bell.

 2, Samuel H. Paden died at Barrtown, Kansas, where his wife lives with several children and grandchildren.

 3, Frank B. Paden and family live in Western Texas. He has one daughter living in Mississippi, a Mrs. Caradine. His children were seven. Both Samuel H. and Frank B. were married twice.

 4, Clarinda Paden married Benj. Clark. Mother of twelve children. This Spartan dame gave the Confederate cause five noble sons; they laid their young lives on the altar of the lost cause. (The Peden historian has not the proud honor of inscribing their names on these pages, but they are enrolled on the heart of the South.) The other seven children are left in Chickasaw County, Miss., save one, Sarah, who married Louis Hooker and lives in Eastland County, Texas.

 5, Elizabeth Paden married John Dawson; both died in Choctaw County, Miss., leaving several children, two of whom live in Vanzant County, Texas.

 6, Marinda Paden married J. M. Moore, who was a native of Abbeville County, S. C, though they were married in Alabama. She was mother of thirteen children; ten are now living, three died young. The ten are in Texas, came in 1867. J. M. Moore died in 1880. Mother preceded him many years dying in 1861. The children: 1, J. P. Moore; 2, J. T. Moore;

 3, L. Moore, lives at Florence, Williamson County, Texas;

 4, Susan P. Moore married Morris; 5, S. F. Moore married Tomlinson; 6, H. A. Moore married Jackson, also live in Florence, Tex.; 7, Clarinda Moore married McVey, lives at Tayter or Taylor, Texas. 8, S. H. Moore and 9, M. M. Moore, who married Harrison, live at Seymour, Baylor County, Texas; while the writer, 10, W. F. Moore, lives in Mexia, Limestone County, Texas, The Moores all have children, save the writer.

 7, Susan Paden married Carroll Thompson; both died at Dodd City, Fannin County, Texas, where their children, number not known, now live.

8, Frances Paden married Dr. J. H. McLendon. Mother of six children, all of whom died in childhood, and their mother did not survive them long, so this entire family is lost to us.

Winston County, Miss., was largely populated by Padens, and their relatives. Rev. Mitchell Peden was their first pastor. The Texas Pedens-Padens are in almost every county of that immense State, but the largest number are grouped near the central part, in Hill, Kaufman and Limestone Counties. All are descended from the same source, preserve the same characteristics, plain, substantial citizens, true to their country and to themselves. None have amassed great wealth. What Irishman ever does? I never knew a bad drinker among the whole relationship; or office seekers, and very few ever held office. Grandfather's family were divided as to creed. John, Clarinda, Marinda and Susan were Missionary Baptists. Samuel, Frank and Frances were Campbellites, Elizabeth a Cumberland Presbyterian; while the originals were all strict Presbyterians, The grandchildren of James, son of Samuel, son of John, the father, numbered seventy-two, though many died young.

(Signed)   W. F. Moore.

V., Sallie married ____ Barnes; settled in Winston County, Miss.
VI., Dillie married ____ Adams; settled in Neshoba County, Miss.
VII., Ellen married ____ Trimm. No records,
VIII., Senie married ____ Trimm. No records.
IX., Penelope married ____ Lynn. No records.
X., Katie married her first cousin, John Morton (house of Jane); he died, she then married his half-brother, Samuel Morrow (house of Jane). No further record.

This closes the incomplete house of Samuel, whose records were furnished by two of his grandchildren, Mrs. Leanna Peden McNiell and Dr. W. F. Moore.

Chapter Nineteen - House of Alexander

"There are countless heroes who live and die,
   Of whom we have never heard,
For the great, big, brawling world goes by
   With hardly a look, or a word,
And one of the bravest, truest of all.
   Of whom the list can boast
Is the man who falls on duty's call.
   The man who dies at his post.
There are plenty to laud and to crown with bays.
   The hero who falls in the strife;
There are few who offer a word of praise,
   To the crownless hero of daily life,

Alexander, sixth son of John, the father, was born in Ireland, April, 1756, and was married to Rebecca Martin April 15, 1784. He was one of the four younger sons, and spent his long, quiet life, after the Revolutionary war, near Fairview, S. C, under the wide, spreading boughs of his immense black walnut tree, which he planted, reared and enjoyed for its "shade, fruit and dyestuff." The roots of this giant furnished the gavel used at the reunion of 1899. Of the immense clan of Peden only a few of his descendants now remain on "their native heath." This being one of the largest and strongest houses.

To Alexander Peden and Rebecca, his wife, were born eleven children. They were as follows: I., Robert; II., Margaret; III., John Thomas; IV., Nancy; V., Rebecca; VI., Mary; VII., Scipio; VIII., Janet; IX., Elizabeth Melissa (died young); X., Sarah; XI., Eliza Alston (died young).

I., Robert married his first cousin, Jane, a daughter of Thomas, one of the seven original brothers. Their children: I, Thomas Alexander, born Sept. 27, 1808; 2, Martin White, born Nov. 28, 1810; 3, Terethiel, born Oct. 13, 1812; 4, Andy Milton, born July 27, 1814; 5, John Simpson, born Oct. 12, 1816; 6, Elizabeth Ann, born Aug. 24, 1818; 7, James Scipio, born March 12, 1821; 8, Mary McDill, born June 29, 1823.

I, Thomas Alexander Peden married Jane Boyd. Their children were: 1, Mary; 2, Jane; 3, Robert; 4, James Boyd; 5, Margaret; 6, Sarah; 7, David; 8, Catherine; 9, John.

1, Mary married Hugh Woods. Her children were: Jane, John, James, Martin, Lucian. No record of their grandchildren.

2, Jane married David Barton. Only one child, Sarah, who married a Babb.

3, Robert never married.

4, James Boyd never married.

5, Margaret married Washington Thomason. One child, Alice, who married a Babb. Her second husband is Neal Putnam. Their children are five: James R., John W., Sallie K., Thomas Alexander, Mary.

6, Sarah married Barnett Babb. No record of children's names.

7, David married twice; first Elizabeth Boyd. One child, J. Robert, who married Norris. They have no children. Name of the second wife and her children unknown.

8, Catherine was the first wife of Barnett Babb who, after her death, married her sister, Sarah.

9, John married Elizabeth Barton. Their children are: Nancy, Mary, Myra or Mysie, Janet, William, Rosa, Ellen, Earl Grace.

2, Martin White Peden married Eleanor Baker, who was of the house of David. In this marriage there is a union of three houses, Thomas, Alexander and David. Their children were: 1, Franklin; 2, Jane; 3, J. Waddie T.; 4, Robert; 5, John; 6, Elizabeth; 7, Andrew; 8, Mollie; 9, David; 10, William; II, Thomas.

1, Franklin laid his life a brave sacrifice on the altar of the Confederacy. He was not married.

2, Jane was twice married; first to Silas Lipsy, second to Shelton Halsell. She was the mother of five children names not given.

3, J. Waddie T. twice married; first to Jane Mooney of the house of Thomas. Her children were: 1, Henry; 2, Dora; 3, David, 1, Henry married Margaret Cook. Their children: Mabel, Lorena, Sunie. Second to Susan Griffin. No children.

4, Robert; unmarried.

5, John was twice married; first to Ellen Marion; second to Rosa Marion, No children.

6, Elizabeth married S. L. Wilson. Their children are ten in number; names not given.

7, Andrew married Katie McJunkin. Seven children; names not given.

8, Mollie married Robert Marion. No children.

9, David married Jennie Mosely. Two children; names not given.

10, William; unmarried.

11, Thomas twice married; first Sophronia Calloway;, second Mary Boyd.

The men of this family were splendid soldiers in the civil war wearing the gray, while the women were devoted to the lost cause.

3, Terethiel; died young.

4, Andrew Milton Peden married Elizabeth Fowler, of the house of Thomas. They were the parents of twelve children: I, Alexander; 2, Nancy; 3, Robert; 4, James M.; 5, Jane; 6, Mary Ann; 7, Matilda; 8, G. Beauregard; 9, Susan; 10, 11, 12 died in infancy.

1, Alexander was a brave member of Hampton Legion, Company E., and was killed in battle early in the civil war.

2, Nancy died.

3, Robert married Ann Terry. Their children were six:

1, Charles T.; 2, Andrew (died); 3, Belle; 4, John; 5, Lou; the sixth died an infant, 1, Charles T. married Alice Delong.

2, Belle married Charles Garraux. Mother of four children: Cora, Annie, Belle, baby's name unknown. 4, John, unmarried; 5, Lou married ____ Bigbee and lives in Texas.

4, James M. married Caroline Babb. Their children are four: 1, Minnie; 2, Emma; 3, Marion; 4, Calvin, 1, Minnie married Wm. Thomason. Two children, names not given. 2, Emma married Sam Turner. Two children, names unknown.

5, Jane went to Texas and married there. Names of her husband and children unknown.

6, Mary Ann married Andrew Chapman. Names and number of children unknown; homes in Georgia.

7, Matilda M. married W. H. L. Thompson. Their children: R. V., A. B., M. S., B. B., L. M., S. L., N. E.

8, Beauregard went to Alabama; married there; name of wife and number of children unknown.

9, Susan married ____ Dempsey. Mother of three children, then died; names and whereabouts of children unknown.

5, John Simpson Peden married his first cousin, Margaret M. Peden, daughter of John Thomas, brother of Robert, both sons of Alexander. Their children were: 1, Thomas; 2, Robert; 3, Mary; 4, David M.

John Simpson Peden met his death at the hands of his neighbor, Enoch Massey, over a land boundary dispute,

1, Thomas married Harriet Harrison and was killed in battle during the civil war, being a member of the famous Hampton Legion; leaving only one child, Corrie, the wife of Wm. P. Anderson. She is the mother of two noble young sons. Frank P., Wm. P., Jr.

2, Robert married Elizabeth Harrison. These two wives were sisters. Their children are William, Thomas, Elizabeth. The two youngest are married.

3, Mary has never married.

4, David M. married M. J. Stoddard, Their children are: Leila, W. L., Essie, Maggie, Stacie. Robert, Mary.

Some years after the tragic end of her husband, the wife of John Simpson Peden married Miles Garret. Two children: Callie, Davis, these are also recorded in the mother's line, that of John Thomas Peden.

6, Elizabeth Ann married Moses T. Fowler and their children, grandchildren and great-grandchildren are recorded in the house of Thomas, to which Moses T. Fowler belonged in right of his mother, Nancy Peden, also by courtesy of seniority, this being one of the families of the "distaff of spindle side," meaning descent through the female line.

7, James Scipio and Elizabeth Stenhouse were married Nov. 30, 1854. Children: 1, Adam Stenhouse, born June 20, 1856; 2, John Stewart, born June 20, 1859; 3, Rixie, born Nov. 18, 1861; 4, Janet, born April 11, 1864.

1, Adam S. Peden married Nannie Stewart, daughter of Rev. C. B. Stewart, Nov, 13, 1883. Children: Bessie Belle, born Feb. 14, 1885; Annie Stewart, born Sept. 10, 1886; James Clark, born Oct. 20, 1889.

2, John Stewart and Mamie (Mears) Wright were married Oct. 5, 1892. Children: Samuel, born Aug. 14, 1893; Robert Lee, born Aug. 28, 1894; Henry Burwell, born July 12, 1897; Lila and Lizzie, born March 26, 1899.

3, Rixie and W. Stewart Peden were married Dec. 21, 1882. Their children are recorded in the line of John Thomas Peden, from whom W. Stewart Peden descends (same house).

4, Janet E. married Wm. M. Stenhouse Jan. 27, 1897. They have one child, Margaret Elizabeth, born June 27, 1899; the youngest guest at the Peden reunion during August, 1899.

James Scipio Peden gave his life for the Confederate cause, dying nobly on the field of battle, 1864.

8, Mary McDill Peden married David Boyd. Children: 1, Jane Ann; 2, Elizabeth Curtis; 3, James Scipio; 4, Salhe Simpson; 5, Mary McDill; 6, Robert Peden; 7, Louisa Tarethiel; 8, Catherine Ehender; 9, Nannie Alethia.

I, Jane Ann Boyd married George F. Terry. Lives at Lickville, S.C., Children: 1, Mollie Elizabeth; 2, Nannie Alethia; 3, Sallie Jane; 4, Cannie Louisa; 5, Leila Boyd; 6, Mettie Eugenia; 7, Josie Stella, 1, Mollie E. Terry married Thomas R.

Goldsmith. Lives at Cedrus, S.C. Children: Jane Hellen, Sarah Woodside, Thomas George, James Edwin. 2, Nannie A, Terry married John A. Norris. Lives at Woodville, S.C. Children: Cleo, Jessie, Walter, Frank, Annie C. 3, Cannie L. Terry married Robert L. Simpson. Lives at Piedmont, S.C.

2, Elizabeth Curtis married John H. Boyd. Lives at Grandview, Tex. Children: 1, Lula; 2, Kate; 3, Johnie; 4, Allen; 5, Jo Stella; 6, Curtis; 7, Moss, 1, Lula Boyd married Prof. Garrison. Lives in Grandview, Tex. Children: Zollie. 2, Kate Boyd married a Lovelady. Lives in Cleburne, Tex. 4, Allen Boyd married; names unknown; one child. Live in Cleburne, Tex.

3, James Scipio Boyd married Julia Campbell. Lives in Jonah, Tex. Children: 1, Walter Edgbert; 2, Annie; 3, Jennie Lou. 1, Walter E. Boyd married Lillie Bowers. Lives in Jonah, Tex. 3, Jennie Lou Boyd married Burt C. King. Lives in Jonah, Tex.

4, Sallie Simpson Boyd married John Stewart. Lived in Texas; now dead. Children: Ada, May, Dee. All three are married and have homes in Texas.

5, Mary McDill Boyd married Wm. Terry. One child: 1, Lou Ella. At the death of Wm. Terry she married James Pullin. Lives in Bee County, Tex. Have eight children, names unknown, 1, Lou Ella Terry, daughter of above married Wm. Keese. Lives in Lyon, Tex. Children: Bertha, Arthur, David, Lommie Lee and Leila Lou (twins).

6, Robert Peden Boyd married Addie Campbell. Lives in Towenville, Tex. Children: Eddie, Dee, Edgar, Alice.

7, Louisa Tarathiel Boyd married Wm. Wylie. Lives in Auburn, Tex. Children: 1. Lola; 2, Mamie; 3, Johnny; 4, Charles, 1, Lola Wylie married Thomas Nation; at his death married ____ Crowley. Has one child; name unknown. 2, Mamie Wylie married Prof. Holland. Lives at Ozra, Tex. Children: Lucile, T. Y. 3, Johnnie Wylie married E. B. McClelland. Lives at Grandview, Tex.

9, Nannie A. Boyd married Charles Ingle.

II., Margaret married her first cousin, Moses White Peden, her records are found in the house of Thomas. She was the mother of eleven children, of whom traces have been found, save of Mary Ann, who married James Thompson (house of Mary).

IV., Nancy married her first cousin, John Peden, eldest son of David, therefore her records are found in the house of David. She was the mother of eight children.

In these sisters the pioneer spirit was dominant. They went with their families first to Georgia, later to Mississippi, helping to establish the County of Gwinnett, and Fairview Presbyterian church, in the same county, along with the Alexanders and a large number of other Pedens. Later they moved to Mississippi, establishing the County of Kemper, and founding the Presbyterian church of Smyrna, where the burdens of this life were lifted and they laid down to sleep, far from the tombs of their own parents. Tradition says they were very beautiful women, of the rich brunette order, and devotedly attached to each other. "In life inseparable, in death they were not long separated, having attained to a great age."

III., John Thomas Peden married his first cousin, Elizabeth Martin. Their children were ten: 1, Margaret M.: 2, Rebecca; 3, Mary T.; 4, Jane E.; 5, David Martin; 6, Nancy T.; 7, Alexander J.; 8, Robert N.; 9, Sarah F., 10, Martha C.

1, Margaret M. married her first cousin, John Simpson Peden, same house; recorded in line of Robert (house of Alexander).

2, Rebecca married twice; first, a cousin, R. Montgomery Morton (house of Jane). Their children were: James, Elizabeth. No trace save they went West. Her second husband was James Thompson, another cousin, of the house of Mary. Their children are: Alexander, John Thomas, Joseph, Mary, David, Jefferson. These all moved to Alabama.

3, Mary T. married Thomas Austin. Their children: Jane, John Thomas, James, Ellen. No records, save of Ellen, who married H. F. Whiten. Their children: Alvin C, Cora, Nannie. Her second husband was Beverly Garrett. Their children: Linnie, Callie, Eliza, Beverly, Jr. No further record.

4, Jane E. married James McDowell. Their children: 1, Mary; 2, T. Whitner; 3, Callie; 4, Phrona; 5, Reed; 6, Ella; 7, Wister. 1, Mary married J. M. Richardson. Their children: T. W., Furman, Pearl, Carrie. 2, T. Whitner married Jane Harrison. Their children: John L., James S., Corrie E., Laura E., Thomas S. His second wife was Elizabeth E. Garrett. No children. John L. married Gertrude Babb. One child, Frank H. 3, Callie married M. P. Nash. Their children: L. B., N. J., S. R., Essie, E. M. 4, Phrona also married a Richardson. Their children: James, Walter, Maggie, Manie. 5, Reed married an Armstrong. No further record. 6, Ella married ____ Armstrong. Their children: Jane, Ernest, Charles, John. 7, Wister married Eugenia Wasson. Their children: Eva, Jennie, Peden, Minnie, Hettie.

5, David Martin Peden of sainted memory, a man of sterling worth, with few peers in his generation. Of him it might be truly said, as of Enoch of old, "he walked with God." The briefest acquaintance with him betrayed the fact that he lived in close communion with his Saviour.

He was prosperous in the goods of this world above the average of his race, and while his fervid piety was of the same type of his forefathers, the outside world knew little of him or his worth. This noble man, who would have died for a principle, was a quiet forceful character. A brave Confederate soldier even to the end of the struggle in 1865.

He married Caroline Harrison who, with four children, survive him. The children: 1, John Thomas; 2, Laura E.; 3, W. Stewart; 4, Sue. John Thomas — "Big Tom" — is large of physique but larger of heart, a worthy son of his good father. He married Mary Dorroh. Their children: David Dorroh, Charles Lindsay, Carrie Sue, Samuel L., Thomas Eugene, Lucy Allen. 2, Laura E. married James L West. Their children: Charles D., Casper S., Ethel, Eleanor Morris, Annie May, Peden. 3, W. Stewart married his cousin, Rixie Peden (same house). Their children: Fred S., Nettie, Laura Belle, David M. 4, Sue P. married Jones R. West. Their children: Geneva, Eleanor, Mabel, Robbie Jones, Wm. David Peden.

6, Nancy L. married John S. Hammond. Their children: 1, Tocoa; 2, T. Herbert; 3, Adelia; 4, Mary T.; 5, Samuel G. I, Tocoa married J. J. Vernon. No children. 2, T. Herbert married. Wife's name unknown. Their children: A. P., Ethel P., Leila M., Nannie E., Ernestine, Edna Louise. Mary Ella, John H., Marjie Belle, Marion F., Thomas Alexander. 3, Adalia; unmarried. 4, Mary T. married F. M. Hardin. Their children: Mary T., Frank H. 5, Samuel G. married Minnie E. Oeland. Their children: J. Oeland, Edmund B., Samuel R., Margaret E., S. G.

7, Alexander J. died young of fever.

8, Robert N. died at the same time of fever.

9, Sarah Frances married Marion West. Their children: Mary, Robert, Sarah.

10, Martha C. married T. McDuffey Templeton, who was also a noble sacrifice to the lost cause. One child, a son,

Laurence Hayne Templeton, who married Mary J. ____.

Their children: Lutie McD., Lula M., James H., David Peden, Corrie E.

The family of John Thomas Peden furnished many a brave soldier to the Confederate cause and gave a number of young lives in the service of the South.

V., Rebecca Peden married John Stenhouse. Their children: 1, Jane; 2, Rachel; 3, Alexander; 4, Adam; 5, Rebecca; 6, Mary.

I, Jane married James Harrison. Parents of eight children: Rebecca, Mary, Sarah Ann; Rachel, Margaret, Virginia, William, Turner. This entire family moved to Kemper County, Miss., which was settled almost entirely by Pedens and their branches of other names, and as frequent intermarriages have taken place the names of Stenhouse and Harrison will occur among other lines of this immense house.

2, Rachel married James Anderson. Their children: 1, John (died); 2, Stewart (died); 3, Lou; 4, Sallie; 5, 6, Calvin and Pinkney (twins); 7, Anna; 8, Laurens; 9, 10, twins who died unmarried. 3, Lou Anderson married J. Wister Stewart and left three children: Leila, Catherine, Anderson. 4, Sallie Anderson married Lawrence Garrett and left two sons: Talmadge, Joe Hitch. 5, Calvin Anderson married Hettie Sprouse. No children. 6, Pinkney Anderson died unmarried. 7, Anna Anderson married Charles Smith, Died leaving no children. 8, Laurens Anderson moved to Texas, married and has four children: Ora B., Marion C, Lang, Forest.

3, Alexander Stenhouse married Virginia Knox and moved to Mississippi. No further trace.

4, Adam Stenhouse also married in Mississippi (Kemper County). No trace.

5, Rebecca Stenhouse married J. T. Paden (house unknown). Moved to Kemper County, Miss. No trace.

6, Mary Stenhouse married Samuel McKittrick. Their children: 1, John; 2, Addie; 3, Mattie; 4, S. Turner; 5, Jefferson D. Three died in infancy (unnamed), 1, John McKittrick married Mollie Sprouse. Seven children: Pallie, Samuel, Nicholls, J. H., Mary, Lake; last child's name not given. 2, Addie McKittrick married John Simpson. No children. 3, Mattie McKittrick married

Warren Sprouse. Three children: Carrie, Annie, William. 4, S. Turner McKittrick married Tempie Scott. Four children: Fred Stenhouse, Mary, Samuel, Sue Turner. 5, Jefferson D. McKittrick married Nannie Thackston. No children.

VI., Mary married her first cousin, William Thomas Peden (of the house of Samuel). Their records are found in that house.

VII., Scipio Peden, third son of Alexander and Rebecca Peden. Born Feb. 9, 1799. Married his cousin, Martha McVey, 1819. Only one child, John McVey. They settled about two miles south of Cedar Falls, on the east bank of Reedy River, and spent their lives on this farm. Scipio died 1867. His wife, Martha, died (at the home of her son) in 1874.

John McVey, son of Scipio and Martha Peden. Born July 27, 1821. Married Miss Nancy Eliza Smith, 1856. They settled one half mile west of Fairview Presbyterian church, on the Fork Shoals road, and reared the following family: 1, Martha Eugenia; 2, Mary Theresa; 3, John Elliott; 4, Irene; 5, Archie Lee; 6, James Walter; 7, Oscar McVey; 8, May Eliza.

1, Martha Eugenia married Dr. H.B., son of Rev. C.B. Stewart, March 4, 1880. Is living three miles south of Fairview church and has the following heirs: Frennie Fair, Bessie Britt, Allie Amanda (dead), Clifford Calhoun, Mack M., Hoke Harry Howe, Rosa Ross, Calvin Boardman.

2, Mary Theresa married Rev. D. S., son of Mr. G. B. Thomason, Dec. 12, 1878. Is living one mile from Fairview church, on Fork Shoals road and has the following heirs: Clarence Gideon, Daisy, Samuel.

3, John Elliott married Nana Richardson in August, 1886. Is living near Piedmont, S.C. Heirs: Blanche, Mary.

4, Archie Lee married Janie Willis March 5, 1887. Is living on McKittrick Bridge Road, about two miles southwest of Fairview church, and has the following heirs: Earle, Floree, Harry Lee.

J. McPeden died July 26, 1891. He was a member of Fairview church from early manhood. Served through the whole of the Confederate war. Come home foot-sore and hungry and lived a quiet life on the farm until the end.

(Signed)   H. B. Stewart.
Historian for line of VII., Scipio Peden.

VIII., Janet Peden married her first cousin, James Martin. Their children: 1, Rebecca; 2, David; 3, Alexander; 4, Serena; 5, James, 1, Rebecca married Franklin Baker, her cousin, of the house of David. They moved to Chickasaw County, Miss. No further records, but they have kept up the time honored custom of intermarriage, so they will be found among the branches of the Peden tree. 2, David married ____ Marion, of Chickasaw County, Miss. 3, Alexander went to Mississippi but no record of wife or children. 4, Serena married ____ Wilson, also of Chickasaw County, Miss. No trace or record. 5, James found a home with his family in Chickasaw County, Miss. This county too was colonized by Peden branches.

IX., Sarah married William Harrison. Mother of two sons. 1, John A.; 2, W. Thomas W. 1, John A. never married but died for the Confederacy. 2, W. Thomas W. married Nannie E. Pegg. Their children: 1, Sallie, who died young. 2, Hollie married George Smithson. Mother of two children: Louis, Pearl. 3, Thomas Samuel married Nannie E. Pool. Their children: Miriam, Albert, Iris. 4, Thomas; 5, Elizabeth; 6, Ruth; 7, William Henry; 8, Margaret; 9, John Alexander; 10, Evelyn; aged nine.

X., Elizabeth Melissa died very young.

XI., Eliza Alston died also in early womanhood The Peden historian hopes no blame will be attached to her for the apparent smallness of this, one of the largest houses. It would seem the women were specially attractive to their cousins of the other houses, as that of Thomas absorbs Margaret, that of David absorbs Nancy, that of Samuel absorbs Mary, all three of whom had large families. Of the other sisters, Rebecca (Stenhouse or Stennis), Janet (Martin), impossible to obtain full records. There were only three sons, and on them depends the representation.

As a fitting close to this house is added the following from the tomb of its father:

    Sacred to the Memory of Mr. Alexander Peden.

    Born April, 1756 and died 21st January, 1841.

Mr. Peden was a soldier in the Revolutionary war and for 53 years an inhabitant of Greenville District, and a member of the Presbyterian church at Fairview.

    As a Patriot Beloved;

    As a Citizen Esteemed;

    And as a Member of the Church Exemplary.

Like a shock of corn fully ripe, he was gathered to sleep with his fathers in the dust. His name will ever be dear to and his epitaph read with the deepest emotions of regard by a large circle of friends and relatives.

"The memory of the just is blessed
But the name of the wicked shall rot."

Chapter Twenty - House of David

David, seventh son and youngest child of John and Margaret McDill Peden, was born in Ireland, November 1, 1760. He was therefore only a few weeks old when King George H. died and his weak, tyrannical son, George HI. reigned in his stead.

Born in the midst of troublous times, yet none the less welcomed into that already overflowing household. His mother was already grandmother to a host of small Alexanders, Mortons and Pedens when he arrived, and as she merrily said afterwards, "Yes, Davie came when my nose and chin 'thritened ither,'" referring to her age and loss of teeth.

David was about ten years of age when the long voyage across the Atlantic took place. He remembered its perils, its few pleasures, its incidents and talked of them freely, but of his Irish home he never spoke, in deference to his father's wishes, or rather his commands.

After serving faithfully through the entire period of the war for American Independence, 1776-1783, entering the army at the age of sixteen, under protest of both parents and all his brothers, he learned to be a miller with Robert Goodgion. Then receiving a grant to lands in the newly acquired territory, now Greenville County, S.C. took possession and founded his house. The grant referred to (signed by Govenor Pinckney) is in the posesion of his lineal descendant, Capt. D.D. Peden, and shows his holding to have been between 900 and 1,000 acres. The old boundary lines have been furnished the writer as follows:

"1st corner a little east of Raeburn creek, just below and including the old mill site, running due north thence to 2nd corner, in what is now known as the M.T. Fowler place, running thence west across Raeburn creek to 3rd corner, of the once Mooney place, now that of D.M. Peden; thence south to the 4th corner, on the old Ramsay, now Wm. Thomason place; thence back to the old mill, now proprety of Hon. J.R. Harrison, forming almost a perfect square. This tract, with the exception of the old homestead, number acres not known, and belonging to Mr. L. Brownlee, and five acres owned by Dr. G.W. Wasson, is still in the possession of the Peden descendants, but not those of David Peden."

As his children grew up and married he gave them off a certain number of acres each, which in time they disposed of and migrated West, except Thomas, the fifth son, and Eleanor, the youngest daughter, who married James Dunbar. David Peden died in October, 1823, leaving the three children of his last wife minors; they chose James Dunbar as their guardian. He bought the old stead for his wife, Eleanor, and in time the shares of her two brothers, whom he reared to manhood. The old home place of David Peden has passed through the following ownerships since 1823: first James Dunbar, who sold it to his son-in-law, Dr. J.W. Hewell, in 1862-1863, he sold it to ____ Marchant in 1865, who in turn sold it to Josiah Wasson, date unknown, and a number of years ago, possibly ten or fifteen, it became the property of its present owner.

Of the great host of David Peden's descendants there are now in South Carolina only fourteen souls, and none of them own a foothold of the old homestead.

David Peden married first Eleanor Goodgion, a daughter or sister of that brave soldier and noted Whig, Capt. Robert Goodgion. Their children were: 1, Margaret, born Feb. 15, 1787; II., John, born Sept. 3, 1788; III., Robert, born July 15, 1790; IV., James, born Jan. 17, 1792; V., Penelope, born Nov. 29, 1793; VI., William, born April 3, 1795; VII., Thomas, born Feb. 11, 1799; VIII., Rebecca, born March 15, 1800; IX., Samuel, born Oct. 15, 1802; X., Alexander, born Sept. 12, 1804. These compose the elder branch, or line of the house of David.

In 1806 or 1807 he married Margaret Hughes, daughter of Thomas and Annie Hughes, and granddaughter of Samuel Miller, all of patriotic Whig record in Upper South Carolina. Their children were: XI., Eleanor Goodgion, born June 16, 1809; XII., Andrew Gilliland, born Oct. 28, 181 1; XIII., David Hamilton, born Aug. 12, 1813; XIV., Dan Morgan, born , 1815. The last lived only a few months. These comprise the younger branch.

I., Margaret married her second cousin, James Alexander, son of Maj. John Alexander, according to the Alexander records, into which house, that of Mary, she becomes merged. The meager records found of her and her children are included in that house, for according to good old Scottish usage and custom, when "a. woman by marriage and change of name, lost her identity with her father's house, she ceased to be recognized as one of them;" moreover the children rightfully belong to the name and lineage of the father.

II., John, first son and second child of David and Eleanor Goodgion Peden, was born at the old home, Fairview, S.C. Married his first cousin, Nancy Peden, second daughter of the house of Alexander. They moved from Fairview, Greenville County, S.C., to Fairview, Gwinnett County, Ga., in 1828; thence to Kemper County, Miss., 1845, where he died at the ripe old age of fourscore and nine. Their children were: 1, Eleanor, Nov. 26, 1812; 2, Rebecca, March 23, 1815; 3, Margaret, Oct. 7, 1816; 4, David (historian of this line), April 3, 1820; 5, Mary, July 14, 1823; 6, Sarah, May 18, 1826; 7, Eliza, Dec. 26, 1829; 8, Nancy Aug. 18, 1833.

1, Eleanor married W.P. Dunbar. Only one child, a son named James, who lives at Ennis, Miss., but made no response to numerous inquiries.

2, Rebecca Peden married J.F. Cousar. They are the parents of: 1, Martha Cousar, Jan. 5, 1837; 2, David Cousar, Oct. 26, 1840; 3, John Cousar, July 9, 1845; 4, Nancy Cousar, May 5, 1848; 5, Thomas Cousar, Feb. 20, 1854; 6, Maggie Cousar, Nov. 28, 1857.

I, Martha Cousar married J.W. Mooney. Have two children: Olivia Mooney, July 9, 1859. Married B. C. Margrave.

They are parents of seven children. Alice Mooney, May 17, 1861. Married E.L. Brady. They have four children.

2, David Cousar married M.M. Rea. Six children.

3, John Cousar married Mary Arnold. Ten children.

4, Nancy died unmarried.

5, Thomas married Mollie Carter. Five children.

6, Maggie married W.M. Stout. Five sons.

All of John Peden's daughters are gone, only his son, David, is left; they rest in Mississippi, except Rebecca (Peden) Cousar and Nancy (Peden) Peden, they sleep in Parker County, Texas, near Knob.

3, Margaret, born Oct. 7, 1816; died 1827.

4, David, the only son, married his first cousin. Margaret Eveline Peden, daughter of James, brother of John (same house). They are childless and are the honored historians of of their families, John and James, through the courtesy of their niece, Harriet Eveline Jarvis, who has done their writing, and who is making the last stages of their long pilgrimage happy in her warm, loving heart and home.

5, Mary born July 14, 1823; died 1827.

6, Sarah, born May 18, 1826. Married W. P. Knox. One child, a son, Sarah, died April 31, 1849.

7, Eliza, born Dec. 26, 1829; died 1865.

8, Nancy, born Aug. 18, 1833. Married David T, Peden, first cousin, son of Alexander (same house). Nine or ten children who are in Parker County, Texas,

III., Robert, second son of this house, was born at Fairview, S.C. Married Mary, or Polly, Miller, of Spartanburg County, S.C., in 1813; her birth date being Jan. 15, 1795. After the birth of two children, sons, they turned their faces westward towards the newly opened lands of Cherokee, in North Alabama. Their children were: 1, Robert Miller, born Oct. 23, 1814; died in 1859 or 1860. 2, James Alexander, born Dec. 3, 1816; lost in California. 3, Jane Dodds, born Nov. 15, 1819; died Sept. 17, 1878. 4, John P., born May 8, 1822. Killed in the Confederate cause during a skirmish near home, 1861 or 1862. 5, David R., born April 13, 1825; died Jan, 29, 1849. 6, Nancy K., born Feb. 25, 1828. Lost in Missouri. 7. William T., born Jan. 15, 1831; died May 3, 1856. 8, IVrary E., born May 7, 1837; died Oct. 7, 1840. 9, Joseph F., born Aug. 13, 1840. Lost in Missouri.

W. P. Black's very interesting narrative is inserted here. He is a grandson.

My mother, Jane Dodds Peden's people, are scattered from South Carolina to California. Most of them are lost to us, as far as knowing their locations exactly. My mother was a daughter of Robert and Mary Peden, I never saw but two of her family, my uncles, James and David. My mother often had letters from them up to the civil war, but after that time very seldom.

She loved her family dearly, would often tell me of their pleasant associations and fun making expeditions around Spartanburg, and later in Cherokee County, Alabama. At the latter home she left them. Came on a visit to Kentucky to her mother's brother, William Miller, in 1838; she then met my father, James Shaw Black, and they were married in this neighborhood in the early part of 1839. They visited her family in Alabama in 1840. She never saw any of them afterward, except the two brothers before mentioned,

I was in Alabama in 1870 and met some of her people; among them one very old man, James Alexander, who was related but I do not know how. Their county seat then was at Center (since that time Cherokee County has been divided into several counties). Two of my mother's brothers remained in Cherokee County until they died. The oldest, Robert Miller Peden, in 1859 or 1860; left a wife, but no children. The other, John P. Peden, was killed in the Southern army, not far from home in 1861 or 1862. He left a family of children living near the Georgia line. Uncle David died here (Crider, Ken.,) in 1849, soon after his return from the Mexican war. Uncle James visited my mother during 1849-1850, He had been living in Mississippi prior to that time for some years, but had determined to go to California, and made a farewell visit before starting. He wrote back several times from Sonoma Valley, Cal. We never heard from him after the civil war.

My grandfather, Robert Peden, removed from North Alabama to Missouri; date lost, so do not know whether before or after grandmother's death, which occurred in 1853, but am inclined to think she died in Missouri. He married again in that State. Was quite old when he died, ninety or ninety-one years of age, making death date about 1880 or 1881.

My aunt, Nancy K. Peden, married a Mr. Pilant, living near Independence, Missouri, when last heard from. My mother's youngest brother, Joseph F. Peden, lived at Ozark, Mo., at last hearing. Records sent are copied from my mother's Bible.

Jane Dodds Peden, eldest daughter and third child of Robert and Mary Miller Peden, married James Shaw Black in 1839. Mother of two sons: David Alexander, born Jan., 1840, died July, 1857. W.P., born July 16, 1843, on the old Kentucky homestead, where he now lives, and hopes to die, Crider, Ken. Was first married to Evaline Brelsford. After almost a brief, happy year she died in June, 1865. In Feb., 1867, was again married to Mary Wilson, who died Sept., 1897, leaving two children: Jane Ella, Thomas W. Both at home, unmarried, and with their father constitute the "Kentucky trio."

(Signed)   W. P. Black.

IV., James, third son of this house, was born at the old home, Fairview, S.C. Served as a soldier in three wars, Creel: and Seminole, "1812," and Texan Independence, 1845-1846. He married Mary Baker, noted for her devoted piety. She was born Feb. 22, 1792. Their children, seven in number, went with their parents to Kemper County, Miss., being among the pioneer Pedens of that State, also founders of Smyrna Presbyterian church. James Peden was a successful farmer, and blacksmith by trade; after a long useful life died and is buried at Smyrna church, Kemper County, Miss.

Their children are in the States of Mississippi and Texas useful and important citizens. They are as follows: 1, Eleanor Olivia, Jan. 13, 1819; 2, Margaret Evehne, Nov. 18, 1820; 3, John Tillinghast, Oct. 22, 1822; 4, James Dunbar, June 25, 1825; 5, Mary Ann, Nov. 13, 1827; 6, Andrew Hugh Hamilton, April 4, 1831; 7, William M., Aug. 22, 1834.

1, Eleanor Olivia (Peden) married her brother-in-law, Thomas Pearson. Mother of two children: Frank, 1858; Mary Ann, 1860. They moved to Parker County, Texas, in 1860 and both died in 1899.

2, Margaret Eveline (Peden) married her first cousin, David Peden, only son of John, the eldest son of this house, of which he is their acknowledged historian. They were married Sept. 18, 1843.

3, John Tillinghast Peden married Rebecca Stennis (house of Alexander). They were parents of: Mary Ann, 1844; Margaret Eveline, 1848. Both sisters married brothers named Lovelady, and went to Texas. James Alexander,

1846. married Winnie Allen. Name of fourth child not on the record. John Tillinghast Peden died, 1856, in the prime of life.

4, James Dunbar Peden married his kinswoman Laura Ann Peden, of the house of Samuel. She became the mother of: 1, John Richmond Peden; 2, Harriet Eveline; 3, James Thomas; 4, Martha Elizabeth; 5, Alary Rebecca; name of the other child not on record. Laura Ann (Peden) Peden died in 1862.

In 1865 James Dunbar Peden was married to Matilda Fowler, originally Matilda Peden, a kinswoman, being a widow with two children. She became mother of the following children: 7, Matilda Josephine, 1866; 8, George Madison, 1869, 9, Samuel Wilson, 1872; 10, Annie Laura, 1874; 11, Flugh Hamilton, 1878; making eleven children in this household.

I, John Richmond Peden, 1850, and his wife, Matilda Jarvis, Their twelve children: Martha Ann, 1875; James Jarvis, 1876; Indiana Florence, 1878; Mabel Clare, 1879; Ada Pearl, 1881; William Kertis, 1883; John Thomas, 1885; Bonnie Ruth, 1887; Battie Dot, 1889; Matilda Inez, 1891; Seth, 1893; Clifton Carlyle, 1895.

2, Harriet Eveline (Peden) wife of E. T. Jarvis, writer for historian this line, was born 1855; married 1874. Their children are seven: Laura Eugenia, 1875; Sarah Elizabeth, 1878; William David, 1880; Ida Josephine, 1883; Martha Ann, 1886; Mary Leona, 1888; Kate Eveline, 1891. The three grandchildren of this couple, being in the seventh generation from John, the father of the house of Peden, are those of their daughter Sarah Elizabeth (Jarvis) wife of John T. Peden, of the house of Samuel, they are, Lois, 1898; Ruth, 1900; John T., 1902.

3 James Thomas Peden, 1856, and his wife Nancy Houston, 1858, are parents of four children: Jessie, 1882; Albert, 1883; James, 1887; Clay, 1890.

4, Martha Elizabeth (Peden), 1858, wife of John Thomas Peden (house of Samuel). Their children are: Annie Laura, 1892; Mary EveHne and Earle Alexander (twins), 1894.

5, Mary Rebecca (Peden), 1860, wife of Dewitt Vandervander. Two children: Jessie, 1892; Virgie, 1894. She then married the second time Palmer. Three children:

Henry and Herbert (twins), Laura Edna.

6, Matilda Josephine (Peden), 1866, wife of Milton Smith, 1869. Their children are: Frank, 1888; James, 1891; Ernest, 1893; Clyde, 1895; Mary M., 1897.

7, George Madison Peden, 1869.

8, Samuel Wilson Peden, 1872, and his wife, Madie Clark, Their children: Vera, 1894; Elizabeth, 1896.

9, Annie Laura (Peden), 1874, wife of Henry Sanford, 1873 No children.

10, Hugh Hamilton Peden, 1878, and his wife, Alberta Jarvis, 1882. One child, Guy, 1900.

5, Mary Ann (Peden), born Nov. 13, 1827; married Thomas Pearson in 1848. Was mother of: James Wilson, 1850; David Andrew, 1853; Sarah Eleanor, 1856; name of youngest missing. She died and her eldest sister married her husband and took charge of her children.

6; Andrew Hugh Hamilton Peden, born April 4, 183 1; married Catherine Stewart. Childless. He died for the Confederate cause, 1862.

7, William M. Peden, born Aug. 22, 1834. Died in Confederate service, 1862.

James Dunbar Peden was a successful farmer. He died in 1887, aged sixty-two years. He served through the entire civil war on the Confederate side.

V., Penelope, second daughter of this house, was born at Fairview, S.C. She grew up "fair, fat and rosy, with a merry heart and sunny temper," and married Samuel H. Baker, a man eminent for his beautiful Christian life and character. Says an old record: "The removal of Samuel H. Baker from this (Fairview) church is a great blow." This removal took place in 1836, first to Anderson County, S.C., where the wife and mother died, leaving the father and tne children to make the second removal to Mississippi. There were seven sons and three daughters: Franklin, Whitefield, Wilson, Samuel, David, James, Lindsay, Eleanor, Esther, Ann.

All of these save Lindsay and Ann went to Mississippi and sleep at Friendship Presbyterian church, near Van Vleet, Chickasaw County, except James, who was lost in the civil war, a brave soldier of the Confederate cause, and whose body was never recovered, whose soul went up to his Maker through the smoke and din of a fierce battle. Esther moved to Texas with her family and is buried at Corsicana, Texas. (Of Lindsay there is no trace given here.)

Ann married John Brownlee, lived and died at Westminster, S.C. No trace of her family.

Wilson Baker's sons live in Chickasaw County, Miss. There are only two living out of a large family.

Franklin Baker's family are in Texas. They number seven.

Esther Baker married her kinsman John M. Peden (houses of Thomas and Alexander). Two of her sons are living, Hugh Peden, in Chickasaw County, Miss., White Peden, in Vandale, Ark.

Eleanor Baker married a kinsman, Martin W. Peden (houses Thomas and Alexander). Six of her children are living'.

Both these sisters are, with their families, included in the houses of Thomas and Alexander.

(Signed)   J. W. T. Peden.

VI., William, fourth son of this house, was born in the old Fairview home. He was a child of unusual promise and great beauty. His devout father, at his baptism, set him apart solemnly consecrating him to the "holy ministry of the Presbyterian Church." William however had other views, he was "a soldier born," so after passing successfully through "three wars" he came home and married his pretty first cousin, Cynthia Peden (house of John). They soon after moved to Roswell, Ga., where they spent many years. Their children were: 1, Eleanor; 2, Louisa; 3, Jane; 4, Rebecca; 5, Margaret; 6, William; 7, Cynthia; 8, Samuel.

1, Eleanor Peden never married.

2, Louisa Peden never married.

3, Jane Peden married ____ Arnold. Their children were five in number: 1, John; 2, Eliza; 3, William; 4, Anna; 5, Lula,

1, John Arnold married Martha Tribble. Three children: James, Jane, Claude.

2, Eliza Arnold married Dr. Harvey Lewis. Three children: Thomas, Eva, Mary. Of these Thomas Lewis married. Wife's name unknown. One child. Eva Lewis married ____ Knox.

Names and numbers of children unknown.

3, William Arnold married Ella Drake. Five children: Howard, Ben, Frank, Laura, Ella.

4, Anna Arnold married H. Mitchell. Three daughters: Hattie, Mamie, Annie. Hattie Mitchell married ____ Ingraham. Mamie Mitchell married ____. Annie Mitchell married Bennett.

5, Lula Arnold married Dr. Geo. H. Vincent. No children. 4, Rebecca Peden married Aaron Butler. Four children; 1, George; 2, Mary; 3, Ervine; 4, Fannie

1, Rev. George Butler, M.D., missionary of the Southern Presbyterian Church to North Brazil. Married Kilpatrick. Five children, names unknown. They have been in their present field since 1876, and have been greatly blessed in the battle with Romanism.

2, Mary Butler married Andrew Stewart. No children of her own, but has reared and educated a number of nieces and nephews.

3, Ervine Butler married Fannie Stewart. Four children: Lena, Maude, William, Kittie. Maude married; name unknown.

4, Fannie Butler married Henry McNeely. Three children: Aaron, Walter, Claude. Aaron McNeely married Ola Webb. One child.

5, Margaret Peden married Englebert Flake. No children.

6, Cynthia Peden married first George Wrigley. Three children: Edward, Helen, Eva. The two first are not married. Eva Wrigley married Dr. H. Rice. Three children: William, Elkin, Louise. Name of second husband is unknown.

7, William Peden died in the Confederate cause after a hard fought battle in Virginia, 1863, one of the bravest, most daring sons of the house of Peden.

8, Samuel Peden married Mary Albritian. Two sons: John, William. Both married and have four children each; names unknown.

Both these brothers, William and Samuel, were members of the first Atlanta company to go to the front during the civil war. William gave his life. Samuel went to the bitter end,

(Signed)   Margaret Paden Flake.

VII., Thomas, fifth son of this house, was born at Fairview, S.C. He was a gun and locksmith by trade, and married Nancy, daughter of "That redoubtable, old Whig rebel, Bill Hanna, who escaped unhung," (Allaire's Diary), one of the heroes of Cowpens, S.C.

They settled near the old home on the mill tract, later exchanged for a better place on Reedy River, where he built his shops and spent his life. The Peden historian recalls this old couple among her earliest memories, standing in great awe of Aunt Nancy, who was a precise house wife with a horror of children. Her hair, which was "ruddy gold," rolled away from her broad brow in a Pompadour of short natural curls. Her caps were snowy white and had no frill the curls forming a natural trimmnng. Her face was handsome. Dear "Uncle Tommy" was the historian's grandmother's champion on more than one occasion. He and Aunt Nancy, who was a devoted Methodist, are buried at Fairview. Their only child, a son, was David Thomas Peden, who was born 1840. He was also a gunsmith, and during the civil war first enlisted as a member of Company E., Hampton Legion, but was sent home in 1863 to engage in the manufacture of ammunition in the Confederate government works at Greenville, S.C. (A few hundred yards from the historian's home stands the site of this once famous "gun foundry.")

He was married about 1855 to Lucinda Terry, daughter of Charles and Pamela Terry. To this couple was born one child, a daughter, the mother dying a few weeks after her birth. She was never replaced. There were the two good grandmothers, and "Aunt Ellen," as the historian's own grandmother was called.

David Thomas Peden answered the higher roll-call of the Christian soldier in 1875-1876. The old home is still the property of Alice Peden Brooks, his daughter.

Alice (Peden) Thomason Brooks was born 1858, and was married in 1878 to Francis Thomason. Their children were: David Edward Thomason, Nina Lee Thomason, Annie May Thomason, Francis Capers Thomason. After a few years of widowhood she married Capt. Brooks, of Simpsonville, S.C. Their children are: Bertie Lee Brooks, Marie Brooks, Gertrude Brooks, Carl Peden Brooks.

VIII., Rebecca, third daughter of this house was born at the old home, Fairview, S.C. She never married, and after the death of her father, found home and welcome among her numerous brothers and sisters, living to a good, old age, and leaving a host of nephews and nieces to lament her and miss her ministrations. Her last resting place is in Georgia, or Kemper County, Miss.

IX., Samuel, sixth son of this house, was born at Fairview, S.C. He like the others grew up to manhood in the old place and married his first cousin, Malinda or Linnie Peden (house of John). They moved to Gwinnett County, Ga., and were parents of four children, three daughters and one son: 1, Elizabeth Ann; 2, Eleanor; 3, Susan; 4, James.

1, Elizabeth Ann married James R. Jackson. Six children: Hugh Hamilton, Virginia, Elbert, Samuel, Amanda, Sarah. Of these the first three married, but there are no further records and all trace is lost.

2, Eleanor married Riley Bracewell. Three children, all of whom died in early childhood.

3, Susan married S. Gwinn. Four children. No further record.

4, James, the only son, fought bravely through the civil war; rose to the rank of captain. One authority states that he laid his life down for the Confederate cause in one of the battles near Atlanta, Ga. Another that he survived the war and married; wife's name not given; then removed to Mississippi, where he soon after died, leaving no children.

The records of this line are very incomplete, these few were kindly given by Andrew Jackson, a former friend and neighbor.

X., Alexander, seventh son of this house, was born at Fairview, S.C. He is described by one of his descendants as "being of fine physique, and handsome of face." He went to Georgia with his brothers. There he met and married Rebecca Durham. After a few years in Georgia they went to Kemper County, Miss. For him the town of Peden, Miss., is named. In 1875 there was a exodus of Pedens to Texas, among them Alexander Peden and all his sons. They all settled near each other in Parker and Tarrant Counties. He lived only four years after this move, dying suddenly of rheumatism of the heart, in 1880.

"He was a grand, old man, robust, jovial, but famous for what we call 'Peden temper,' though a kinder, more generous-hearted man never lived, full of fun and always ready to play a prank or practical joke on some one," so writes his granddaughter, Kate D. Stafford.

In this household there were twelve children, seven sons and five daughters; of this happy band seven remain, four of the sons and three daughters. Their names are as follows: 1, Mary E.; 2, Susan M.; 3, David T.; 4, John A.; 5, Matilda F.; 6, Rebecca J.; 7, James D.; 8, Andrew H.; 9, Lacy G.; 10, Levi F.; 11, George D.; 12, Josephine.

1, Mary E. Peden married Wm. Deaton. Their children: 1, Alex. Peden; 2, Susan M.; 3, Mary E.; 4, Thomas; 5, John B.; 6, Frances; 7, George D.; 8, Mina D.; 9, Pat Dimock; 10, Lillie J. and a baby boy who lived only a few days. Out of this dear household of eleven, seven have gone. The dear "boy cousins" Alex., Tom and John, Mina and Pat died when very young. The sisters are left save Fannie, and of the boys only George. 2, Susan M. married Capt. Joe Perry and 3, Mary E. married T.L. Carruthers. These sisters were also extremely handsome women, the eldest has been a widow for more than twenty-five years, and the youngest nearly as long. 10, Lilly Josephine has been married twice; first husband was ____ Birdsong; the second Fisher. If these sisters have children no record has reached the writer.

2, Susan Marion Peden married Rev. C.P. Sisson, of the Baptist Church, they had no children "they were beautiful in their lives, and in death were not divided."

3, David T. Peden married Nancy, his first cousin, daughter of John, eldest son of this line. They had a number of daughters and only one son, Marion Peden, who lives at Reno, Parker County, Texas.

4, John A. Peden also married his cousin, Matilda Fowler. He was killed in the Confederate army, leaving her a widow with two daughters: 1, Louella Peden, the eldest, married Daniel Clark. They have six children: Effie, John

George, Josephine, Gladys and Hutton. 2, Johnsie Peden, the youngest, married David Pearson, who died a few years ago. Her children are with her at her mother's home, Cottondale, Tex.

5, Matilda F. Peden married Rev. W. J. Collins, eminent Baptist minster. Their children were thirteen: 1, Kate D. 2, William T.; 3, L. Henry; 4, Eva Deaton; 5, Lois Judson 6, Alex.; 7, Charles Marion; 8, Frank Peden; 9, Claude W. 10, Elia C.; 11, Ada M., 12, Luta L. The little baby died.

Two of the brothers are living: 2, Wm. T. Collins and, 7, Charles Collins. The first has been married twice. Has seven children. Charles unmarried.

4, Eva D. Collins married G. W. Hudson. Has no children. Her husband is county judge of Anderson County, Texas.

II, Ada M. Collins married W. G. Smith. One child.

5, Lois J. Collins; 10, Elia C. Collins, and 12, Luta L. Collins, are unmarried.

I, Katie D. Collins, the eldest and historian of this line, married W.U. Stafford. They have ten children, seven are living: George Ervin, Wm. Reagan, Katie Lois, Henry H., Peden Wallace. Annie M., Charles W. Bruce.

6, Rebecca T. Peden married William Young. Is the mother of eight children: 1, Samuel A.; 2, Anna E.; 3, Rebecca M.; 4, John W.; 5, Frances J. (who died at six years); 6, Henry D.; 7, Mary E.; 8, James D. Three married, 1, Samuel A. Young married Lizzie Bennett, 1880, who died shortly afterwards. 4, John W. Young married Mattie Franklin, 1891. They have had four children: Clyde, born 1893; Floyd, born 1895; Henry, born 1897; Samuel, born 1899 (died). 7, Mary E, Young married John T. Mitchell, 1895. Three children: Eva, 1897: Deaton, 1899; Essie, 1900.

7, James Dunwoody Peden married a distant cousin, Margaret Stennis, during the civil war. They reared a large family. No record.

8, Andrew Hamilton Peden married Mary Chambers. No children.

9, Lacy Peden married Ellen Terry. They have several children. No record.

10, Levi Franklin Peden; killed in Confederate service during civil war, unmarried.

11, George D. Peden married; wife's name not known; Hve in Indian Territory.

12, Josephine Peden died in young womanhood.

XI., Eleanor Goodgion, youngest daughter of David, and eldest child of Margaret, his second wife, best known as Ellen, was born at the old home, Fairview, S.C. Married James Dunbar, who came over direct from Randallstown, Ballymena, "County Antrim, Ireland, during the summer of 1820. Their marriage took place on her "fifteenth birthday," June 16, 1824. She died May 12, 1899, having survived her parents, all her brothers and sisters, her husband and two daughters a number of years, and the sun went down on this long Christian pilgrimage of nearly ninety years, spent at Fairview, the beloved home place of the Pedens. She sleeps, but on that brighter shore has heard the glad "well done!" Their children were three daughters: 1, Elizabeth McConnell, born August 29, 1825. "The sun being about an hour high." Thus chronicles her father. 2, Margaret Emily, born December 9, 1834. 3, Jane Caroline, born Oct. 1, 1837; died Jan. 24, 1864.

I. Elizabeth McConnell Dunbar married Dr. J.W. Hewell, of Merriwether County, Ga., Aug. 22, 1848, while on a visit to her uncles in Pike County, Ga., near Pedenville, Rev. Andrew G. Peden performing the ceremony, at the home of his brother. David H. Peden. Their children: 1, Eleanor M., Peden historian, born in Lafayette, Ala., Feb. 7, 1853. 2, Eugenia Dunbar, born in Lafayette, Ala., Oct. 5, 1857. . 3, J. Dunbar, born in Tuskeegee, Ala., July 17, 1859; died April 9, 1860. 4, John Witherspoon, born Feb. 2, 1865, at Fairview S.C.

1, Eleanor M. and, 2, Eugenia D. unmarried.

4, Dr. John W. married Meta, only daughter of Capt. C. Marion McJunkin, June 19, 1893. Their children: Marion McJunkin, born June 10, 1898, in Greenville, S.C. Elizabeth, born March 23, 1900, in Greenville, S.C. Barbara, born April 18, 1902, in Greenville, S.C.

2, Margaret Emily Dunbar married William G. Britt, of Pike County, Ga., Dec. 18, 1851, at the old home, Fairview, S.C. Their children: 1, Marion Cassius, born Oct. 10, 1852, in Pike County, Ga. 2, Mary Ida, born Oct. 8, 1855, in Pike County, Ga. 3, William Hewell, born Sept. 2, 1860, in Pike County, Ga.

1, Rev. Marion C. married Elizabeth Hurt, of Atlanta, Ga. No children.

2. Mary Ida Britt married, Nov., 1879, A. M. Weir, known all over the South as "Sarge Plunket," of the Atlanta Constitution Their children are: 1, William S.; 2, Marion Britt; 3, Mary Withrow; 4, Addison Milton, Jr.; 5, Kate; 6, Robert; 7, Ernest.

1, William S. Weir married Clara Mull, of Atlanta. Their children: Willie May, Thomas Patrick, Margaret Emily. These are in the seventh generation from John Peden.

2, Marion Britt Weir married Samuel J. Clark, of Atlanta. No children.

3, William Hewell Britt married Hattie Denmark. One child, Emma-Jo.

XII., Rev. Andrew Gilliland Peden. This noble son of the house of David was born at the old home, Fairview, S. C, and "passed beyond our ken" on the 19th of Jan., 1896. His memorial appears elsewhere on these pages. He married first Margaret Dantzler, descended like himself from a Revolutionary ancestry. Their children: 1, David Dantzler; 2, Mary Crawford (died); 3, Elizabeth Miller; 4, Alexander Vernon (died).

I, David Dantzler Peden, of whom a sketch appears elsewhere, is a native of the grand old "Spartan District," S.C. He married Frances Dickey Plowden, of South Carolina, one of the rarest of women, of whom no eulogy could be extravagant, and who went to be with Jesus January 19, 1897, from out of the grief stricken home circle at Houston, Tex., leaving two sons a legacy to the Peden name: 1, Edward Andrew, born March 5, 1868; 2, Dickey Dantzler, born , 1874.

I, Edward Andrew Peden married Ione Allen, of Houston, Tex., in February, 1894. Their children: Allen Vernon, born Jan. 5, 1899; David Edward, born Jan. 20, 1901; Ione Hortense, born October 19, 1902. There was not life for both, the mother died that the child might live, so "in the gray dawn of October 21, God called the pure and loving spirit of her whom we knew as Ione Allen Peden to put off its clothing of corruptible flesh. Truly the ways and reasons of the rulings of the Lord's law are to mere mortals 'past all finding out;' and blessed is he who can devoutly cry: 'Thy will, O Lord, not mine, be done.'

"The wife of Mr. E. A. Peden and daughter of Mrs. Sam Allen, Mrs. Peden's life was made, by the tender ministrations of her family circle as well as by the prompting of her own loving heart and dutiful disposition, 'one grand sweet song.'

"Those of Mrs. Peden's family to whom her friends hearts go out in affectionate sympathy, beside her husband, her mother and three sweet little children, are her brothers, Percy, Baltis and Eugene, and especially her sisters, Mrs. Menefee and Misses Jennie and Ruth Allen.

"The tremendous quantity and exquisite loveliness of the flowers sent to the Peden residence on Tuesday morning as tokens of loving regard and tender sympathy has never been surpassed in Houston. The beautiful body of our now-silenced singer lay almost embowered in their masses of sweet purity. All the clubs to which Mrs. Peden belonged sent handsome tributes and some to which she did not belong sent them, too, because she had so generously sung for them. "Music is the only one of the arts practiced on earth which we have Biblical authority for believing we carry to heaven with us when we die, so Mrs. Peden's God-given voice makes now a part of the angelic glorias." — Houston Daily Post, Sunday, October 26, 1902.

3, Elizabeth Miller Peden married J. R. Tolbert, Oct 20, 1860. Their children are: 1, Peden Tolbert, born 1862; 2, John, born 1864; 3, Andrew Vernon, born 1867; died Jan. 3, 1886, in Georgia, at his grandfather Peden's; 4, Harry Lee, born 1867; died Feb. 3, 1900; 5, Charlie Luther, born 1872; died May 5, 1895; 6, Maggie Lizzie, born 1875; 7, Eugene Russell, born 1878; 8, David Dantzler, born 1880; 9, Mary Estelle, born 1884.

T, Peden Tolbert and Miss Lucy Turner were married 1891. Their children are: Mary Elna, born 1893; Peden, Jr., born 1895; Tom, born 1897.

4, Harry Tolbert and Miss Fannie Nation were married 1893. They also have three children: Una Blanche, born 1894; Andrew Vernon, born 1895; Mamie Ione, born 1898.

5, Charlie Tolbert and Aliss Bertha Houston were married in 1892. Their children are: Carl, born 1893; Charlie Luther, born 1895.

The second wife of Rev. A. G. Peden was Mary Isabella Britt, of Marion County, S. C, who died in 1852, leaving no children.

The third wife was Margaret C. Davis, of Winnsboro, S.C. Their children are: 1, Leonora Estelle; 2, Eleanor Eudora; 3, Arthur Davis (died in infancy).

1, Leonora Estelle married J. W. Sullivan. Their home is in Houston, Texas. The children of this household are: Leonora, Alargaret Peden, Luther McCall, Andrew Peden, William Edward, Frances Eudora.

2, Eleanor Eudora married Clark Sullivan. Their home is at Pedenville, Pike County, Ga. There are six happy children in their home: Malcolm Dubose, Annie Eudora, Ruth Peden, Margaret Lucile, William Bartlett, Julia Estelle.

XIII., David Hamilton Peden, youngest son of the house of David, was born at Fairview, S.C.; married Oct. 10, 1837, Lucilla Jones, of Abbeville County, S.C., who died June 30, 1852, leaving four children, three sons and one daughter. He was married the second time to Julia Wrigley, of Macon, Ga., who survives him. He went to be with Jesus from his lovely home in Griffin, Ga., from the midst of a host of friends, sorrowing grandchildren and devoted wife, Nov. 9, 1891. His sons died in the flush of early manhood leaving no families. The eldest son, Andrew Stephen (1842), was lost in one of the battles near Winchester, Va., where he fills an unknown grave. The second, Alpheus (1845), died when almost home on a sick furlough (1861). The youngest, James Albinus (1850), died just as he reached stalwart manhood, 1886-1887.

His daughter, Henrietta Jane (1840), married Mr. Andrew Weir Blake, of Greenwood, S. C., in 1864. Their children: 1, David Peden; 2, William Newton; 3, Andrew Stewart; 4, Lucilla Jones; 5, Walter Julian.

Henrietta Jane (Peden) Blake preceded her father to the home in heaven almost a year, she went hence in the autumn of 1890.

1, David Peden Blake married Genevieve Hemphill. Their children are: Andrew Eugene, David Pierson, Wilton McKay, Myrtle Josephine.

2, William Newton Blake married Cora Malaier. Their children: John, Rennie, Andrew Joshua, David Peden.

3, Andrew Stewart Blake married Mattie Daniel. Their children are: Otis Daniel, Arthur Copeland.

4, Lucilla Jones Blake married George Coppedge, Griffin, Ga. Their children are: Jennie Blake, Julia Amelia.

5, Walter Julian Blake married Georgia Guinn. Their children are: Guinn Weir, Julia.

Chapter Twenty-One - In Reminiscent Mood

"Should you ask me, whence these stories?
Whence these legends and traditions?
I should answer, I should tell you —
I repeat them as I heard them."

In using these reminiscences of her grandmother, the Peden historian explains that it is not intentional to enlarge upon, or exalt this house above the others, or give it more space than is seemly, though it is one of the largest. This chapter really gives an insight into the inner life of these early pioneer homes, therefore what is true of one is true also of all — a pen picture with different personel that is all. These traditions drawn from the well-stored memory of Eleanor G. Dunbar, one of the youngest members of the household of David, are strictly true, not over-drawn, she being a woman who abhorred falsehood as she did murder or other crime. Little dreamed she of storing the mind of future historian of her race; neither did the eager little listener imagine that some day she would rehearse these tales of a grandmother for the benefit and pleasure of future generations of Pedens. "Thus are honors thrust upon us." Being one of those tiresome, troublesome children endowed with the faculty of asking endless questions, a still, nervous child, with an insatiable appetite for stories, true stories, she often taxed the patience of her elders. While her young companions delighted in fairy-lore, unless a tale was true it lost interest for her, so naturally her mind turned to history very early, the introduction being "Scott's Tales of a Grandfather."

This grandmother of sweet memory, though naturally a silent woman, was very indulgent to the young listener when in reminiscent mood. So the signal for the telling of some old time tale was usually when she sat down in her low seated, straight, high-backed chair, drew her knitting from a bag hanging from the fire-board, her pipe and tobacco from their places on the shelf and filled her pipe with the fragrant weed, packing it in well with fore-finger and thumb, then adroitly inserting it among the embers to crown it with a glowing coal. Matches were not plentiful in South Carolina during the dark days of 1864-1865. Besides, she was of an economical turn of mind and hated waste. She was extremely industrious too for her fingers were always employed, "never idle, never still." After the breathless ceremony of pipe lighting ended, the knitting adjusted, the story would begin; very often the writer would bear her company with her own very grimy, tear-stained soldier's sock, or her own small stocking, not for the love of the work, oh no, but as a punishment for some childish misdemeanor she was doomed to knit at least ten or twelve tiresome "rounds," sitting beside grandmother, in the "stiff, little blue chair;" but the keen edge of the hated task was taken off by some story she dared not ask for vohmtarily. After a few long, delicious draws and whiffs, how she enjoyed and coveted that pipe - "Well, Ellie, who must we talk about this time?" Ellie generally knew. Sometimes the dear dark eyes would dim with unshed tears; sometimes brim over with fun; sometimes flash with fire, and the nostrils dilate with courage, according to the nature of the story told.

Many, very many, of these fireside tales were of the fathers and came direct to her from her own father, tales of adventure, persecution, battle, and of intense interest; then later of her own day and time, some sad and some bright. One specially enjoyable was the first wedding that occurred in the household of David, which is rehearsed here to show the spirit of the times. It took place about 1811 or 1812. The eldest daughter of the house, Margaret, or Peggy, said to be a reprint of Peggy McDill, "only having her father's black hair," was the bride. Now a marriage in the early homes of the Pedens was a very serious affair, in solving all the "kith and kin," so as soon as it was hinted among the women by the expectant bride's mother (in this case stepmother), during the "intermission" at "meeting," there were knowingnods and wise "I told you so," or incredulous, "Did ever I hear?" which must have been exceedingly trying to the young woman if she was present, which she generally was for there was no avoiding "meeting;" yet she bore the friendly banter quietly, knowing it was kindly meant if the match was approved; if otherwise the hint was received in stern silence, and sombre head shakes, "but never a word sard they." Oft-times the reception of the information unfavorably had the desired effect, most frequently not, and then they made the best of the affair, "Run-away" matches were very rare among the early Pedens, as their marriages were among themselves. From the "hint" to the wedding day there was suppressed excitement. All the house-mothers went to work to help with the trousseau and an article of household stuff to help out Margaret's kist which was already filled to overflowing, thanks to her own industry and skill, also her stepmother's help. Homemade blankets, sheets, pillow "slips," valances, counterpanes, all trimmed with lace and fringes, quilts, coverlets galore. All saved eggs, fowls and fattened turkeys, laid by butter and sweet meats and laid aside the choicest ham for the feast.

The men were not silent onlookers or sneerers, they held no consultations with their "women folk" but went steadily to work to help build the new home, whether they approved or not, made no criticism, made the simple new furniture, including the three-cornered cupboard from David Morton's shop, and looked over their flocks and herds for a pig or yearling cow for the new barn yard. The groom-elect was taken into the secret, but the bride was supposed to be entirely unconscious, and propriety forbade her asking any questions, or taking interest outside her wedding gown. This, in the earliest homes, was of fine Hnen made at home, but in the case of Margaret Peden was of some dainty fabric woven in foreign looms, and with attendant veil, gloves and high-heeled slippers emerged mysteriously from the depths of her father's big market wagon when it stopped on the way home from market at Elizabeth Gaston's door. Said one neighbor to another: "Davie Peden stopped at the Gaston's the day, is any of they folks sick?" "Och dinna ye ken woman, Margaret is to be married till Jimmie Alexander?" was the reply. This dainty robe was evolved by the skillful fingers of Elizabeth Gaston, with a silken dress for the "infair," a great dinner given at the groom's father's next day. David Peden gravely disapproved the marriage of cousins, but he could not hold out against the genial warmth of this fair and debonair son of Alexander, who possessed the irresistible charm of his race. "Yes," Elizabeth Gaston declared, "Jimmie Alexander is all right, and, Davie, if he canna marry Margaret in your house, he shall in mine." This argument was final, so Davie said no more and bonny Margaret went from her father's door as fair a bride "as ever the sun shone on."

As to the wedding and the feast all the "kith and kin" were bidden, so the "big pot sat in the little pot." All the women came to assist. Aunt Elizabeth was in the lead, the mother was not strong so she was set aside, the bride banished up stairs with orders not to cry and spoil her eyes, neither was she to tell her beads and say her prayers but to rest and be out of the way, and dream happy dreams of the future. As for Jimmie, that restless young man was strictly forbidden the premises for two whole weeks, nor was he to have a glimpse of his bride. To say he fretted under this restraint would be useless. He was 'no unworthy Alexander without resources of his own. Uncle Davie's spring proved very attractive. He had to pass the house to reach it and fair Margaret was far sighted; moreover she was very thirsty, she wanted to have her water fresh; also there was a grape-vine swing where she could rest. "Well 'twas ever thus, and love still laughs at the locksmith." At the house and in the big kitchen all was bustle and stir. There were cakes to bake and frost by the score. Aunt Violet, the sister of the mother, a famous cook in her day, took charge of the cakes and sweets. Aunt Polly Alexander took the breads, while Aunt Jenny Savage looked after the fowls and pastry, and Granny Hughes attended to the broiling, roasting and frying. The appetizing odors filled the autumnal air. Aunt Polly constructed her famous pyramids of golden butter and Aunt Elizabeth made the "syllabub," modern whipped cream, flavored with wine; there was boiled custard flavored with peach leaves or the "kernels," late cider and a drink made of honey.

Aunt Elizabeth took charge of the table. Her china and silver were brought out to adorn this occasion, and all the glass attainable. The long table, composed of several borrowed ones, covered with snowy cloths and adorned with cedar boughs dipped in egg then sprinkled with flour, candles in lilies, made of waxed paper, shone brilliantly, bringing the loaded board into full relief. There were no flowers, they were regarded as unlucky at a wedding because so short lived. A hush fell over the assembled guests as Aunt Elizabeth came down the narrow stairs with the blushing bride, whom she transferred to the care of her father, and by him was given to the waiting Jimmie Alexander. Soon the few words were spoken that made them one. The feast began soon after the ceremony and lasted into the small hours.

Next morning the young couple departed on horseback, Jimmie riding proudly in front, while his bride was safely perched upon a pillion behind him, the entire company following as an honorary escort over to his father's, Maj. John Alexander's, where the great "infair" dinner was to take place. After a week of dinners at various places, among them Aunt Elizabeth Gaston's, they went to their own humble abode on the creek, which had been slyly fixed in apple pie order against their arrival by the bride's family.

The last wedding superintended by the loved Elizabeth Gaston, the last bride arrayed by her skillful hands, was the grandmother, who gave the tradition. The tall, queenly, beautiful Eleanor Peden.

She thus describes her father, whom she seems to have loved with a devotion almost worshipful: "Father was one of the tallest of the seven brothers, very erect and carried himself like a soldier; he was spare of build, his face was rather long and narrow, skin clear with the red showing underneath; he was always clean-shaven, scorning a beard; his eyes were almost black, keen and bright, his mouth very firm; his nose just like mine, (which was aquiline and clean cut); his hair was fine as silk, black as a crow's wing, and as straight as an Indian's. His manner was serious most of the time, though he inherited a keen sense of humour from his mother. He was not a great talker. While seemingly a stern man he was almost worshipped by his family. Of all the seven brothers he was most like old John Peden in appearance, while in character he was more like his mother, Peggy McDill. Of his own children those most like him were my brothers John, 'Robbie,' 'Tommie' and myself."

Among other reminiscences of him she told of the long, perilous journey down from Pennsylvania with his parents and brothers, John, Samuel and Alexander, to join other friends at Nazareth, in Spartanburg District, S.C. Here he remained with his parents sharing with them the vicissitudes of frontier life. When his father and brothers were away on the hunt, or serving soldier duty against the Indians, he was sent with his mother to one of the blockhouses or forts, where he made himself useful bringing water and wood amid whistling arrows, moulding bullets and loading muskets in case of sudden attack by Indian and Tory. Thus he entered the training school of war at the age of ten or twelve, sometime before his actual services were demanded by his adopted country. At the outbreak of the Revolution, 1776, indeed, prior to this date, he was bearing arms, though but sixteen, or some authorities say fourteen, he was "as thorough a Whig patriot as ever shouldered gun." When his brothers, with their father, went to join Dan Morgan with the other "Tyger Irish," Davie marched too, greatly against the wishes of both father and brothers. He laughingly told how "they would have none of his company." But, for once he proved obstinate, tears and threats were of no avil, until the brave Peggy McDill took his part and joined the determined lad in the conspiracy, so she did naught to hold back her "baby boy." He soon found favor with his officers and while he never rose in rank, he became a great favorite with his soldier comrades. He was with the Hamptons part of the time; again he followed the fortunes of Hughes, a soldier of great courage. He told of the winter at Valley Forge, of Brandywine; then in the State of his adoption several important partisan battles under different leaders. He was, after Gates' defeat, with Sumter, and many a tale of hairbreadth adventure and narrow escape did he tell; of his life among the swamps and mountains, and of hardships in hiding, want of food, subsisting on green corn and sweet potatoes, until the rally of 1780. Then of Cowpens, where he was with Pickens; King's Mountain (1781), Guilford C.H., and finally the grand culmination at Yorktown. Then the young soldier turned southward, half clad and shoeless, to encounter other perils on the way, yet to reach home and mother safe and sound, with father and all his brothers.

Davie then went to learn the trade of miller with a Goodgion, presumably his fellow soldier, Robert Goodgion. There he met and won the sister or the daughter of the miller. Tradition locates this mill in several different places, near the present town of Gowensville, at the foot of the Saludas, and in Laurens County on Raeburn Creek, where Goodgion's mills still exist. The name Goodgion is a corruption of an old French name, but of the history of this family the writer is in profound ignorance, only in these days it ranks well socially, its women for fifty years have been noted for beauty of mind and person, while the men are successful in the business world.

Eleanor Goodgion was a sprightly, vivacious girl of sixteen when she became the bride of David Peden "in the humble pioneer cabin home at the foot of the mountains," he having stated his willingness to serve seven years for her, such was his love for her, but his love was not so severely tested for she came with him to his home-building at Fairview to help rear their pioneer home in 1785. In addition to her beauty she had boundless pluck and energy, but in her fiery French blood there lurked "a demon of a temper," which blazed forth at times. David only remarked calmly, "that a little thunder cleared the air," and went his unruffled way. This is the legend of Peden temper, but, this hot temper is not confined to the descendants of Eleanor Goodgion. She was the fond idol of David Peden's life, its guiding star, high priestess of his hearthstone, and she brought

"To her husband's house delight and abundance.
Filling it full of love and the ruddy faces of children."

She died in the year 1804 or 1805, leaving a desolate home and ten children, having attained only thirty-six years of age.

The habits of this colonial household were very simple. David rose "long before light," made the fire by uncovering huge "chunks" from a bed of ashes. In those days fires were not allowed to go out for great annoyance and delays would have been the result. Matches did not exist and the nearest neighbor was miles away, still there was the "flint and steel" for emergencies. Then swung the kettle from the crane, soon the good wife followed, they employed themselves busily until "light." David lighted his candle of tallow, hung the stick by its hook to a chair (this old relic still exists), and busied himself in making shoes for his many boys and girls; Eleanor teased wool, or carded the fleece into long rolls for spinning until time for breakfast. While this was preparing, David "fed and milked." When the corn cakes and rashers of bacon and eggs were ready, mush and milk for the little ones prepared, the children roused and simply clothed, they all sat down to a frugal meal with thankful hearts. Then prayers and each set about the daily task.

After the first few hard years, there was milk and butter in abundance, fowls were plenty, wild game still abounded in the woods. In a few years David Peden had so prospered that he had set up a "double mill" down on the creek, one for lumber and the other for grist. Had also planted extensive orchards of peaches and apples.

Early in 1800 the cultivation of cotton was introduced among them, one brother bringing the seed home from Charleston, their only market, to and from which they made two or four long journeys each year, in their big wagons, drawn by four horses or mules. These brothers so arranged their marketing that they were never all absent at once. These trips being taken about Christmas, before planting time (March), after crops were laid by (July), and when they were gathered, harvestime. Two generally sufficed, but occasionally four were necessary. In this way they kept in touch with the outside world. True, the county courthouse was established in 1818, but did not furnish much attraction for these old wagoners, who clung to old ways and loved to camp out and sleep under the stars.

They too had acquired a number of slaves, who were more like friends in these homes. David had, among others, two very curious characters, Joe, who claimed to be a king, and Delphi or Delfy, who proved a capable nurse and cook, so was invaluable aid to the housewife whose health was giving way under the strain of a large household of children. She was known as "Granny," living to a great age. Not a few marvellous tales are told of the little, old, shriveled, black woman. Joe, after a short servitude, disappeared mysteriously, the supposition being, that he, in trying to find his way back to the coast, had been destroyed by wild beasts, Indians, or was drowned in trying to cross some deep stream.

As years passed on it became necessary to add to the one main room. Others were shedded on. The big room, within the memory of the writer, held the grandfather's chair, a small stand, on which his Bible, hymn-book and case containing his spectacles lay, in the opposite corner the three cornered cupboard, in another the huge four-poster with its snowy covers, valances and pillow-cases, all trimmed with elaborate laces, or fringes, at its foot stood a tall table, also draped in white, on this were a few toilet accessories; while above it hung the small mirror, or shaving glass, presumed to have been brought over by his father, John Peden, from Ireland, and used by his son. David, for like purpose; in another corner stood the steep, crooked staircase to the low, cosey chamber above; and on one side stood a book-case, then very new, and greatly valued. The long, narrow room just back was the dining-room where was placed the table with its long bench against the wall, on which the children sat to eat their meals and were gradually promoted to chairs on the other side, as one after another left the mother's lap, for a place on the bench. The other three rooms were sleeping apartments.

The out-houses were the loom-house, kitchen, and negro cabins, the barns, gin-house and shops.

As the pipe would sometimes die out the writer would offer to rekindle it but always met the gentle, but firm refusal, "No, that is how I learned to smoke, child, and I don't want you to learn how, it is a bad habit and grandmother is ashamed of it. When did I learn? well, when the women were on the looms it was troublesome to keep getting off to light their pipes, so I would do it for them.'"

In 1807 David Peden married Margaret Hughes, of Spartanburg County, S.C. She was the daughter of that remarkable character Anne Hughes, who deserves a high place among the Women of the Revolution. That she has not adorned the pages of history is owing to the palpable neglect of her descendants, for she was not only a famous house-wife and cook, well skilled in wood-lore, but a patriotic soul devoted to the Whig cause. She lived to a great age and her life would fill a volume of romance and adventure.

Margaret Hughes was no longer in her first youth when she took pity on David Peden and his big houseful of children. She was a small body, with a big heart. She is described as a fair woman, all smiles and dimples, sunny of temper, and warm of heart; rather silent but full of energy and industry, and soon brought order out of chaos, being a fine manager and skillful housewife. Moreover, she brought a goodly store of household stuff with her as a dower. If the reader will turn to the last chapter of Proverbs and find there the best portrait of Margaret Hughes. She soon won and made life-long friends of most of her step-children as letters in the hands of the writer prove, and is held in reverent respect by their descendants.

Margaret never rallied from the shock of her husband's death. She too was very ill with the same dread disease when he died, and did not regain consciousness until after he had been laid to rest some days. The date of her death is uncertain, either December 21, 1824, or April 9, 1825, this being her anniversary and forty-seventh birth-day. The heads of this large house sleep in the rock-walled God's acre at Fairview, awaiting the resurrection. Through the filial generosity of Capt. D. D. Peden, neat monuments now (1900) mark the tombs of David Peden and both his wives, within the shadow of the Peden monument.

Of her brothers the grandmother never tired telling and had many reminiscences of them. The writer does not recall any of the three eldest, Johnny, Jimmie and Robbie. These all married and left the home nest while she was very young. Billie and Tommie were evidently her favorites. Billie, handsome Billie, as she called him, was a boy of great promise, but too full of fun to be studious, while his father designed him for a scholar, and a future preacher. At the country school "Billie was a great dunce at his books." The father exacted his attendance, and a certain amount of study. Billie was jolly, good-tempered, but incorrigible. He was specially kind to the trio of half-brothers and sisters, denying himself oftentimes to gratify them.

On one occasion a traveling show stopped at the Squire's (Alexander's), store, or "double-cabins" of later times, and Billie had worked hard to earn the money to go, so he very kindly offered to take the "young ones." Their mother consenting they set out on the three-miles tramp, Davie, aged two, on Billie's broad back, Andy swinging to one hand, while Ellen timidly clung to his "coat tails." It was a long remembered occasion. Among other things the "ginger cake stall," so Billie out of his small store gave each of the "young ones" a dime to spend. Ellen and Andy proceeded to invest and eat, but Davie held fast to his dime and cried for a cake, this so amused Billie that he bought a cake for him allowing him to keep the dime, doing without himself, refusing the share Ellen offered of hers. Repeating the story to his father when they reached home he expected him to enjoy the joke. Father looked at him very gravely and said, "Billie will never gather money, it burns his fingers, but Davie will hold his dollars 'til the eagle screams." A prophecy literally fulfilled in the lives of the brothers, for Billie was always poor while Davie amassed a fortune.

Again, instead of carrying out his father's wishes regarding preparation for the gospel ministry, amid the bitter lamentation of the "young ones," handsome Billie mounted his big "chestnut roan" and rode off to be a soldier, and a soldier he was to the heart's core. After the war ended he came home safe and sound with his brothers James and Robert, only to further vex his father's soul by wedding his fair, first cousin, Cynthia Peden (house of John).

Thomas, or Tommie, had a weakness for drink. Not often, but on occasions he would "take too much" and then was very hilarious, and his high-spirited wife declined to allow him to enter their well-ordered house in that condition. He was never past finding his way to Ellen's, her husband being of like mind with Tommie's wife, she always managed to hide him away, until he sobered sufficiently to make his appearance. He was devoted to Ellen and she to him all their days, spent near each other. In the dark days before her marriage all her other half-brothers and sisters opposed the step, but defying them all "Tommie stood by me, and I never forgot." So of all her older brothers Tommie was the one she loved best, despite his weakness. She said, "he had the best heart."

Life in these primitive homes was not at all the colorless monotone it seems to the eyes of today. There were the annual camp-meetings, which were a kind of religious dissipation, when all the households packed into the big market wagons the necessary outfit and went into camp, either at Fairview or some other meeting house, far or near.

The regular general or "old field" muster, which was a dissipation of quite another kind, where the old soldiers fought their battles over, and the young men were fired with enthusiastic admiration and desire to become soldiers also.

The neighborhood frolics, such as log-rollings, barn-raisings, corn shuckings, where labor and pleasure were combined, and where the housewife furnished forth assumptions out of door dinner or supper.

The old-time quiltings, where every quilter was expected to be in her place as the sun peeped over the eastern rim of the horizon. Oft-times arriving in time for the early, appetizing breakfast, composed of fried ham, eggs, chicken, hominy, johnny cakes, wheat biscuit, "raised" bread, butter, honey and hot steaming coffee, or cold, delicious buttermilk. These took place always in summer during the long, light days. The dinner was a test of the skill and inventive powers of the hostess. As many quilts were turned off as possible, the more the better pleased was she. Now these being for the use of every day, were not those beautiful creations of the quilters art, those marvels of wonder, which excite the admiration of later generations. They required the leisurely work of weeks. To be a rapid, or skilled quilter, was quite as much of an accomplishment as music or art is now. When the last quilt was cut from the frames, the men folks arrived to take the quilters home, after the bountiful supper, the younger members sometimes remaining to indulge in romping games.

The sweet, little poem which closes the annals of the house of David was composed by that living light, that pillar of the church, eminent for devout, humble Christianity, Samuel H. Baker, one of the three Baker brothers whose lives left so sweet an incense to their descendants. The lines were written for his daughters Esther and Eleanor, one of whom worked them on a "samplar," from which they were kindly copied for this work by her lineal descendant, John M. Peden.

The Land for Me

Farewell! farewell to all below,
My Savior calls me I must go,
I launch my barque upon the sea,
This land is not the land for me.
I find the winding paths of sin,
A rugged way to travel in.
Beyond the chilling waves I see
The land my Savior bought for me.

Farewell! farewell I cannot stay.
The home I seek is far away.
Where Chirst is not, I cannot be.
This land is not the land for me.

Praise be to God my hopes on high
Where angels sing and so will I —
Where angels bow and bend the knee,
O that's the land; the land for me.

No night is there, 'tis always day.
And God will wipe all tears away,
And saints their Savior's face shall see,
O that's the land, the land for me.

Where kindred spirits meet again,
Secured from sorrow and from pain,
May feast on pleasures full and free,
O that's the land, the land for me.

O sinners why will you not go —
There's room enough for all below?
Our boat is sound, our passage free.
And that's the land, the land for me.

Milton Keynes UK
Ingram Content Group UK Ltd.
UKHW010630290424
441924UK00001B/149